# THE PRICE OF
# EVERYTHING

# EDUARDO PORTER

# THE PRICE OF EVERYTHING

## THE COST OF BIRTH, THE PRICE OF DEATH, AND THE VALUE OF EVERYTHING IN BETWEEN

WILLIAM HEINEMANN: LONDON

Published by William Heinemann 2011

4 6 8 10 9 7 5

Copyright © Eduardo Porter 2011

First published in Great Britain in 2011 by
William Heinemann
Random House, 20 Vauxhall Bridge Road,
London SW1V 2SA

www.randomhouse.co.uk

Addresses for companies within The Random House Group Limited
can be found at www.randomhouse.co.uk/offices.htm

The Random House Group Limited Reg. No. 954009

A CIP catalogue record for this book
is available from the British Library

ISBN 9780434019786

The Random House Group Limited supports The Forest Stewardship
Council (FSC®), the leading international forest certification organisation.
Our books carrying the FSC label are printed on FSC® certified paper.
FSC is the only forest certification scheme endorsed by the leading environmental
organisations, including Greenpeace. Our paper procurement policy can be found at
www.randomhouse.co.uk/environment

Design by Pauline Neuwirth
Printed and bound in Great Britain by
Clays Ltd, St Ives PLC

*For Gisele and Mateo*

# Contents

# CONTENTS

# Prices Are Everywhere

**ANYBODY WHO HAS** visited a garbage dump in the developing world knows that value is an ambiguous concept. To most people in the developed world, household waste is worthless, of course. That's why we throw it away. Apparently, Norwegians are willing to pay about $114 a ton for somebody else to sort their recyclables from the general garbage. A survey of families in the Carter community of Tennessee several years ago found they were willing to pay $363 a year, in today's money, to avoid having a landfill nearby.

But slightly beyond our immediate experience, waste becomes a valuable commodity. In Kamboinsé, outside Ouagadougou, Burkina Faso, farmers pay municipal trash haulers to dump unsorted solid waste on their sorghum and millet fields as fertilizer—bits of plastic included. The going rate in 2003 was 400 francs per ton. In New

Delhi, a study in 2002 found that waste pickers earned two rupees per kilo of plastic soda bottles and seven rupees per kilo of hard plastic shampoo bottles. A child working on foot on Delhi's dumps could make twenty to thirty rupees per day.

Waste, in fact, confronts us with the same value proposition as anything else. The price we put on it—what we will trade to have it, or have it go away—is a function of its attendant benefits or costs. A bagful of two-rupee plastic bottles is more valuable to an Indian child who hasn't eaten today than to me, a well-fed journalist in New York. What she must do to get it—spend a day scavenging among the detritus of India's capital, putting her life and health at risk—is, to her, not too high a price to pay because life is pretty much the only thing she has. She has little choice but to risk it for food, clothing, shelter, and whatever else she needs. I, by contrast, have many things. I have a reasonable income. If there's one thing I have too little of, it is free time. The five cents I could get for an empty plastic bottle at the supermarket's recycling kiosk are not worth the trouble of redeeming it.

The purpose of this comparison is not to underscore that the rich have more opportunities than the poor. It is that the poor choose among their options the same way the rich do, assessing the prices of their alternatives. The relative costs and benefits of the paths open to them determine the behavior of the poorest Indian girl and the richest American man. These values are shaped by the opportunities they have and the constraints they face. The price we put on things—what we will trade for our lives or our refuse—says a lot about who we are.

The price of garbage provides a guide to civilization. Pollution is cheapest in poor countries. Their citizens are more readily willing to accept filth in exchange for economic growth. Yet the relative price of pollution rises as people become richer. Eventually it becomes expensive enough that it can alter the path of development. China is a dirty place. Yet underlying its dismal air and foul water is a choice that balances the costs of pollution in bad health, poisonous rivers, and so forth against the cost of cutting back production or retooling plants to control their effluvia. It is a different choice from that of Switzerland, where preserving environmental assets—clean air, trees, wild animals—is considered more valuable than providing manufacturing jobs to unemployed farmers. Twice as many Swiss as Chinese are members of environmental organizations. More than a third of the Swiss population believes environmental pollution is the most important problem facing the nation; only 16 percent of Chinese feel the same.

But as China grows, the price of building one more coal-fired power plant, measured in terms of its contribution to acid rain, global warming, and the rest will one day exceed the value the Chinese place on the extra output. As it keeps growing, it will likely evolve out of the most noxious industries, like steel and chemicals, into less polluting sectors, like medical and financial services. It may even one day buy its steel and chemicals from poorer countries with a higher tolerance of foul water and air. In other words, it will behave more like Switzerland or the United States. One study concluded that emissions of sulfur dioxide peak when a country's income per person reaches around $8,900 to $10,500. In the United States, sulfur-dioxide emissions soared until the passage in 1970 of the Clean Air Act. Since then, emissions have fallen by half.

HEREIN LIES THE central claim of this book: every choice we make is shaped by the prices of the options laid out before us—what we assess to be their relative costs—measured up against their benefits. Sometimes the trade-offs are transparent and straightforward—such as when we pick the beer on sale over our favorite brand. But the Indian scavenger girl may not be aware of the nature of her transaction. Knowing where to look for the prices steering our lives—and understanding the influence of our actions on the prices arrayed before us—will not only help us better assess our decisions. The prices we face as individuals and societies—how they move us, how they change as we follow one path or another—provide a powerful vantage point upon the unfolding of history.

Nearly two decades ago, when he was chief economist of the World Bank, Lawrence Summers, President Barack Obama's former top economic adviser, signed his name to a memo suggesting it would make sense for rich countries to export their garbage to poor ones. Because wages are lower in poor countries, he said, they would suffer a lesser loss if workers got sick or died. "I think the economic logic behind dumping a load of toxic waste in the lowest wage country is impeccable and we should face up to that," it said. Moreover, pollution mattered less in a poor country with other problems: "The concern over an agent that causes a one in a million change in the odds of prostate cancer is obviously going to be much higher in a country where people survive to get prostate cancer than in a country where under 5 mortality is 200 per thousand."

Leaked a few months before the 1992 United Nations Earth Summit in Rio de Janeiro, the memo confirmed to critics that the World Bank believed poor countries were dumps. The reasoning "is perfectly logical but totally insane," wrote the late José Lutzenberger, then Brazil's environment minister, in a letter to Summers. Furious, Vice President Al Gore torpedoed Summers's chance to become chairman of then-president Bill Clinton's Council of Economic Advisers. Summers apologized, explaining the memo as an attempt to offer "sardonic counterpoint" to sharpen analytical thinking about the trash trade.

Lutzenberger had a point. Wages are not the only benchmark of people's value. The price of dealing with garbage in impoverished countries is often zero not because their citizens care nothing about pollution, but because their governments don't enforce pollution-related laws. But Summers had a powerful point too: in poorer countries, an untainted environment is less valuable than other things that are more abundant in richer nations—schools, for instance. Many developing nations would serve their interests best by trading trash for the chance to build an extra one.

## THE PRICE OF CROSSING BORDERS

Most of us think of prices in the context of shopping expeditions. In the marketplace, prices ration what we consume, guiding how we allocate resources among our many wants. They prompt us to set priorities within the limits of our budgets. Just as prices steer our purchasing patterns, they steer the decisions of the companies that make what we buy, enabling them to meet our demand with their supply. That's how markets organize a capitalist economy.

But prices are all over the place, not only attached to things we buy in a store. At every crossroads, prices nudge us to take one course of action or another. In a way, this is obvious: every decision amounts to a choice among options to which we assign different values. But identifying these prices allows us to understand more fully our decisions. They can be measured in money, cash, or credit. But costs and benefits can also be set in love, toil, or time. Our most important currency is, in fact, opportunity. The cost of taking any action or embracing any path consists of the alternatives that were available to us at the time. The price of a five-dollar slice of pizza is all the other things we could have done with the five dollars. The price of marriage includes all the things we would have done had we remained single. One day we succumb to the allure of love and companionship. Years later we wonder what happened to the freedom we traded away at the altar. Economists call this the "opportunity cost." By evaluating opportunity costs, we organize our lives.

Just to be born, the scavenger girl in Delhi had to overcome Indian parents' entrenched bias against girls—which has led to widespread abortions of female fetuses. The Indian census of 2001 recorded 927 girls aged six or less per 1,000 boys. This compares to 1,026 girls per thousand boys in Brazil and 1,029 in the United States. The bias is due to a deeply unfavorable cost-benefit analysis: while boys are meant to take over the family property and care for their parents in old age, daughters must be married off, which requires an onerous dowry. To redress the balance of incentives, regional governments across India have been experimenting with antipoverty programs aimed at increasing parents' appetite for girls. In 2008, Delhi launched a program to deposit 10,000 rupees into the account of newly born girls in poor families—making subsequent deposits as they progress in school. The objective is to build a cushion of resources for them to marry or pursue higher education. A social insurance program launched in 2006 in Haryana pays parents who only have daughters 500 rupees a month between the age of forty-five and the age of sixty, when it is replaced by the general public pension.

I REMEMBER A conversation I had a few years ago with an illegal immigrant in Stockton, California. I worked at the *Wall Street Journal* writing about the Hispanic population of the United States. The immigrant was educating me about the relative merits of having his two young children smuggled from Mexico *por el monte*—a grueling hike across the desert—or *por la línea,* across a regular checkpoint using forged documents. The choice was hard. He couldn't have made more than $8 or $9 an hour, picking asparagus, cherries, and everything else that grew in California's San Joaquin Valley. He would have to pay about $1,500 each for a "coyote" to guide his kids across the desert. Yet he figured that getting a smuggler with fake documents to bring them across a border checkpoint would put him back about $5,000 per child. The conversation laid in stark relief the type of bare-knuckle cost-benefit analyses that steer people's lives.

Over the last decade and a half, the Border Patrol's budget has grown roughly fivefold. Average coyote fees increased accordingly, to about $2,600 in 2008. Yet the price that rose most sharply is measured in the odds of dying on the way, as a border crossing that used to take less than a day around San Diego became a three- to four-day trek through the Arizona desert, evading thieves and the Border Patrol, lugging jugs of water. In 1994, 24 migrants died trying to cross the border. By 2008, the death toll was 725. The calculation of the immigrant I spoke to was straightforward enough. To bring his children into the United States through a checkpoint, he would have to work longer to earn the price of passage. But it would lower the risk that his children would perish along the way.

The debate among Americans about illegal immigration is itself a discussion about prices. Critics charge that illegal immigrants lower the price of natives' labor by offering to do the job for less. They argue that immigrants impose a burden on natives when they consume public services, like education for their children and emergency medical care.

These arguments are weaker than they seem. Most illegal immigrants work on the books using false IDs, and have taxes withheld from their paychecks like any other worker. They can't draw benefits from most government programs. And there is scant evidence that immigrants lower the wages of American workers. Some industries only exist because of cheap immigrant labor—California's agricultural industry comes to mind. Absent the immigrants, the farm jobs would disappear too, along with an array of jobs from the fields to the packing plant. We would import the asparagus and the strawberries instead.

Illegal immigrants do affect prices in the United States. One study calculated that the surge in immigration experienced between 1980 and 2000 reduced the average price of services such as housekeeping or gardening by more than 9 percent, mainly by undercutting wages. Still, it had a negligible impact on natives' wages because poor illegal immigrants compete in the job market with other poor illegal immigrants.

Immigration policy has always been determined by who bears its costs and who draws its benefits. Illegal immigrants are tolerated by the political system because their cheap labor is useful for agribusiness and other industries. It provides affordable nannies to middle-class Americans. This suggests that despite presidential lip service to the need to reform immigration law, nothing much is likely to be done. Creating a legal path for illegal immigrants to work in the United States would be politically risky and could provide a big incentive for more illegal flows. By contrast, cutting illegal immigration entirely would be prohibitively costly. The status quo is too comfortable to bear tinkering like that.

The ebb and flow of immigration will continue to be determined by potential immigrants' measuring the prospect of a minimum-wage job—perhaps a first step up the ladder of prosperity—against the costs imposed by the harsh border. The price may occasionally be too high. As joblessness soared following the financial crisis of 2008, many potential immigrants decided to stay at home. The Department of Homeland Security estimates the illegal immigrant population dropped by 1 million from its peak in 2007 to 10.8 million in 2009. But this will prove to be no more than a blip in the broad historical trend.

## PRICES RULE

Considering the capacity of prices to shape people's choices, it is rather surprising that governments do not use them more often to steer the behavior of the governed. For instance, public-health campaigns might be a nice way to educate people about the risks of certain behaviors, such as smoking and drug abuse. But they are nowhere near as effective as prices when it comes to making people stop. Four decades after President Richard Nixon launched his "War on Drugs," drug abuse remains stubbornly popular. Between 1988 and 2009, the share of twelfth graders who admitted having done drugs in the last month increased from 16 to 23 percent. The share of teens who had smoked a cigarette in the same period fell from 28 to 20 percent.

This is a paradox. Though it is illegal for minors to purchase cigarettes, adults can readily get them. Drugs, by contrast, are illegal for everybody. Being caught with even a smidgen of cocaine in the state of Illinois can lead to one to three years in jail. Yet the difference is less paradoxical considering how the price of these vices has evolved. A battery of city, state, and federal taxes has roughly doubled the price of a pack of cigarettes since 1990, to about $5.20 on average. On July 1, 2010, the minimum price of a pack of cigarettes in New York City rose $1.60 to $10.80—of which $7.50 are taxes. By contrast, the retail price of a gram of cocaine on New York's streets cost $101 in 2007, about 27 percent less than in 1991. The price of heroin collapsed 41 percent to $320 a gram. Falling prices reflect the failure of policies to stop the supply of illegal drugs into the American market. But it also suggests a potential solution: at a sufficiently high price, teens would cut back. Compared with a failed drug war, legalizing, regulating, and taxing drugs might be the more effective route to curtail abuse.

Consider what we could achieve by tinkering with the price of gas. In the United States, cheap gas allowed people to move to bigger homes farther from work, school, and shopping. Just in the last decade or so, Americans' median commute to work rose from nine to eleven miles. The typical home grew from 1,750 to 1,807 square feet.

Europe rarely sprawled so. Its cities were constrained by history. They were built hundreds of years ago, when moving long distances was costly in time and effort. During the French Revolution, it took King Louis XVI twenty-one hours to flee 150 miles from Paris to Varennes. Modern sprawl was contained by gas taxes. Europeans pay two to three times as much as Americans for gas. That's partly why Houston in Texas has roughly the same population as the German port city of Hamburg but 2,500 fewer people per square mile.

For all the differences between the configuration of American and Western European cities, they are both strikingly different from development in the Soviet bloc, where market prices played little or no role in allocating land. Seventy years of communist allocation by bureaucratic fiat produced an urban scene pockmarked by old factories decaying on prime locations downtown while residential housing becomes denser farther from the center, through rings of Stalin-era, Khrushchev-era, and Brezhnev-era apartments.

A study by World Bank urban planning and housing finance experts after the collapse of the Soviet Union found that 31.5 percent of the built-up area in Moscow was occupied by industries, compared to 6 percent in Seoul and 5 percent in Hong Kong and Paris. In Paris, where people pay a premium price to live near downtown's amenities, the population density peaks some three kilometers from the center of town. In Moscow it peaked fifteen kilometers away.

Prices make sense of many disparate dynamics over the span of human history. Advances in transportation technology that reduced the cost of distance enabled the first great wave of economic globalization in the nineteenth century. The obesity pandemic was bound to happen when bodies designed to survive in an environment of scarce food by gorging themselves whenever they could found themselves awash in cheap and abundant calories brought by modern technology.

There are few better ways to understand the power of prices than to visit the places where they are not allowed to do their jobs. During a trip to Santiago de Cuba a few years ago I was driven around town by a bedraggled woman who, to my surprise, turned out to be a pediatrician at the city's main hospital. She had a witchlike quality—knotty and thin as a reed. Two of her front teeth were missing. She told me they fell out during a bout of malnutrition that swept through the island after the Soviet collapse in 1991 cut off Cuba's economic lifeline. The doctor owned a beat-up Lada. She was very smart. But otherwise her life seemed no different from that of any street urchin, living off the black market at the limit of endurance, peddling a ride or a box of cigars that fell off the back of a truck. She charged ten dollars for driving me around town all day. I couldn't help wondering how the collective decisions that shaped Cuba's possibilities at the time could make it so a pediatrician found this to be a worthwhile deal.

## WHEN PRICES MISFIRE

As with anything powerful, prices must be handled with care. Tinkering can produce unintended consequences. Concerned about low birthrates, in May 2004 the Australian government announced it would pay a "baby bonus" of three thousand Australian dollars to children born after July 1. The response was immediate. Expectant mothers near their due dates delayed planned cesarean sections and did anything in their power to hold their babies back. Births declined throughout June. And on July 1, Australia experienced more births than on any single date in the previous three decades.

Taxing families based on the number of windows in their homes must have seemed like a good idea when King William III introduced the window tax in England in 1696. Homes with up to ten windows paid two shillings. Properties with ten to twenty windows paid four shillings and those with more than twenty paid eight.

The tax was logical. Windows being easy to count, it was easy to levy. It was fairish: richer people were likely to have bigger houses with more windows, and thus pay more. And it got around people's intense hostility to an income tax. But the king didn't count on people's reaction. They blocked up windows in their homes in order to pay less. Today, blocked-out windows in Edinburgh are known as Pitt's Pictures, after William Pitt, who brought the tax to Scotland in 1784.

Seemingly modest actions can reverberate throughout society by altering, if only slightly, people's evaluations of costs and benefits. Such is the case of the 55 mph speed limit imposed across the United States in 1974 as a way to conserve gasoline in the wake of the first oil crisis, when Arab countries proclaimed an oil embargo in response to the United States' decision to resupply the Israeli military after the Yom Kippur War.

Conserving gas was a reasonable objective at the time. The strategy, however, was fatally flawed because it ignored the value of drivers' time. At the new legal limit, a seventy-mile trip would take about one hour and sixteen minutes—sixteen minutes more than at 70 mph. Considering that the wages of production workers in 1974 averaged around $4.30 an hour, those sixteen minutes to commute to and from work would cost a typical worker about $1.15.

In 1974, a gallon of leaded gas cost fifty-three cents. To break even, an average driver would need to save 2.17 gallons per trip. For this to happen would have required a big leap in fuel economy: a 22 percent increase in the fuel efficiency of a Chevy Suburban, for example, or a doubling of the fuel efficiency of a Honda Civic. Of course, lowering the speed limit did not achieve this improvement. So drivers ignored the new rule.

In 1984, drivers on interstate highways in New York were found to flout the 55 mph limit 83 percent of the time. They dished out $50 to $300 to buy CB radios to warn one another about cops nearby. Between 1966 and 1973 there were about 800,000 CB licenses issued by the Federal Communications Commission. By 1977 there were 12.25 million CBs on the road. Cops then reacted to the reaction, installing radar. Drivers reacted with radar detectors. Some states passed laws making radar detectors illegal. I doubt the United States Congress expected this chain of events when it passed the 1974 Emergency Highway Energy Conservation Act. By 1987 it increased the maximum limit to 65 mph and in 1995 it repealed the federal speed limit altogether.

## WHERE WILL PRICES TAKE US?

Archimedes of Syracuse, the great mathematician from the third century BC, said that to move the earth he needed only a lever, a fulcrum, and a firm place to stand. Moving people requires a price. The marriage rate has fallen not because of changing fashions but because of its rising price, measured in terms of the sacrifice it entails. We have fewer children because they are costlier. Economists suggest that the Catholic Church has been losing adherents not because people stopped believing in God but because membership became too cheap compared with evangelical Christianity, which demands a bigger investment in its churches from members and thus inspire more loyalty.

*The Price of Everything* will take us to the store, where we will discover how price tags operate on our psychology, subtly inviting us to buy. But we will endeavor beyond quotidian commercial transactions, to investigate how other prices affect the way people live. In many cultures, husbands pay for multiple brides to amass as many as possible and increase their reproductive success. In others, parents abort female fetuses to avoid the cost they would incur to marry off their daughters. Many behaviors that we ascribe to "cultural change" arise, in fact, as we adapt our budgets to changing prices. We will ponder why employers pay for workers rather than enslave them. We will discuss why it is that as we become progressively richer, the commodity that increases most in value is our scarce free time. And we will find that despite clinging to the notion that life is priceless, we often put a rather low price on our lives.

And we will find that prices can steer us the wrong way too. We still don't know how much we will have to pay, as a civilization, for the economic distortions caused by the upward spiral in the price of American homes between 2000 and 2006. A century down the road, the cheap gasoline of the 1900s might come to be seen as the cause of incalculable environmental damage. Prices can be dangerous too.

# CHAPTER ONE

# The Price of Things

**OF THE VARIOUS** things I don't fully understand about my life, one is why I pay what I do for a cup of coffee. I'm a fairly heavy drinker— I took it up when I first quit smoking, to fill the space left behind by my previous addiction. It has since become my main source of sustenance: my breakfast, my lunch, and quencher of urges in between.

Several possibilities cross my path as I commute between home and work every day. There's the Dunkin' Donuts across the street from work, which offers a cappuccino for $3.02, and the Illy in-house café on the fourteenth floor, one floor above my office, which proffers cappuccinos for $3.50. The Dean & DeLuca store that opened in the lobby sells a slow yet rich cappuccino for $3.27.

Over the past couple of years I have gravitated somewhat randomly from coffee purveyor to coffee purveyor. While this may appear unremarkable, I find my fickle taste intriguing. My choice of coffee should be a function of the value I get for my money. But the equation is not obvious. Should I even notice the small price differences, trivial amounts when compared with my disposable income? What else, besides the quality of the brew, enters my calculation? My switch from Dunkin' to Illy probably had less to do with price, or flavor, than with Illy's sleek brushed steel, a definite step up from Dunkin Donuts' orange-and-pink, saturated fat aesthetic. Illy also offered meaningful social interactions in the chance encounters with long-lost colleagues from other floors.

Most intriguing of all, there is an undeniable emotional angle to my preferences, which can trump on occasion every other consideration. The best coffee I've had in a long time comes from the tiny pie shop on the corner, half a block from my house. It used to sell a superb cappuccino for the unbelievable price of $2.75. I would stop by for a cup as often as I could. Then, a year or two ago, it abruptly raised the price to $3.50. This made me so furious I decided never to drink coffee there again.

I'm not sure what infuriated me so. The friendly barista offered explanations: they were switching to a premium coffee that cost a dollar an ounce; the new cups were bigger; they were using double shots—more than half an ounce of coffee per cup. Maybe I was disappointed at seeing a bargain vanish. Maybe it was a sense of betrayal that the young, laid-back, indie-rock-loving people at the pie shop on the corner could strategize about prices as ruthlessly as Starbucks. I would grumble that rent, wages, and profit make up a bigger share of the price of a cup of coffee than the cost of the coffee that goes into it. Still, my anger made no sense. Their coffee did not cost much more than coffee I bought elsewhere. And it tasted much better. There was something irrational about my boycott. Fortunately, I forgave them. So I'm drinking great coffee again.

• • •

**BUYING GOODS AND** services makes up a large part of modern life. There's food, clothes, movie tickets, summer vacations, utility bills and mortgage insurance premiums, gas, iTunes downloads, and haircuts. The marketplace is where prices acquire their most straightforward definition, determined by a voluntary transaction between a buyer and a seller who expect to benefit from the trade. Yet despite the routine nature of the standard mercantile transaction, consumers' interactions with prices are fairly complex. This chapter is about this economic interaction, the tango between buyers and sellers as they strive for a deal.

Economists tend to assume people know what they are doing when they open their wallets. They can assess the benefit they will derive from whatever it is they are buying and figure out whether it's worth their money. It's hard to overstate the importance of this assumption. It is one of the bedrock principles upon which classical economics was built over the last 250 years. It is often true, and has yielded deep and far-reaching conclusions about human behavior.

But as a general principle, the assumption is misleading in a subtle yet important way. Markets may be the most effective institution known to humanity to determine the value of goods and services to the people who consume them. Still, the price-setting process is by no means a transparent and straightforward interaction between rational, all-knowing calculators of costs and benefits. That's because market transactions do not necessarily provide people with what they want; they provide people with what they think they want. These two things are not the same. Consumers often have but the most tenuous grasp of why they pay what they do for a given object of their desire. Sometimes they don't know why the object is desirable at all. Moved by any number of unacknowledged biases, they are easy prey to manipulative devices deployed by those who want to sell them things.

Prices help us understand these cognitive lacunae. They provide a road map of people's psychological quirks, of their fears, their unacknowledged constraints. Prices—how they are set, how people react to them—can tell us who people really are.

Most of us have heard of the placebo effect—in which a pill with no therapeutic properties relieves a real ailment by making us believe that we are being cured, setting in motion some inner psychological process. A few years ago, psychologist Dan Ariely from the Massachusetts Institute of Technology and some colleagues performed an experiment that uncovered an interesting variant. They told a bunch of students they were getting a new type of painkiller but gave them a placebo instead. Then the researchers made up the placebo's price. Subjects who were told that the pill cost $2.50 reported much deeper pain reduction than those who were told it was bought on the cheap, at the bulk price of $0.10.

Consider lap dancing. Lust is a reasonable explanation for the popularity of the service, about as close as one can legally get to paying for sex outside the state of Nevada. Yet apparently there are hidden gradations of desire that modulate our willingness to pay. In an exploration of the "gentlemen's club" scene, psychologists from the University of New Mexico found that lap dancers who were not on the pill made much more money in the most fertile phase of their menstrual cycle.

Dancers can't charge explicitly for their services because that would run afoul of laws against solicitation. Instead, they rely on "tips," usually enforced by large, muscled bouncers. In Albuquerque's clubs, according to the study, the average tip for a three-minute dance is about fourteen dollars.

Perhaps dancers smell more enticing when they are at the peak of their fertility. Maybe they grind their hips more enthusiastically or whisper more alluring nothings. The fact is that dancers who are not on the pill made $354 a night when they were at their most fertile, about $90 more than in the ten days before menstruation and about $170 more than during menstruation.

Dancers on the pill made less money than those who were not, and their earnings were much less sensitive to the menstrual cycle. But perhaps the most interesting finding is that neither dancers nor their patrons have a clue of the effect of the menstrual cycle on their pay. It all happens below the radar.

**THE TASTES IN** shopping of my six-year-old are driven by the fictitious character on the label, oblivious to price, flavor, texture, or even the purpose of the desired item. At his behest, I've bought Dr. Seuss shampoo, Spider-Man toothbrushes, and Cinderella toothpaste. He alternates between Dora the Explorer and SpongeBob yogurt. His tastes are not unique. A study by the people who make *Sesame Street* found that young children who are offered a choice between chocolate and broccoli are more than twice as likely to choose the vegetable when it has an Elmo sticker.

Grown-ups are expected to know better. Yet we indulge in more extreme follies, paying often-stratospheric prices for things of debatable value. People will travel across town to save $20 off a $100 sweater but not to save $20 off a $1,000 computer, an odd choice considering that both actions are priced equally: $20 for a trip across town. And, unlike my six-year-old son, who couldn't care less what toothpaste costs, I may be more willing to buy something if it is expensive than if it is cheap.

Buying wine is an exercise that combines flavor, smell, and other physical attributes with an array of difficult-to-measure qualities— from how well it projects our self-image to whether it brings forth pleasant memories of a European vacation. Americans will pay more for a French wine than an Argentine wine of similar quality, the same grape varietal, and the same age. Simply stamping "Product of Italy" on the label can raise the price of a bottle by more than 50 percent.

Economists will tell you that, other things being equal, people will always prefer the cheaper option. But drinkers like a bottle of wine more if they are told it cost ninety dollars a bottle than if they are told it cost ten. Belief that the wine is more expensive turns on the neurons in the medial orbitofrontal cortex, an area of the brain associated with pleasure feelings.

Wine without a price tag doesn't have this effect. In 2008, American food and wine critics teamed up with a statistician from Yale and a couple of Swedish economists to study the results of thousands of blind tastings of wines ranging from $1.65 to $150 a bottle. They found that when they can't see the price tag, people prefer cheaper wine to pricier bottles. Experts' tastes did move in the proper direction: they favored finer, more expensive wines. But the bias was almost imperceptible. A wine that cost ten times more than another was ranked by experts only seven points higher on a scale of one to one hundred.

Sometimes people pay stratospheric prices for humdrum items because doing so proves that they can. As the price of oil soared to around $150 a barrel in the summer of 2008, Saeed Khouri, a twenty-five-year-old businessman from Abu Dhabi, made it into *Guinness World Records* for having bought the most expensive license plate ever. Khouri paid $14 million for the "1" tag in a national license plate auction that drew Rolls and Bentley owners from around the kingdom. The number one is, to be sure, a nice digit to have stamped on a piece of plastic attached to the front and back of a car. But it is hard to argue that the number alone merits a premium of $13,999,905 over the standard fee for a regular license plate.

This behavior is surprisingly common, however. Paying high prices for pointless trinkets is just an expensive way to show off. In his famous *Theory of the Leisure Class*, the nineteenth-century American social theorist Thorstein Veblen argued that the rich engaged in what he dubbed "conspicuous consumption" to signal their power and superiority to those around them. In the 1970s, the French sociologist Pierre Bourdieu wrote that aesthetic choices served as social markers for those in power to signal their superiority and set themselves apart from inferior groups. Anybody can buy stocks. Oligarchs, emirs, and hedge-fund managers can pay $106.5 million for Picasso's *Nu au Plateau de Sculpteur,* which sold in only eight minutes and six seconds at an auction in New York in May of 2010. Had Mr. Khouri paid ninety-five dollars for a license plate, he could have been anybody.

Over the last three decades, evolutionary biologists and psychologists picked up on Veblen's and Bourdieu's ideas and gave them a twist. The point of spending huge sums on useless baubles is not merely to project an abstract notion of power. It serves to signal one's fitness to potential mates. Wasteful spending on pointless luxury is not to be frowned upon; it is an essential tool to help our genes survive into the next generation. Sexual selection puts an enormous value on costly, inane displays of resources. What else is the peacock's tail but a marker of fitness aimed at the peahens on the mating market? It is a statement that the bird is fit enough to expend an inordinate amount of energy on a spray of pointless color.

A diamond ring has a similar purpose. N. W. Ayer, the advertising agency behind "A Diamond Is Forever," which crafted the marketing strategy for the global diamond cartel De Beers in the United States, persuaded American women to desire big diamond engagement rings, and men to buy one for them, by convincing them that these expensive bits of rock symbolized success. They gave big diamonds to movie stars and planted stories in magazines about how they symbolized their indestructible love. And they took out ads in elite magazines depicting paintings by Picasso, Derain, or Dalí to indicate that diamonds were in the same luxury class. "The substantial diamond gift can be made a more widely sought symbol of personal and family success—an expression of socio-economic achievement," said an N. W. Ayer report from the 1950s. Today 84 percent of American brides get a diamond engagement ring, at an average cost of $3,100.

In 2008 Armin Heinrich, a software developer in Germany, created the ultimate Veblen good: he designed an application for the iPhone called I Am Rich. It did nothing but flash a glowing red gem on the screen. Its point was its expense: $999. Maybe stung by criticism over its banality, Apple removed it the day after its release. But before it could pull it, six people had bought it to prove that, indeed, they were.

## A HISTORY OF PRICES

Value—what confers it, what it means—has captivated thinkers at least since ancient Greece. But the concept then was different from that of contemporary economics. For hundreds of years, the analysis of value began as a moral inquiry. Aristotle was sure things had a natural, just price—an inherent value that existed before any transaction was made. And justice was the province of God.

Throughout the Middle Ages, when the Catholic Church regulated virtually all corners of economic life in Europe, scholars understood value as a manifestation of divine justice. Inspired by Saint Matthew's notion that one should do unto others only what one would have them do unto oneself, Thomas Aquinas stated that trade must convey equal benefits to both parties and condemned selling something for more than its "real" value.

In the thirteenth century, the Dominican friar Albertus Magnus posited that virtuous exchanges were those in which the goods that were transacted contained the same amount of work and other expenses. This idea was refined into the principle that the inherent value of goods was set by the work that went into them.

The Church gradually lost its grip on society as trade and private enterprise expanded throughout Europe. Religious dogma lost its appeal as an analytical tool. Still, the penchant to view prices through the lens of justice survived the development of capitalism, thriving well into the eighteenth century. Adam Smith and David

Ricardo, the two foremost thinkers of the classical age of economics, struggled with the notion of inherent value, which they viewed as a function of the labor content of products, distinct from the market price set by the vagaries of supply and demand. Smith, for instance, argued that the labor value of products amounted to whatever it cost to feed, clothe, house, and educate workers to make them—with a little extra to allow them to reproduce.

But this line of argument got stuck. For one, it had no role for capital. Profits were an immoral aberration in a world in which the only value could come from a worker's toil. Moreover, it didn't seem to square with common sense. In Ricardo's day critics were harsh on the labor theory of value. Some pointed out that the only thing that made aged wine more valuable than young wine was time in a cellar, not work. But before the idea could die, Karl Marx took it to what seemed like its logical conclusion. He used the labor theory of value as a basis for the proposition that capitalists used their leverage as the owners of machinery and other means of production to filch value from their workers.

A product, Marx maintained, is worth all the labor that went into making it, including the labor used to make the necessary tools, the labor in the tools used to make the tools, and so forth. Capitalists made money by usurping part of this value—paying workers only enough to guarantee their subsistence and keeping the rest of the value they created for themselves. This line of thinking could easily lead a thinker astray. Marx concluded that despite appearances, the value relation between different things—their relative price— had nothing to do with the properties of these things. Rather, it was determined by the labor time that went into them. "It is a definite social relation between men that assumes in their eyes the fantastic form of a relation between things," he wrote.

This shares some of the cool strangeness characteristic of mystic thought, where things are representations of some deeper phenomenon underneath the skin of reality. But it sheds no light on why

I find a glass of cold beer so much more valuable than a glass of warm beer on a hot day. I will buy a head of lettuce if its use value to me—because it is crunchy, fresh, and healthy—is higher than its price, what I have to forgo in order to get it. But if some desperate lettuce lover accosts me on my way home to offer twice what I paid, I will sell it to her at that higher price. There is no mysterious relationship between its intrinsic value and its market price. There are just two people who take different degrees of satisfaction from eating lettuce.

There's a cool trick that teachers have used for years to expose students to the power of this transaction. First they distribute bags with assortments of candies among their students and ask them how much they value the gift—what would they be willing to pay for their stash? Then they allow them to trade candy among themselves. If students are asked again after the exchange to assess the value of their booty, they will invariably give it a higher value than the first time. That's because trading allowed them to match their lot to their preferences. They traded things they valued less for things they valued more. Nobody worked, yet the value of the entire allotment of candies grew.

The realization that things do not possess an absolute, inherent value seeped into economic thought in the nineteenth century. Marx's labor theory of value eventually faded into irrelevance as nobody could figure out how his concept related to the prices at which people voluntarily bought and sold real things. Things are costly to make, of course. This puts a floor on the price at which they are supplied. But the value of a product does not live inside it. It is a subjective quantity determined by the seller and the buyer. The relative value of exchanged things is their relative price. This realization lifted prices into their rightful spot as indicators of human preferences and guides of humankind.

## TAMING PRICES

Two people will be willing to trade one good for another as long as the perceived benefit from owning one more unit of what they get—the *marginal* gain—is at least as much as the lost value of what each trades away. This gain, in turn, is determined by the buyer's endowment of goods: money, time, and whatever else might come into her calculation. The more one has of a given thing, the less one will value having one more. This single principle is the organizing force of markets, which determines the prices of goods and services around the world.

In a market, sellers' priority is usually to squeeze as much money as possible from buyers. Buyers, in turn, will try to get stuff they want as cheaply as they can. They each operate within a set of constraints: for buyers a budget; for sellers, the cost of producing, storing, advertising, and bringing to market whatever they make. While producers can raise prices if consumer demand for their good grows faster than its supply, consumer demand will wane as prices rise. Above all, producers' space to raise prices is constrained by competition. In a competitive market consumers can safely assume that prices will be kept in check as rival producers vying for consumers' custom force them down to their marginal cost, the cost of making one more unit.

There are lots of exceptions to this dynamic, however. To begin with, fully competitive markets are rare. In markets for new inventions, legal monopolies called patents allow companies to charge higher prices than they would in a competitive field in order to recover the up-front cost of their invention. Local monopolies are common—think of the popcorn vendor inside the movie theater. Even in markets for run-of-the-mill products, producers will do their best to keep competition at bay. A tried and tested tactic is to convince consumers that their product is unique, muddying comparisons with rivals' wares. Another is to lock in consumers with a cheap product that, it later becomes apparent, only works in conjunction with some higher-priced good. Another is simply to hide their prices from consumers' view.

Unacknowledged motivations cloud the assessments of value that drive our daily decisions. My monthly dues of $58.65 at the New York Sports Club next to the office mean that each of my twice-weekly visits costs just under $7—a reasonable price for a two-hour session, less than what I would pay to see a movie or have a quick lunch. But there are those who will pay much more than I do for a session on the Stairmaster. Paradoxically perhaps, they aren't the fitness freaks. The uncommitted couch potatoes pay the highest prices. That's because they are paying for more than a workout. They are buying a commitment-booster too.

A study of visitors to sports clubs that offered monthly subscriptions for just over seventy dollars or single passes for just over ten found that monthly subscribers paid more than they had to. They visited the gym 4.8 times per month, on average, paying some seventeen dollars per visit. Still, having a membership might improve their health, giving them a monetary incentive to work out.

Every day we commit to buying goods and services without paying careful attention to their cost. In 2009, the HP DeskJet D2530 printer might have seemed a steal at $39.99. But the price, displayed prominently on the HP Web site, was almost irrelevant. The more relevant numbers were $14.99 for a black ink cartridge, which prints about 200 pages, and $19.99 for the color cartridge, which prints 165. For those printing photos at home, the crucial number was $21.99 for the HP 60 Photo Value Pack, a set of cartridges and 50 standard sheets of photo paper. At the Rite-Aid drugstore, 50 same-day prints cost $9.50.

The worldwide printing business depends on selling cheap printers and expensive ink. According to a study by *PC World,* printers will issue out-of-ink warnings when the cartridge is still up to 40 percent full. HP, Epson, Canon, and others have sued providers of cheap ink refills, charging them with false advertising and patent infringement to make them stop. But the best ally of the printer business is consumer ignorance about what they are really paying to print.

Just setting the printer default to "draft" quality would save consumers hundreds of dollars a year. Yet few consumers do. Though many companies still sell cheaper ink refills, refills account for only 10 to 15 percent of the market. That means that 90 percent of printing is still done using ink that, according to the *PC World* analysis, costs $4,731 per gallon. You might as well fill your ink cartridges with 1985 vintage Krug champagne.

**CONSUMERS CAN ALSO** strategize keenly to fit their wants and needs to their budgets. As gas prices surged, drivers drove some 7 billion fewer miles on American highways in January 2009 than they did a year earlier, a decline of about twenty-two miles per person. During a run-up in gas prices between 2000 and 2005, economists at the University of California at Berkeley and Yale found that as the price of gas doubled from $1.50 to $3, families became more careful shoppers, paying between 5 and 11 percent less for each item. The typical price paid for a box of cereal at one large California grocery chain fell 5 percent. The share of fresh chicken bought on sale jumped by half.

But businesses are usually a step ahead. Nobody understands for sure what drove surging prices of agricultural commodities in 2007 and 2008. Analysts have mentioned drought in important growing areas, rising transportation costs and fertilizer prices, the diversion of maize and other crops to produce fuel, and even improving diets in big developing countries like India and China. Whatever the reason, food companies were remarkably adept at protecting profit margins by quietly reducing the size of their portions while keeping the price the same. Wrigley's took two sticks of gum out of its $1.09 pack of Juicy Fruits. Hershey's shrank its chocolate bars. General Mills offered smaller Cheerios boxes.

Then, as recession took hold in 2009 and agricultural prices started falling, firms resorted to the opposite tactic: giving consumers more for less and announcing it loudly. Frito-Lay packed 20 percent more Cheetos into each bag, stamping the bags with a "Hey! There's 20 percent more free fun to share in here." French's tried competing against itself to convince customers it offered a killer deal. It launched a twenty-ounce bottle of its Classic Yellow mustard for $1.50, less than the $1.93 at which it sold its fourteen-ounce bottle.

What really tames prices is the presence of more than one producer in the marketplace. If munchers had no other option but Frito-Lay products, the company would have less of an incentive to put more Cheetos into the bag and trumpet it to the world. Had there been no other confectioners around, Hershey's might have raised the price of its chocolate bars even after shrinking them. But the price of a product must mesh within a universe populated by other brands of sweets and snacks. How well it fits will determine its overall success. This is consumers' most significant defense against corporations' power: competition.

The power of competition is writ all over the cost of a phone call. In 1983, shortly after the government broke up AT&T's monopoly of the American telephone market, AT&T charged $5.15 for a ten-minute transcontinental daytime call. By 1989 it charged $2.50 for the call. Today an AT&T subscriber on the $5-per-month international plan can call Beijing for eleven cents a minute and London for eight cents.

In Britain, it was the government that held a monopoly over telecommunications. But in 1981 the government of Margaret Thatcher allowed Mercury Communications, a private company, to offer competing phone service, and in 1984 it spun off the state-run British Telecom. On February 1, 1982, the rate of a three-minute call from London to New York was cut from £2.13 to £1.49. Today, as long as one keeps each call at under an hour, BT's international package offers an unlimited number of calls from London to New York for £4.99 per month.

Competition can protect us from runaway printing prices. Fat profits from overpriced ink allow companies like HP to compete by selling printers at less than what it costs to make them. Others employ different tactics. Kodak's ESP printers are about 30 percent more expensive than similar models, but the ink cartridges cost as little as ten dollars and print about three hundred pages. Regardless of the mix of tactics, the overall price of printing should fall as printer makers vie to win market share.

**CONSIDER WHAT HAPPENS** when there is little or no competition in a market. Steve Blank, a former Silicon Valley entrepreneur who teaches a customer development class at the University of California at Berkeley, used to tell his students about Sandra Kurtzig, the founder of a company that in the 1970s designed the first business enterprise software for small companies that could run on microcomputers rather than huge mainframes.

When she walked in to make her first sales pitch, Ms. Kurtzig had no idea of what to ask for her system, so she mentioned the biggest number she thought a rational person would pay: $75,000. But when the buyer wrote the number down without flinching, she realized she had made a mistake. "Per year," she added quickly. The company man wrote that down too. Only when Ms. Kurtzig added maintenance at 25 percent per year did the buyer object, so she cut it to 15 percent. According to Mr. Blank, the company buyer said, "Okay." Ms. Kurtzig could do this because she was offering a unique service in a specialized industry with few competitors, and thus had great freedom to set her prices. But where there are many rivals it is impossible to achieve this kind of market power. The mere threat of competition can move companies to respond. Indeed, for many years the threat that Southwest Airways would start flying on a given route would prompt other carriers to lower fares on that route, to preemptively buy customers' loyalty.

Walmart drove supermarkets to despair when it expanded into groceries in 1988, offering prices 15 to 25 percent cheaper than the competition. The opening of a Walmart supercenter caused sales at other grocers in the neighborhood to fall 17 percent, on average, according to one study, amounting to $250,000 worth of forgone revenues each month. To remain in business, its rivals were soon forced to follow its lead. A study of retail prices in 165 cities across the United States between 1982 and 2002 found that the opening of a new Walmart in the long run forced rivals in the area to cut prices on products like aspirin, shampoo, and toothpaste by 7 to 13 percent.

Like most businesses, Walmart cuts prices only when there are competitors around. One study found that it charged 6 percent more in Franklin, Tennessee, where it had virtually no competition, than in Nashville, where it had to compete with rival Kmart. Critics argue that Walmart decimates communities, forcing local retailers into the ground. The company's relentless push for the cheapest products has driven many suppliers to relocate to low-cost China, contributing to the decline of American manufacturing. Still, Walmart's competitive drive has definitely benefited Americans in their roles as consumers. Its impact has been so powerful that, according to one study, the Department of Commerce overstates American inflation by about 15 percent because the sample it uses does not include Walmart's low food prices.

## KEEPING COMPETITION AT BAY

In 2005 Detroit's automakers—General Motors, Ford, and Chrysler—used a novel tactic to unload their bloated inventories and revive their flagging finances. They offered customers an unprecedented deal to buy a car at the same discounted price they usually reserved for employees. When GM launched its "Employee Discount for Everyone" program in June, sales jumped 40 percent. When Chrysler launched its "Employee Pricing Plus" in July, it sold the most cars ever.

But upon closer inspection, the promotions weren't such a great deal. A study by economists at the University of California, Berkeley, and the Massachusetts Institute of Technology found that many cars could have been purchased for less before the employee discount program was launched. For a majority of GM and Chrysler models, and a substantial share of Ford's, customers paid more in the two weeks of the promotion than they could have in the two weeks before its launch. They were simply told they were getting a bargain and they believed it.

If competition is a consumer's best friend, corporations' favorite countervailing strategy is to keep consumers from figuring out where they can get the best available deal. Unlike the competitive utopia described in economic models, where consumers can effortlessly compare competing products to make their choices, the real world is plagued with what Nobel laureate George Stigler called search costs. It is difficult for consumers to find out what a given product costs in all the shops in town—let alone everything available on the Internet. It is even tougher if the goods are not identical. This is a shortcoming that businesses can exploit.

For many companies, evading competition is a question of survival. Makers of everything from cars and computer chips to shoes and TV sets experience what is known as increasing returns to scale: each additional microchip costs less to make than the preceding one. Companies can obtain raw materials and parts more cheaply the more they buy. They also share the cost of investments in machinery and the like among more products, reducing the cost per unit. This dynamic presents companies with a challenging conundrum: competition, when operating properly, would drive the price of TV sets and microchips relentlessly down until they were barely above whatever it cost to make the last one. If this were to happen, makers of chips and TV sets would go out of business. At that price, they wouldn't be able to recover all their costs. Fortunately for them, there are ways to wriggle free to some extent from competition's constraints. One of the best-known techniques is to make it difficult for customers to understand where they can get the best value for their money.

At the Fairway supermarket in Brooklyn where I take my son shopping on weekends, the pricey organic section is segregated from everything else, lest a price-conscious shopper decide to get the cheaper plain cereal this time. Similar items are strategically placed far from each other across the vast space, discouraging price comparisons. There's fancy fresh cheese at a counter on my way in and cheap packaged varieties on my way out. There are at least two different sections for cold cuts and for olive oil. Prepared pasta sauces of different brands seem to be peppered throughout the store. Even fruits are segregated.

Frequent sales and markups also serve as tools to keep customers from working out where the cheapest box of cereal is sold. A study in Israel of four similar products sold across a range of stores from 1993 to 1996 found an enormous variation in prices. Not only did the same can of coffee or bag of flour cost more than twice as much at the most expensive store as at the cheapest; it wasn't always cheapest in the same store. Retailers kept moving the prices around to keep shoppers on their toes.

Even the Internet, a technology that was meant to empower the twenty-first-century consumer by allowing us to compare prices around the world at the click of a mouse, can cloud consumers' understanding. Online retailers of computer chips will muddle product descriptions and offer dozens of different versions to make it tough to comparison shop. They add large and hidden shipping and handling costs, surround products with a cloud of add-ons that have to be stripped out, and offer low-quality products to lure customers to their Web sites and, once there, get them to upgrade.

Some retailers have even figured out how to trick the shop-bots used by price search engines to make them think they are giving the product away for free and appear at the top of the search rankings. Rather than foment transparency, the Internet has encouraged retailers to cheat. Whoever offered a decent product at a fair price would be buried under a pile of "cheaper" superspecial offers by less honorable rivals.

## SEARCHING FOR FOOLS

The killer tactic to identify and reel in the highest-paying customer in a crowd remains the auction. Auctions are designed to find the customer who places the highest value on whatever item is on the block. Daniel Kahneman, the Israeli psychologist who won the Nobel Prize for economics for researching the behavioral quirks that can lead our economic judgment astray, called auctions a tool to "search for fools." That's why sellers love them but buyers don't. A 2006 poll of private equity firms found that 90 percent of them preferred to avoid auctions when buying a company, but 80 to 90 percent favored using them when selling one. The fabled American investor Warren Buffett never omits the warning in Berkshire Hathaway's annual report: "We don't participate in auctions."

They are not necessarily a bad deal for buyers. But buying at auction can be tricky when the value of what's for sale is unknown. For instance, consider a government auction for the right to exploit the airwaves or drill oil wells. If all the bidders know what they are doing, chances are the average bid will reflect the value at which the average oil company or telecommunications firm could profitably exploit the rights. But that means that the winning bid—which will necessarily be above average—will exceed this value. If this is the case, the odds are high that the winner will lose money. That's why it's known as the winner's curse.

The auction, however, is not the only technique available to lure high-paying consumers. In fact, corporations have many subtle and elegant ways to segregate them according to their willingness to pay and exact a higher price from those who value their items most.

Consider, for a moment, how people shop. According to a study of Denver shoppers, families that make more than $70,000 a year pay 5 percent more for the same set of goods than families making less than $30,000. Singles without children pay 10 percent less than families with five members or more. Families headed by people in their early forties pay up to 8 percent more than those in their early twenties or late sixties. Retirees are much more careful shoppers than middle-aged people. They search dutifully for the best deal and end up paying nearly the same amount for the same product. People in middle age, by contrast, buy more carelessly. The prices they pay are thus all over the map.

These patterns arise because of differences in the way people value time and money. Time is relatively more valuable to the rich, who already have money, than for the poor who don't. A janitor in New York making $11 an hour will likely prefer an extra $20 than an extra hour of leisure. A lawyer who makes $500 an hour, by contrast, would probably choose the free time. This affects how each of them will shop. The lawyer will be less inclined to spend hours comparison shopping and instead will pay the first price she sees. The janitor, by contrast, will be more willing to spend a little time to clip coupons, shop around, and get a better deal.

The value of our time also rises with age. That's because wages increase as we proceed on our careers, gain expertise, and acquire seniority. The number of hours in the day, by contrast, does not. As any parent will admit, time actually contracts when one has children competing for attention with household chores, shopping expeditions, and a job. Time is at its most scarce and expensive around age forty-five, when wages and job responsibilities peak while families still have children living at home.

Companies exploit these differences. They charge more for basic staples in supermarkets in rich neighborhoods than in those frequented by lower-income shoppers. Rebates and coupons allow them to sell the same good at two prices—one for poorer coupon clippers and another for the rich who couldn't care less. The technique can be used to discriminate between all sorts of people with different costs of time.

**PEOPLE DIFFER ALONG** dimensions beyond age and wealth. Companies try to target these differences to sell their product to as many customers as possible, extracting from them the maximum price they are willing to pay. Examining the 2008 Zagat restaurant guide for New York City, two economists discovered that restaurants rated as romantic or with a good singles scene charged up to 6.9 percent more for appetizers and up to 14.5 percent more for desserts, relative to the cost of the main course, than did restaurants classified as good places to have business lunches. The reason, they surmised, could well be that couples—if they liked each other—would linger and order an appetizer, perhaps a dessert. It would be unromantic for either to make a fuss about the price. So a restaurant could charge them relatively more for these "romantic" items on the menu.

The technique—called, appropriately, "price discrimination"—is ubiquitous. What else is the student discount at the bookstore, or the cheap matinee ticket on Broadway? Books are published in pricey hardcover months before their paperback edition to capitalize on those who can't wait to read it and will pay more to get it faster. Apple launched an eight-gigabyte iPhone at $599 in June of 2007, to capture the early adopters who would pay anything to be among the first to have one. Two months later it dropped its price to $399.

Airlines are masters at selling seats on a plane at vastly different prices. They honed their techniques over more than thirty years trying to fill flights that cost the same to operate whether they are empty or full. In 1977, American Airlines was the first carrier in the United States to try the gambit, offering cheaper "Super Saver" tickets that required advance purchase and a minimum stay of seven days or more to lure price-conscious leisure travelers. Price variation exploded after airfares were deregulated in 1978, setting off intense competition as airlines strove to fill as many seats on their planes as they could. For a quarter century their most famous technique was the Saturday-night stay rule, used to segregate price-conscious tourists from business travelers who could expense the ticket and would pay anything to get home before the weekend. Today airlines have up to twenty different prices for seats on the same flight, depending on when and where the ticket was bought, how long the trip will last, and several other dimensions. Tickets with restrictions on the days of travel cost about 30 percent less than unrestricted tickets. Travelers who buy their ticket less than a week in advance pay 26 percent more than those who buy it at least three weeks ahead of time. Passengers who stay over a Saturday night pay 13 percent less.

It's a profitable tactic. A study of thousands of pop acts from 1992 to 2005 found that concerts that offered different ticket prices for different sections earned 5 percent more revenue than those that didn't, drawing a more lucrative mix of fans with cheap tickets in the nosebleed section and expensive seats in the front rows. Discrimination works better in cities that are richer and for artists who are older because they generate a more diverse audience: older and wealthier fans who have followed the band since the early days and young new ones who will go hear a band of old-timers provided tickets are cheap. It is now the norm: In 1992 more than half of all gigs sold all seats for the same price. By 2005, only about 10 percent did so.

Some schemes to charge consumers according to their willingness to pay don't work. In the late 1990s Coca-Cola experimented with a vending machine that would automatically charge more for a Coke on warm days. But when Coke chief executive Doug Ivester revealed the project in an interview with the Brazilian news magazine *Veja*, a storm of protest erupted. The *Philadelphia Inquirer* slammed the idea as the "latest evidence that the world is going to hell in a hand basket." An editorial about the idea in the *San Francisco Chronicle* was titled "Coke's Automatic Price Gouging." Pepsi saw the opening and announced it would never "exploit" its hot customers. Ivester defended the plan. He told *Veja*, "It is fair that it should be more expensive. The machine will simply make this process automatic." Still, Coca-Cola dropped the idea.

The Internet is likely to bring price discrimination into every corner of our lives. In September of 2000, Amazon.com was caught offering the same DVDs to different customers at discounts of 30 percent, 35 percent, or 40 percent off the manufacturer's suggested retail price. Amazon said the differential pricing was due to a random price test. It denied that it was segregating customers according to their sensitivity to price, which could be gleaned from their shopping histories recorded on their Amazon profiles. But ever since the incident, consumer advocates have warned that the reams of personal information that people give away when they search, shop, and play on social networking sites online will allow companies to finely tune their prices to fit the profiles of each customer. The less price sensitive, for instance, would be offered pricier versions of articles at the top of a search list. Bargain hunters could be presented with cheaper alternatives first.

The practice isn't evil. Companies prone to economies of scale in competitive businesses often depend on it to raise their average unit price in line with their average unit cost. If they sold everything at the marginal price—the price it cost to make the last single unit—they would not be able to cover their fixed costs and would go out of business. And it can be beneficial to consumers. If Cokes were all sold at the same price, a consumer who would have appreciated a Coke on a mild autumn day if it had been slightly cheaper won't buy it, forgoing what, for him, would have been a profitable acquisition. Allowing Coca-Cola to charge more on hot days and less on mild days would allow more consumers to indulge their taste for a Coke.

Still, price discrimination alone cannot rescue a flawed business model. Airlines prove that it does not even guarantee profitability. For all their efforts at price management, competition has pushed airfares down by about half since 1978, to about 4.16 cents per passenger per mile, before taxes. Most of the major carriers have spent some time in bankruptcy. In terms of operating profits, the industry as a whole spent half the decade from 2000 to 2009 in the red.

## PROTECT US FROM WHAT WE BUY

The understanding of humanity as a set of rational beings able to accurately evaluate costs against benefits, striving to maximize their well-being, remains immensely popular among economists. It is a bedrock belief of the conservative movement in the United States: if we understand our own preferences better than anybody else does, there is no reason for the government to butt into our decisions. It has powerful corollaries. We can't be second-guessed. If we buy something for a given price, it must be worth at least that much to us. The market price of any given thing is the best approximation the world has of the thing's real value to society.

The belief is not empty. It provides a reasonable approximation of real people in many situations. For instance, it provides a satisfactory explanation of why we prefer things we choose to things other people choose for us. Joel Waldfogel, an economist at the University of Pennsylvania, approached a bunch of university students and asked them to compare the value of presents they received with things they had bought themselves. To make the answers comparable, he asked for the minimum amount of money they would demand to give the items up. A total of 202 students responded, providing hypothetical prices for 538 things they had purchased themselves and 1,044 items they had received as gifts. Mr. Waldfogel found that people value what they bought about 18 percent more, per dollar spent, than what they got as a present.

As we will see in subsequent chapters, the model of rational humanity is a powerful tool that can help us understand the behavior of men and women in many walks of life. Yet, at the end of the day, belief in the inerrant ability of our choices to communicate our preferences is inconsistent with how we actually behave. As some of the prior examples might suggest, people often make decisions about prices and values that, upon careful consideration, are inconsistent or shortsighted. We change our minds and rue our actions only minutes later. We knowingly overindulge. We prize what we have more than what we don't.

Students of Duke University, for instance, said they were willing to pay up to $166, on average, for a ticket to the big basketball game—when Duke was one of four teams vying for the championship. But those who had a ticket said they wouldn't sell it for less than $2,411. Economists who trust human rationality see credit as an optimal tool to smooth consumption over our life cycle, allowing us to consume more when we earn less and pay it back later. The rest of us know credit cards can be dangerous. One study found that basketball fans in possession of a credit card would pay twice as much for tickets to a Boston Celtics game as those who had to pay in cash.

And we are often simply inveigled by prices. In the 1960s, the California businessman Dave Gold discovered that charging $0.99 for any bottle of wine in his liquor store increased sales of all his wines, including bottles that had previously cost $0.89 and even $0.79. He left the liquor business, launched the 99 Cents Only chain of stores, and made hundreds of millions. Since then, companies of every stripe have lured us by slapping $0.99 on the price tag. Steve Jobs revolutionized the music industry by persuading us to pay $0.99 for a song. Evidently, the number convinces us we are getting value for money.

Surveying the landscape of our idiosyncratic decision making more than fifteen years ago, Kahneman, the Nobel Prize–winning psychologist, suggested that the government should intervene to curb our tendencies toward the less than rational. We should consider, he wrote, "some paternalistic interventions, when it is plausible that the state knows more about an individual's future tastes than the individual knows presently." Jenny Holzer, an American artist of the 1980s who built her reputation projecting self-evident "truisms" on buildings, building them out of neon signs, and stamping them on T-shirts, addressed the very same human vulnerability on the shiny surface of a BMW race car, emblazoning it with the phrase "protect me from what I want."

# CHAPTER TWO

# The Price of Life

**ONE OF PEOPLE'S** most deeply ingrained convictions is that the price of life is incalculable. An old Jewish teaching holds that if one were to put a single life on one scale and the rest of the world on the other, the scales would be equally balanced. The French novelist Antoine de Saint-Exupéry wondered why "we always act as if something had an even greater price than life" when, self-evidently, "human life is priceless."

I'm not quite sure how this belief came to solidify. It might have been favored by evolution as a spur to avoid predators. Yet while true in the sense that each of us would probably accept parting with all of our worldly possessions in order to avoid certain death, this narrowest of definitions fails to account for the continuous pricing and repricing of life that has taken place since life first crawled out of the primeval swamp. More than a single price, life has a menu.

Government is impossible without a grasp of what the lives of the governed are worth. The guidelines of the United States Environmental Protection Agency, last updated in 1999, value a life at about $7.5 million in 2010 money. Britain's Department of the Environment says each year of life in good health is worth £29,000. A World Bank study in 2007 about the cost estimated that a citizen of India was worth about $3,162 a year, which amounts to a little under $95,000 for an entire life.

Indeed, we are all ready to accept that life has a price tag as long as it's not our own. The ethicist and philosopher Peter Singer suggested a nifty exercise to prove the point: ask yourself how much you would be willing to pay, through insurance premiums say, so the health-care system would cover a treatment to extend the life of a stranger by one year. Would you pay $1 million? $10 million? The moment you say no you have put a ceiling on the price of that person's life. Unsurprisingly, prices like this one tend to be controversial.

## PAYING FOR THE DEAD

Consider the September 11th Victim Compensation Fund, which Congress approved to compensate the injured and the families of those who died in the terrorist attacks against the World Trade Center and the Pentagon in 2001. Moved by generosity, mixed in with concern that victims and their relatives would bury United and American Airlines in lawsuits, Congress established the fund with an unlimited budget. Conscious of cost, however, it set tight criteria for payments, to be based on the "economic and non-economic" loss to a victim's family. This principle set victims' lives along a scale of values. It gave them a price.

Appointed to run the fund was Kenneth Feinberg, a lawyer and former chief of staff of Democratic senator Edward Kennedy, who had an impressive track record as a mediator in tough cases. In 1984 Feinberg brokered the $180 million settlement paid by the manufacturers of the defoliant Agent Orange to some 250,000 Vietnam veterans who had been sickened by exposure to the toxic chemical that was sprayed on Vietnamese fields. He was one of three lawyers who determined the $16 million price paid by the government to the heirs of Abraham Zapruder for the original 26.6-second film he took of the assassination of President John F. Kennedy in Dallas, Texas, on November 22, 1963. Years after he had completed his work for the compensation fund, he was tapped by President Obama to become the White House's "pay czar" and set compensation limits for top executives at the big banks that were bailed out by taxpayers following the financial crisis of 2009. In 2010, he was appointed to administer the $20 billion fund created by oil giant BP to try to repair the damage caused by millions of barrels of oil released into the Gulf of Mexico following the explosion of its Deepwater Horizon rig.

For Feinberg, determining the noneconomic loss of the 9/11 victims was easy. He settled on $250,000 a head plus $100,000 per dependent, which he recognized as absolutely arbitrary. Measuring economic loss was more difficult. The concept of economic loss was meant to capture the forgone earnings of a dead worker, adjusted for his or her age, marital status, and number of dependents. This ensured big gaps between awards. It pitted the multimillion-dollar paycheck earned by executives at the brokerage Cantor Fitzgerald working on the 105th floor of the World Trade Center's North Tower against the $17,337 a year made by an illegal immigrant from Peru who worked as a cook at the Windows on the World restaurant five floors above them.

Senator Kennedy, his former boss, gave him some advice: "Ken, just make sure that 15 percent of the families don't receive 85 percent of the taxpayers' money." But despite the suggestion, victims' value in death reflected the inequality they experienced while alive. Bankers were deemed to be worth more than janitors and the young more than the old. Men in their thirties were priced at about $2.8 million. Men over seventy, by contrast, were deemed worth less than $600,000. The women who worked and died in the World Trade Center and the Pentagon earned, on average, less than men. That implied that their value in death—the sum total of what Mr. Feinberg estimated they would have made during their lifetimes—was also lower. The average compensation to their families amounted to about 37 percent less, on average, than men's. The fund ultimately paid about $2 million, on average, to the next of kin of 2,880 victims who died in the attacks. But each of the families of the eight victims who earned more than $4 million a year got $6.4 million, while the cheapest victim was valued at $250,000.

This cold accounting is about as far as one can get from Saint-Exupéry's musings about life's unfathomable worth. The values attached to those who died in the terrorist attacks were determined as a function of their forgone economic output—what they could no longer produce because they were dead. Tort law in the United States uses such techniques to determine compensation for victims of wrongs. But to families of the victims, they represented a distortion of what was really lost.

Family members offered all sorts of personal metrics to inflate the value of their loved ones, relative to the others. One widow said her loss of a husband of thirty-six years had to be worth more than the loss of a spouse to a newlywed. Another claimed her husband's death was worth more because he took a long time to die, as evinced by the many calls he made from his cell phone, and so suffered more than someone who died instantly. The fund to compensate families of the dead of 9/11 produced a head-on collision between family members' notion of the value of their loved one and the collective view that while lives are very valuable they must fit within a finite budget. It was almost guaranteed to leave everybody unhappy.

In *What Is Life Worth?*—a memoir of his experience at the head of the fund—Feinberg suggested that if Congress were ever again to craft a compensation plan of this sort it should pay all the victims the same amount. "The family of the stockbroker and that of the dishwasher," he wrote, "should receive the same check from the United States Treasury." If part of the idea was to keep the rich from suing, however, this is unlikely to have worked. Indeed, the families of the ninety-six mostly wealthy victims decided not to participate in the fund at all and sued the airlines instead, hoping to get more money from the courts. Though this required paying for expensive lawyers, and it took them longer to get their money, they did get a bigger payoff. Years later, the ninety-three families that settled got an average of $5 million.

## VALUING CITIZENS' SAFETY

Courts, government regulators, and insurance companies replicate the sorts of calculations Feinberg made all the time. Governments can't help setting prices on their citizens' lives as they allocate resources among competing priorities. Simply setting the budget for a fire department puts an implicit value on life, putting some disasters beyond firemen's ability to help and condemning those whose death would be too expensive to avert. Every time a rule is passed on product standards or workplace safety, the government is making a call that the lives saved from injury or death by the new regulations are worth the costs imposed on producers, consumers, and taxpayers.

In 2006 the Consumer Product Safety Commission approved a new flammability standard for mattresses on the basis that it would save 1.08 lives and prevent 5.23 injuries per million mattresses.

Valuing each life at $5 million and each injury at $150,000, it concluded that the benefits would amount to $51.25 per mattress. The cost to industry from the change would amount to only $15.07, so it was worth the expense. By contrast, nearly two decades earlier a panel of the National Academy of Sciences contracted by the Department of Transportation recommended against a federal mandate to require seat belts in all school buses on the grounds that this would save one life a year, at a cost of $40 million apiece.

Measuring up costs against benefits is indispensable in a world where limited funds must be allocated between competing priorities. Still, it inevitably challenges people's beliefs of what's reasonable or fair. Cost-benefit analysis has come under withering criticism from consumer safety advocates and environmental activists who tend to believe that we should protect the world's natural bounty at any cost. In the United States, the Clean Air Act of 1970 explicitly forbade the Environmental Protection Agency from taking into account the costs of compliance when setting air quality standards.

A 1958 amendment to the Federal Food, Drug, and Cosmetic Act sponsored by New York congressman James Delaney required that food have no trace of any additive known to induce cancer in humans or animals, regardless of the cost of removing it or of the magnitude of the risk of contracting cancer by ingesting it. Until the Food Quality Protection Act of 1996 loosened the restrictions, the Delaney Clause implicitly accepted that protecting a consumer from food-borne carcinogens was worth an unlimited amount of money.

Opponents of tallying the costs and benefits of government interventions focus on the inherent uncertainty involved in putting a price tag on an ecosystem, or estimating the benefit in dollars of a decline in the risk of contracting cancer. In the United States, critics remember how cost-benefit analysis was deployed in the 1980s during the administration of President Ronald Reagan, a strong-willed free marketeer who flat out opposed government meddling in the economy. During his first inaugural address in 1981, Reagan stated: "Government is not the solution to our problem; government is the problem." Shortly thereafter he determined by executive order that all federal regulations would have to be submitted to cost-benefit analysis to determine whether they were providing value for money, and used these evaluations in a systematic campaign to dismantle regulations across the board.

But the alternative to cost-benefit analysis is resource allocation by fiat. In the seven years that followed the attacks on September 11 of 2001, the United States government spent $300 billion bolstering its homeland security apparatus. Yet an analysis of the number of deaths likely to be averted by foiling potential future attacks concluded that the cost of each life saved by this bulging security investment came somewhere between $64 million and $600 million.

As a reaction to the attacks, Australia deployed about 130 air marshals on domestic and international flights, at a cost of about 27 million Australian dollars a year. The marshals were not entirely useless. They were called upon to act once, to wrestle down a sixty-eight-year-old man with a knife on a flight between Sydney and Cairns. But according to a study in 2008, the program cost taxpayers 105 million Australian dollars per life saved.

It is only natural that societies will try to protect themselves from risks. But it is easy to go overboard when we ignore the costs involved. Because the truth is, we can't afford it all. While the price of protecting ourselves may be hidden from view—when we insist on eliminating even the tiniest risks, the price tag can be staggering. When we fail to account for the costs and benefits of public policies, we often find ourselves spending enormous amounts in an intervention that will save a handful of lives while neglecting others that would provide more life for the money.

During the administration of George W. Bush, John F. Morrall III, an economist at the White House's Office of Information and Regulatory Affairs, published a study of the costs and benefits of dozens of regulations. Some turned out to be astonishingly expensive: a 1985 rule by the Occupational Safety and Health Administration to reduce occupational exposure to formaldehyde would save only 0.01 lives per year, at a cost of $72 billion per life.

The 1980 law that established the "Superfund" to clean heavily polluted sites across the United States assigned some of the highest values ever placed on human beings. Since 1980 the fund has appropriated $32 billion to clean hundreds of polluted sites that could constitute a hazard to human life. But in many cases there were few or no humans at the sites. The EPA determined the need to clean them up by assuming people would settle on them in the future. The lives of these hypothetical settlers were expensive.

A study in the mid-1990s of population records around ninety-nine Superfund sites concluded that only one presented a substantial risk of pollution-induced cancer, one of the most important areas of risk evaluated by the EPA. But while cleaning the PCB-laced site of the old Westinghouse transformer plant in Sunnyvale, California, would avert 202 lifetime cancers, according to the analysis, cleaning up the other ninety-eight sites would prevent only two deaths from cancer in total. At six sites the implicit cost of the program ranged from $5 million to $100 million per each life saved. At sixty-seven sites, the cost of saving a life exceeded $1 billion. And at two sites no deaths were prevented—so the costs were infinite.

While these programs might be nonetheless beneficial to the environment, this price tag might seem high in a world with other, perhaps more pressing needs. Flood protection in New Orleans comes to mind, or fighting malaria. A World Bank study determined that continuing with the World Health Organization's strategy to combat tuberculosis in sub-Saharan Africa would cost $12 billion between 2006 and 2015. But in Ethiopia alone the program would save 250,000 lives. Today, about 92 of every 100,000 Ethiopians die of tuberculosis each year.

## PRICE YOUR OWN LIFE

If the government must tally costs and benefits to evaluate public policies, the obvious question is how should human lives be valued? Feinberg's approach—measuring our life's worth by our contribution to GDP—is perhaps too cold-blooded. But there is an alternative, famously articulated nearly sixty years ago by the comedian Jack Benny.

In March 1948, *The Jack Benny Show* broadcast one of the most famous comedy skits in American radio history: a mugger—voiced by fellow comedian Eddie Marr—accosted Benny as he was walking home from his neighbor's. "Now, come on. Your money or your life," the mugger demanded. Benny, a notorious scrooge, didn't immediately answer, so after a long silence, the robber repeated his threat. "Look, bud," he said. "I said your money or your life." Benny snapped back: "I'm thinking it over."

Benny's skit suggests a solution to this toughest of evaluations. In their efforts to perform better cost-benefit analyses to guide rule making and allocate public resources, governments only have to let people determine the value of their own lives.

We may not be willing or able to put a price on our entire lives, but every day we put a price on small changes in our chance of dying. We do it every time we cross the street, trading a slight chance of being run over by a truck against our wish to get to the other side. Deciding not to fasten a seat belt, smoking, or ordering the potentially poisonous blowfish at the Japanese restaurant involves choosing a higher probability of death than buckling up, not smoking, or picking the salmon. The Toyota Yaris delivers seven miles to the gallon more in city driving than the Toyota Camry—not an insubstantial saving. It also is about $7,000 cheaper. But according to a report by the Insurance Institute for Highway Safety, the chance of dying in a car crash is about 20 percent higher in the tiny Yaris than in the midsized sedan.

In 1987, the federal government allowed states to choose the speed limit on interstate highways, freeing them from the 55 mph yoke imposed in 1974. A study of driving in twenty-one states that revised their speed limits up to 65 mph found that drivers increased their average speed by 3.5 percent. This both shortened their commutes and increased their chances of suffering a fatal crash. The researchers calculated that for each life lost, drivers were saving about 125,000 hours in shorter commutes. If each hour were valued at the prevailing wage, the drivers saved $1.54 million, in 1997 dollars, for each additional death.

In the 1960s, the American economist Thomas Schelling suggested using people's willingness to pay for safety to determine the price tag they put on their lives. "Proponents of the gravity of decisions about life-saving can be dispelled," he wrote, "by letting the consumer (taxpayer, lobbyist, questionnaire respondent) express himself on the comparatively unexciting subject of small increments in small risks, acting as though he has preferences even if in fact he has not. People do it for life insurance: they could do it for life-saving."

A study of parents' willingness to buy bike helmets for their kids concluded they valued their lives at anywhere from $1.7 to $3.6 million. An analysis of how home prices drop the nearer they are to a polluted Superfund site concluded homeowners were willing to pay up to $4.6 million to avoid the risk of getting cancer. Another way to measure life's value is to look at people's choice of jobs, deducing the value of life from the fact that riskier jobs pay more: say a worker accepted $100 more per year to take a job that increased his risk of death by one in 100,000. An economist would conclude from this that the worker valued his life at 100,000 times $100, or an even $10 million.

These techniques have gained traction in many countries to determine the costs society is willing to bear to avoid injuries and deaths. With their appeal to citizens' own preferences they have a more democratic flavor than calculations based on economic loss or other objective criteria. If the Department of Transportation determines that Americans are willing to pay no more than $5.8 million to prevent death in a traffic accident, it can make a reasonable case against spending more than $5.8 million for each life it expects to save through road improvements that would reduce the risk of fatal crashes.

The Department of Agriculture used to value life much the way the 9/11 fund did, tallying lost productivity from premature death. But in the 1990s it switched its metric to value life according to people's willingness to pay. Today, it has a nifty calculator where one discovers that 1.39 million cases of salmonella that afflict the United States in a year impose a social cost of about $2.6 billion. The biggest chunk of the cost stems from the 415 people killed by the disease, each of whose lives the agency values at $5.4 million.

Health agencies prefer to measure the value of living one more year, rather than that of an entire life, on the not unreasonable assumption that we are all going to die anyway and all government action can do is push death back a bit, not prevent it. The most sophisticated analyses take into account the quality of each life saved, assuming that a year of life suffering an affliction or disability is worth less than a year in full health. This has led to the creation of a new unit of measurement: the quality-adjusted life year, known as QALY.

To decide whether to redesign or rebuild a road, for instance, the Department of Transportation values injuries along a scale: a minor injury costs 0.0002 percent of a statistical life; a critical injury is worth more than three quarters. The FDA estimates that the victim of a coronary disease loses thirteen years of life, on average, which is worth—to the victim—about $840,000.

These tools have become the standard in several countries to evaluate and shape government policies. In 2003, for instance, the economic analysis unit of Australia's health department proposed changing warnings on packages of tobacco products. It based its analysis on the fact that it would save about four hundred lives a year—which added up to a benefit of some 250 million Australian dollars a year—at an annual cost of about 130 million Australian dollars in lost excise taxes because Australians would smoke less.

These techniques provide a new measure of the wealth of nations. Economists at the University of Chicago added up the value to Americans of their increased life expectancy to conclude that increases in longevity between 1970 and 2000 added $3.2 trillion per year to the national wealth of the United States.

## DO WE KNOW HOW MUCH WE ARE WORTH?

Despite its democratic appeal, this metric too is troubling. Using people's own choices to determine the price we are willing to pay to save lives could lead society down some uncomfortable paths. Given the choice between pulling a dozen thirty-year-olds from a blazing fire or saving a dozen sixty-year-olds instead, it might be an odd choice to save the seniors from the point of view of social welfare. For starters, saving the young would save many more years of life than the old.

Cass Sunstein, the legal scholar from the University of Chicago who currently heads the White House's Office of Information and Regulatory Affairs, which oversees these valuations, has proposed focusing government policies on saving years of life rather than lives, even though that would discount the value of seniors. "A program that saves younger people is better, along every dimension, than an otherwise identical program that saves older people," he wrote. But just try making this case to somebody over sixty-five. Not only do they value their remaining lives as much as the young do, they have enormous political clout and will vote against anyone who says otherwise.

In 2002 the Environmental Protection Agency introduced a novel element into its analysis of how the Clear Skies Act—which regulated soot emissions from power plants—reduced premature mortality. Rather than evaluate every life saved at $6.1 million, as it had done in the past, it applied an age discount—implying that the life of somebody over seventy was worth only 67 percent of the life of a younger person.

The backlash by the American Association of Retired People and others was so fierce that EPA administrator Christine Todd Whitman was forced to abandon the approach. "The senior discount factor has been stopped," she said. "It has been discontinued. E.P.A. will not, I repeat, not, use an age-adjusted analysis in decision making." When the EPA again adjusted the value of life by age to measure the benefits of regulating exhaust from diesel engines, it bent over backward to please seniors. To come up with a system that valued the life of retirees the same as that of younger Americans, it had to price each year of remaining life expectancy at $434,000 for people over the age of sixty-five and only $172,000 for those younger.

The risks of relying on people's choices to put a value on their lives can be seen in opinion polls showing Americans believe a life saved from a terrorist attack is worth two lives saved from a natural disaster. This bias may explain the indifference with which the United States government responded to hurricane Katrina in New Orleans in 2005, compared with the massive investment to avoid a repeat of the terrorist attacks against the United States in 2001.

Above all, these valuations perpetuate economic inequities. Schelling cautioned about this: "Just as the rich will pay more to avoid wasting an hour in traffic or five hours on a train, it is worth more to them to reduce the risk of their own death or the death of somebody they care about. It is worth more because they are richer than the poor." The fact that the *Titanic* didn't have enough lifeboats for all passengers would be reasonable under this line of thinking. The distribution of deaths—37 percent of first-class passengers, 57 percent of those in second class, and 75 percent of those traveling steerage—would be uncontroversial.

Yet if people thought the compensation by the 9/11 fund was unfair, what would they think of directing lifesaving government programs to the rich simply because they have more resources to invest in their own health and safety and are less willing to take risky jobs than the poor? This system ignores the fact that while the rich are willing to pay more to protect life and limb than the poor, the poor value each dollar they have more than the rich. For a family that subsists on the fringe of poverty, an investment in a doctor's visit could signal a lower tolerance for risk than all the pricey medical treatments of a corporate executive.

This method of self-valuation ignores the fact that people's choices are not always freely chosen. If one were to measure people's worth by their willingness to trade money for safety in the workplace, one would conclude that blacks believe they are cheaper than whites. They suffer more workplace fatalities in almost every industry and the extra wages they get for the extra risk are lower. One study concluded from this data that a white blue-collar worker's life was worth $16.8 million, more than twice the value of that of a similar black worker. But we would have good reason to mistrust this valuation. Rather than reflecting a higher appetite for risk among blacks, it suggests that blacks have fewer job opportunities and so must settle for less.

By this metric, life in the poor world is very cheap. A 2005 study based on wages of Mexico City workers valued their lives at a maximum of $325,000. A 2005 study of what Chinese were willing to pay to avoid sickness or death from air pollution calculated that, at the official exchange rate, the median value of a statistical life could be as little as $4,000. This kind of valuation would lead to some untenable decisions about allocating resources across the world. Representatives of developing countries were outraged when a report of the Intergovernmental Panel on Climate Change in 1995 assessed the impact of global warming valuing statistical lives at $150,000 in poor countries and at $1.5 million in rich ones. Did this mean, they asked, that protecting people in poor countries from climate change provided less bang for the buck than protecting citizens of the rich world? So the panel backtracked, threw out its sophisticated economic analysis, and settled for the politically tenable notion that we are all worth the same, $1 million whether in rich countries or poor.

## THE PRICE OF HEALTH

Cervical cancer is one of Mexico's most lethal ones, killing 8 out of every 100,000 women every year. When GlaxoSmithKline and Merck Sharp & Dohme developed vaccines against the human papillomavirus, the leading cause of cancer of the cervix, Mexico was among the first countries to consider a program of universal vaccination for twelve-year-old girls.

It appeared to be extremely cost-effective. At some 440 pesos a dose, about the price quoted by Glaxo, offering a three-dose course to 80 percent of girls would cost just over 42,000 pesos per each healthy year of life that would be saved by the procedure, according to a 2008 analysis by researchers at the Mexican national health department. This is less than half Mexico's gross national product per capita, and thus considered a good investment by experts at the World Health Organization.

But because Mexico is a relatively poor country, these findings produced a conundrum. A universal vaccination plan would cost about 1.4 billion pesos, almost as much as the entire budget for the government's series of seven mandatory childhood vaccines. So the government took a Solomonic approach. It decided to offer the vaccination program only in poor areas of the country with a relatively high incidence of cervical cancer, which would cut the total outlay by more than half. More controversially, rather than provide the three doses within a period of six to eight months, as suggested by the pharmaceutical companies, the health ministry chose to provide the third dose only after five years.

"All our studies of the vaccines' effectiveness were based on a plan of three doses—the third must be taken eight months after the first," said Miguel Cashat-Cruz, the head of vaccines for Merck's Mexican subsidiary. But Eduardo Lazcano-Ponce, a researcher at the National Institute of Public Health, said pecuniary interests drove pharmaceutical companies' protests. "They say it won't be useful, but they make no effort to reduce the price of the vaccine."

The provision of health is awash in such cost-benefit calculations, as governments allocate limited budgets among new drugs and therapies streaming out of the world's labs. In 2005 New Zealand's Ministry of Health declined to fund a universal vaccination program against pneumococcal disease that would cost about 120,000 New Zealand dollars for each year of life gained in good health by the inoculation. It approved funding two years later, when the manufacturer proved that a program could be carried out for 25,000 New Zealand dollars per year of life.

The British government, which since World War II has provided health coverage for its citizens free of charge, has been the trailblazer in systematically applying cost-benefit analysis to its expenditures on health. It started in the late 1990s, when the erectile dysfunction drug Viagra appeared on the market and officials at the National Health Service worried that the new wonder drug would bust the government's health budget.

These days, the National Institute for Health and Clinical Excellence—or NICE—follows a standard set of guidelines to determine which drugs and procedures will be covered. Anything that costs less than £20,000 per year of good-quality life is approved. And except in very rare cases, the health service will not pay more than £30,000 per year of added life. The practice has spread around the world. The Canadian Agency for Drugs and Technologies in Health makes recommendations to the nation's provincial drug plans on the cost-effectiveness of new drugs. From Australia to the Netherlands to Portugal, economic evaluations are mandatory for the approval of treatments.

The World Health Organization has developed general thresholds for countries around the world. It deems treatments very cost-effective when each year gained in good health costs less than the nation's economic product per person, cost-effective when such a quality-adjusted life year costs one to three years of GDP per capita, and not worth the investment when it costs more than that. This metric would suggest that governments in countries like Argentina, Brazil, or Mexico should afford treatments if they cost less than $29,300 per QALY, in 2009. Their poorer neighbors, like Bolivia and Ecuador, should only afford interventions costing up to $13,800. The rich countries in the hemisphere, the United States and Canada, should be willing to invest up to $120,000 per year of good life gained.

Yet decisions based on cost-benefit calculations are never easy. In 2008 it seemed straightforward for NICE to reject paying for Sutent, Pfizer's newfangled pill for kidney cancer that cost about £3,139 for a six-week regimen and usually extended life by less than a year. This meant it generally cost more than the agency's £30,000 limit per "quality adjusted" year of additional life.

But the storm of public protest that ensued was deafening. A British tabloid, the *Daily Mail*, called it a "death sentence" for those suffering kidney cancer. And NICE backtracked, approving Sutent for some patients on the grounds that "although it might be at the upper end of any plausible valuation of such benefits, in this case there was a significant step-change in treating a disease for which there is only one current standard first-line treatment option." The investment, in fact, would not be too large. Fewer than seven thousand Britons suffered this kidney cancer and Sutent would be suitable for only about half of those. Moreover, Pfizer also offered to pick up the tab for the first six weeks.


**IT'S HARD TO** overcome the belief that we are entitled to all the health care we need. During President Obama's push to reform American health insurance, the White House reminded its allies never to use the dreaded word "rationing." Democrat Max Baucus, who as chair of the Senate Finance Committee was one of the leading legislators crafting the bill, said: "There is no rationing of health care at all" in the proposed reform.

Of course, rationing is pervasive across the American health-care system. For starters, in 2009, 46 million Americans lacked health insurance. A study of victims of severe traffic accidents who landed in hospital emergency rooms in Wisconsin found that those without health insurance received 20 percent less care than the insured. They were kept only 6.4 days in hospital, on average, compared to 9.2 days for those with insurance. And hospitals spent on average $3,300 more on the insured than the uninsured. The uninsured, of course, were 40 percent more likely to die. The study found that if hospitals had treated the uninsured equally to the insured, each life saved would have cost $220,000, which amounts to about $11,000 per additional year. This is a bargain compared to Sutent; well within the limits imposed by Britain's NICE.

Nonetheless, Obama's political tactics made sense in the face of accusations from American conservatives that the government wanted to take over the decision of who lived and who died. The president got a foretaste of the opposition's tactics when a White House proposal to study the relative effectiveness of new drugs and therapies, to decide which were most worthwhile, drew a furious reaction. An editorial in the *Washington Times* compared the proposal to a program called Aktion T-4 put in place in Nazi Germany to euthanize elderly people with incurable diseases, critically disabled children, and other unproductive types.

The rhetoric was effective because it tapped into the belief that life is priceless, that when it comes to matters of life and death we should spare no expense. As Joy Hardy, the wife of a British cancer victim who was temporarily denied Sutent by the NHS, said: "Everybody should be allowed to have as much life as they can." This belief has burdened the United States with a uniquely inefficient health-care system. In 2009 health care consumed 18 percent of the nation's income. And without any mechanism to ensure cost-effectiveness, it could swallow more than a fifth of the economy by 2020. Yet all this spending does not buy better health.

Somehow Americans have a lower life expectancy at birth than the Japanese, French, Spanish, Swiss, Australians, Icelanders, Swedes, Italians, Canadians, Finns, Norwegians, Austrians, Belgians, Germans, Greeks, Koreans, Dutch, Portuguese, New Zealanders, Luxembourgeois, Irish, British, and Danes. We achieve this while spending, collectively, much more on health care than any of them: about $6,714 a year for every American. In Japan, by contrast, health-related expenditures amount to about $2,600 per head, and in Portugal to only $2,000. What's more, allocating health care by patients' ability to pay rather than an analysis of the costs and benefits of treatment ensures that the American distribution of health, and life, is as inequitable as one can get in the industrial world. More than half of Americans who earn less than the average income report not being able to get needed health care due to its cost. This compares to fewer than 10 percent of the British or the Dutch.

Americans are inveigled by a powerful mirage: that markets don't ration. In 2007, the Congressional Budget Office issued a report about how the nation might bring spiraling health-care costs under control by measuring the cost-effectiveness of medical treatments, as several other countries do. The report warned that putting a price on life might be politically tricky in the United States. "Many people find the notion uncomfortable if not objectionable," noted the CBO, incompatible with "the sentiment that no expense should be spared to extend a patient's life." The invisible hand of the market is as ruthless in denying health care to the needy as the most coldhearted central planner. Our unwillingness to acknowledge life's price does not mean it doesn't have one.

# CHAPTER THREE

# The Price of Happiness

**ONE OF MEXICO'S** most famous cultural exports, alongside mariachi bands and drunken spring break in Cancún, is the 1979 telenovela titled *Los Ricos También Lloran,* or *The Rich Also Weep.* Dubbed into two dozen languages, the epic soap opera's tale of the trials and tribulations of a lovely young heiress, Mariana, captivated millions of viewers in more than a hundred countries.

The show was exported to China and Saudi Arabia. It gave Russia a first taste of capitalist pop culture, drawing an audience of 100 million after making its debut there in May of 1992, shortly after the demise of the Soviet Union. President Boris Yeltsin was a fan. According to the Russian newspaper *Pravda,* soldiers from Abkhazia and Georgia would reach a tacit truce during showtimes in order to watch the show.

The telenovela's plotline is of byzantine complexity. Mariana, the heroine, is ejected from the family ranch by an evil stepmother. A wealthy benefactor takes her in. The benefactor's handsome son woos her. Her love for the young man is thwarted by a rival, consummated, tested by jealousy. Somehow—don't ask—Mariana decides to give their baby son, Beto, to a woman who sells lottery tickets. Only after she encounters Beto years later and prevents his father from shooting him will she be happy.

Despite the idiosyncratic plot twists, and the actors clad in bell-bottoms, the telenovela appealed to millions because it tapped into a romantic archetype, that of the helpless heroine who falls into the lap of luxury yet cannot find happiness until she finds true love. Its message—though delivered in a style of high camp—resonates across time around the world: we may think wealth provides happiness, but they are unrelated.

The point had been made over a century earlier by the philosopher Arthur Schopenhauer, who argued that "money is human happiness in the abstract; he, then, who is no longer capable of enjoying human happiness in the concrete devotes himself utterly to money."

In March of 1968, three months before he was shot to death, Robert Kennedy delivered a scathing critique of the nation's fixation on economic growth: "Gross National Product counts air pollution and cigarette advertising, and ambulances to clear our highways of carnage. It counts special locks for our doors and the jails for the people who break them. It counts the destruction of the redwood and the loss of our natural wonder in chaotic sprawl," he said.

"Yet the gross national product does not allow for the health of our children, the quality of their education or the joy of their play. It does not include the beauty of our poetry or the strength of our marriages, the intelligence of our public debate or the integrity of our public officials. It measures neither our wit nor our courage, neither our wisdom nor our learning, neither our compassion nor our devotion to our country, it measures everything in short, except that which makes life worthwhile."

This age-old conviction is undergoing a bit of a revival. As people around the world struggled with the fallout from the global financial crisis and a worldwide recession, the sense that there is something wrong with our unbridled pursuit of material riches coalesced among some policy makers into a belief that nations should pursue something other than economic growth. Our narrow drive to maximize GDP, many seem to believe, brings only disaster.

In 2008, as the French economy slipped toward recession, French president Nicolas Sarkozy drafted two Nobel Prize–winning economists, Amartya Sen and Joseph Stiglitz, and the domestic economist Jean-Paul Fitoussi, to prepare a report on how to better measure people's socioeconomic progress. "The time is right for our measurement system to shift emphasis from measuring economic production to measuring people's well-being," the report concluded. Government, it suggested, should supplement standard economic data with other information, including citizens' sense of happiness with their lives.

The tiny Buddhist kingdom of Bhutan, high in the Himalayas, has stretched the idea further—devising a quantity it calls "gross national happiness," which it plans to use to evaluate policies and keep track of the country's well-being. King Jigme Singye Wangchuck coined the term in 1972, but it became a reality only after he abdicated thirty-six years later, when Bhutan had its first-ever democratic election, and the Bhutanese approved a new constitution that established the world's first GNH index.

The index has six dozen variables, grouped into nine dimensions— including psychological well-being and community vitality, ecology, good governance, and time use. And it sets values to behaviors. People score happiness points if they pray and meditate often and understand their family, and lose points if they feel selfish. Yet more isn't necessarily better. Playing Langthab, for instance, a game in which opponents head-butt each other into submission, is assumed to make Bhutanese happy. But it is enough to play it once or twice a month. Playing more doesn't increase the happiness stock. Similarly, money adds to happiness—but only up to 70,597 ngultrum—or about $1,550—per household per year.

**YET DESPITE ITS** growing popularity, the belief that money has little or nothing to do with happiness is misleading. Like Schopenhauer's musings and Mariana's troubles, the sweeping rhetoric about the emptiness of material wealth supports a dubious proposition that the pursuit of economic progress is somehow a waste of time because it does not deliver what is most important in life. Despite the skepticism about run-of-the-mill economic growth, despite the angry denunciations of materialism, it is usually better to have a big gross domestic product than a small one. Just ask one of the more than 3 billion people—half the world's population—how happy they are making do with less than $2.50 a day.

In fact, surveys find that richer people tend to be happier than poorer people. That's because money provides many of the things that improve people's lot. Richer countries are generally healthier and have lower child mortality and higher life expectancy. They tend to have cleaner environments, and their citizens often have more education and less physically demanding and more interesting jobs. Richer people usually have more leisure time, travel more, and have more money to enjoy the arts. Money helps people overcome constraints and take control over their lives. Whatever Kennedy said, gross national product does allow for the health of our kids.

Researchers in Britain found that an extra £125,000 a year increased people's sense of satisfaction with their lives by one point on a scale of one to seven. A study in Australia pored through surveys to understand how people's feelings of happiness responded to life's events. It found that a windfall of $16,500 to $24,500 provided more or less the same boost to happiness as getting married. Losing between $178,300 and $187,600 generated the same level of unhap-piness as that caused by the death of a child. A Gallup survey in 2009 found that 30 percent of Americans earning less than $24,000 a year had received a diagnosis of depression, compared with only 13 percent of Americans making $60,000 or more. Happiness can be bought for a price.

There is a problem with the enthusiasm for replacing GDP with a measure of happiness. Who gets to define what makes people happy? Would it be the very same governments that would benefit if the indicator found a happy citizenry? For instance, media reports from Bhutan suggest the Bhutanese have lost interest in Langthab and other traditional sports. They are nonetheless included among the fonts of happiness. Bhutan is a fairly authoritarian nation. The government banned television until 1999. In 1989 it made it manda-tory for all Bhutanese to speak Dzongkha in public places. In 1985, it passed a new citizenship law that redefined ethnic Nepalese in southern Bhutan who couldn't prove they had arrived by 1958 as nonnationals, and subsequently expelled about 100,000 of them. It has nice things, like 72 percent forest cover and few tourists. But it also has a lot of female infanticide and feticide and a lopsided sex ratio of 89.2 females per 100 males. More democratic regimes might have problems defining the attributes of happiness. While Bhutan may be a happy nation, this probably has less to do with the many dimensions of their index than with their material wealth. In 1980, Bhutan's GDP per person was 10 percent higher than India's. Today it is 75 percent higher. In 2009, as the rest of the world slumped, Bhutan grew 6.9 percent. In 2008 the Bhutanese economy grew by a fifth. Like other countries around the world, it has grown happier as it has grown richer.

The World Values Survey, a set of polls performed around the world over the past twenty years, found that the happiest country in the world is rich Denmark. The least happy is poor Zimbabwe. The 2006 Gallup World Poll asked adults in 132 countries to rank their satisfaction with life on a scale of zero to ten. The citizens of Togo, whose gross domestic product per person is only $832, ranked their satisfaction at just above three. Americans, fifty-five times as rich, put their happiness at seven.

---

## WHAT HAPPINESS IS

Happiness is a slippery concept, a bundle of meanings with no precise, stable definition. Lots of thinkers have taken a shot at it. "Happiness is when what you think, what you say, and what you do are in harmony," proposed Gandhi. Abraham Lincoln argued "most people are about as happy as they make up their minds to be." Snoopy, the beagle-philosopher in *Peanuts,* took what was to my mind the most precise stab at the underlying epistemological problem. "My life has no purpose, no direction, no aim, no meaning, and yet I'm happy. I can't figure it out. What am I doing right?"

Most psychologists and economists who study happiness agree that what they prefer to call "subjective well-being" comprises three parts: satisfaction, meant to capture how people judge their lives measured up against their aspirations; positive feelings like joy; and the absence of negative feelings like anger.

It does exist. It relates directly to objective measures of people's quality of life. Countries whose citizens are happier on average report lower levels of hypertension in the population. Happier people are less likely to come down with a cold. And if they get one, they recover more quickly. People who are wounded heal more quickly if they are satisfied with their lives. People who say they are happier smile more often, sleep better, report themselves to be in better health, and have happier relatives. And some research suggests happiness and suicide rates move in opposite directions. Happy people don't want to die.

Still, this conceptual mélange can be difficult to measure. Just ask yourself how happy you are, say, on a scale of one to three, as used by the General Social Survey. Then ask yourself what you mean by that. Answers wander when people are confronted with these questions. We entangle gut reactions with thoughtful analysis, and confound sensations of immediate pleasure with evaluations of how life meshes with our long-term aspirations. We might say we know what will make us happy in the future—fame, fortune, or maybe a partner. But when we get to the future, it rarely does. While we do seem to know how to tell the difference between lifelong satisfaction and immediate well-being, the immediate tends to contaminate the ontological.

During an experiment in the 1980s, people who found a dime on top of a Xerox machine before responding to a happiness survey reported a much higher sense of satisfaction with life than those who didn't. Another study found that giving people a chocolate bar improved their satisfaction with their lives. One might expect that our satisfaction with the entire span of our existence would be a fairly stable quantity—impervious to day-to-day joys and frustrations. Yet people often give a substantially different answer to the same question about lifetime happiness if it is asked again one month later.

Sigmund Freud argued that people "strive after happiness; they want to become happy and to remain so." Translating happiness into the language of economics as "utility," most economists would agree. This simple proposition gives them a powerful tool to resist Bobby Kennedy's proposal to measure not income but something else. For if happiness is what people strive for, one needn't waste time trying to figure out what makes people happy. One must only look at what people do. The fact of the matter is that people mostly choose to work and make money. Under this optic, economic growth is the outcome of our pursuit of well-being. It is what makes us happy.

This approach has limitations. We often make puzzling choices that do not make us consistently happier. We smoke despite knowing about cancer and emphysema. We gorge on chocolate despite knowing it will make us unhappy ten pounds down the road. Almost two thirds of Americans say they are overweight, according to a recent Gallup poll. But only a quarter say they are seriously trying to lose weight. In the 1980s a new discipline called Prospect Theory—also known as behavioral economics—deployed the tools of psychology to analyze economic behavior. It found all sorts of peculiar behaviors that don't fit economics' standard understanding of what makes us happy. For instance, losing something reduces our happiness more than winning the same thing increases it—a quirk known as loss aversion. We are unable to distinguish between choices that have slightly different odds of making us happy. We extrapolate from a few experiences to arrive at broad, mostly wrong conclusions. We herd, imitating successful behaviors around us.

Still, it remains generally true that we pursue what we think makes us happy—and though some of our choices may not make us happy, some will. Legend has it that Abraham Lincoln was riding in a carriage one rainy evening, telling a friend that he agreed with economists' theory that people strove to maximize their happiness, when he caught sight of a pig stuck in a muddy riverbank. He ordered the carriage to stop, got out, and pulled the pig out of the muck to safety. When the friend pointed out to a mud-caked Lincoln that he had just disproved his statement by putting himself through great discomfort to save a pig, Lincoln retorted: "What I did was perfectly consistent with my theory. If I hadn't saved that pig I would have felt terrible."

So perhaps the proper response to Bobby Kennedy's angst is to agree that pursuing economic growth often has negative side effects—carbon emissions, environmental degradation—that are likely to make us unhappy down the road. Still, it remains true that American citizens—and the citizens of much of the world—expend enormous amounts of time and energy pursuing more money and a bigger GDP because they think it will improve their well-being. And that will make them happy.

## HAPPINESS IS A CONCRETE FLOOR

Happiness doesn't depend solely on money, of course. People who don't have sex report being less happy than those who do. People are unhappier in areas with higher unemployment, more crime, higher inflation, and more sulfur-oxide pollution emitted by coal-fired power plants. Happier people are more likely to be married, less likely to divorce, and have more friends. Right-wingers are happier than left-wingers.

A survey by the Pew Research Center found that even as the Republican candidate John McCain headed for disaster in the presidential election of November 2008, 37 percent of Republicans rated themselves as "very happy," compared with 25 percent of Democrats. A similar trend has held since 1972, when the General Social Survey started asking the question. This is true around the world. Apparently, it has to do with the left's guilt. A study by psychologists at New York University found that the right-left happiness gap increases with deepening income inequality. This suggests people on the right are better at rationalizing inequality as a normal feature of life and feel less guilty about it.

But improve people's economic outlook and chances are you will make them happier. More than a decade after the fall of the Berlin Wall in November 1989, former East Germans remained unhappier than their fellow citizens from the western side. They would have been even less satisfied were it not for the income boost following unification. East Germans' satisfaction with life rose about 20 percent between 1991 and 2001. Much of that jump was due to the freedoms gained with the demise of their police state. But a 60 percent increase in household income also played a part.

The gross domestic product of the Russian Federation declined by a quarter between 1990 and 1995, as the Soviet Union fell apart. Unsurprisingly, Russians' reported satisfaction with life dropped 17 percent. Analyzing the surge in male suicides following the dismemberment of the former USSR, researchers concluded that a $100 increase in per capita GDP lowered the suicide rate among Russian males by somewhere between 0.14 percent and 0.20 percent. Similarly, an increase of one percentage point in the share of the population who held a job reduced male suicides by about 3 percent.

Consider how unhappy you would feel if you had to live with nothing but dirt under your feet. In 2000 the government of the state of Coahuila in northern Mexico launched a program called Piso Firme, or Firm Floor, that offered people living in homes with dirt floors up to fifty square meters of concrete cement flooring, at a cost to the government of about 1,500 Mexican pesos—equivalent to about $150 at the time, one and a half months' income. Families would be told in advance of the delivery date so they could prepare the rooms to be covered. Large trucks rolled through poor neighborhoods, pouring cement from house to house, leaving each family to smooth it down.

A few years after the cement was laid, researchers from the World Bank and two American universities deployed across the shantytowns of Torreón, the state capital, armed with portable scales and medical testing paraphernalia to measure how it changed people's lives. Dirt floors are a breeding ground for worms and several types of protozoa. Children catch parasites from them, suffer from diarrhea, and become malnourished. Anemia is common, as are developmental disabilities. The researchers weighed and measured the kids. They took stool samples. They pricked the kids' fingers to check for anemia. And they subjected them to cognitive development tests. Parents were asked about how well babies recognized basic words for animals, household items, and the like. Older children were made to relate pictures to words. Then the researchers asked mothers about how satisfied they were with their lives.

To assess the impact of the new floors, they compared the health and well-being of families in Torreón with those in its twin city of Gómez Palacio, which is part of the same metropolitan area but happens to lie across the state line in neighboring Durango—where the program wasn't available. The researchers found that paving floors led to a 78 percent drop in parasitic infestations among children. Diarrhea cases declined by half and the prevalence of anemia plummeted four fifths. Children in homes where cement had been laid got the answers right to the cognitive tests 30 percent to 100 percent more often than those still living on dirt. And the moms became much happier. Depression among mothers fell by half. And their stress levels fell. Mothers in homes with new cement floors reported a 69 percent increase in satisfaction with their life. This happiness cost about $150 per family. Unsurprisingly, the Mexican federal government expanded the program to the rest of the country.

MONEY IS MORE abundant in industrialized countries. But even there it will add to happiness. The Eurobarometer surveys have been asking European Union citizens about the satisfaction with their lives for more than three decades. Among the richest 25 percent of the population, almost a third reported being "very satisfied," according to a study in the late 1990s. Among the poorest 25 percent, only about 23 percent are equally pleased.

Results were similar in the United States. The General Social Survey, a set of polls taken since the early 1970s of Americans' behaviors and beliefs, finds that more than 40 percent of Americans in the richest quarter of the population are very happy. But among the poorest quarter of Americans, only 25 percent are equally satisfied.

Money might not ensure happiness forever. But as Robert Frank, an economist at Cornell, put it: "There's no one single change you can imagine that would make your life improve on the happiness scale as much as to move from the bottom 5 percent on the income scale to the top 5 percent."

New York's Eleventh Congressional District, where I live, is of modest means—stretching from fairly poor areas like East Flatbush and Crown Heights to the fairly posh Park Slope. The typical family in the district earns $51,300 a year, according to the census, about

$12,000 less than the national median. It is a grumpy place. In 2009, pollster Gallup, the health-care consultancy Healthway, and America's Health Insurance Plans, an industry lobby group, released a district-by-district index of well-being based on surveys of people's satisfaction with life, work, and health. My district came out in 421st place in the nation, fifteen rungs from the bottom.

The happiest congressional district in the country is about as far from New York's eleventh as one can get without leaving the contiguous United States. California's fourteenth district hugs the Pacific between San Francisco and San Jose, encompassing much of the high-tech corridor of Silicon Valley. It has lovely scenery, and certainly better weather than Brooklyn. It also has a median family income of $116,600 a year.

## THE TREADMILL OF HAPPINESS

There is a limit to the link between money and happiness. It derives from one of the most distinctive human traits: our capacity to adapt. People bounce back from bereavement. A British study found that while people who became disabled reported a big drop in happiness, many recovered much of the lost happiness within a year or two. A study of marriage and happiness in Germany found that German widows recover from the blow of their husband's death within two years.

Bliss doesn't last either. German women become progressively happier in the two years in which their relationship moves from courtship to marriage. Yet after peaking the year of their wedding, happiness drifts back down over the next two years to close to where it was before. The same thing seems to happen to people who strike it rich. Studies have found that the burst of euphoria people experience when they win the lottery fades relatively quickly, even if the prize is in the millions. Within six months of having won, the happiness reported by big winners is back down around where it was before.

In the 1970s, the economist Richard Easterlin of the University of Southern California made what is probably the most intriguing finding in the history of the economics of happiness. Poring through twenty-five years of surveys about happiness, he concluded that despite stellar economic growth, Americans were not significantly happier than they had been at the end of World War II.

Adaptation would explain this trend. Easterlin suggested another complementary dynamic: happiness may not depend on our absolute level of well-being but on how it compares with the well-being of those around us. We feel happy when we are better off than our neighbors.

Other economists since then have found similar examples of the relative nature of happiness. People feel less happy when their neighbors have more money. Roughly speaking, losing $1,000 produces the same sort of dissatisfaction as seeing a neighbor gain $1,000. Suicide rates are higher than average in areas where there is a large gap between the highest earners and average people. Many economists have accepted the notion that money might buy enduring happiness for very poor people, for whom a rise in income could drastically change their living conditions. But beyond a certain satiation threshold it would be pointless to strive for more. The rich may be happier than the poor. But getting richer wouldn't make them happier, at least not for long, because they would soon adapt to their new life one rung up the income ladder and start comparing themselves with richer people.

Adaptation could be a useful trait. Economists Gary Becker and Luis Rayo argue that the ephemeral, context-dependent nature of happiness makes sense in evolutionary terms. If progress boosts our happiness only briefly, we will be motivated to constantly improve. The desire to keep up with the neighbors would work in much the same way. The relentless drive to improve would increase our chances of survival. As Adam Smith put it 250 years ago, the idea that we can achieve happiness amounts to a "deception, which rouses and keeps in continual motion the industry of mankind."

But surely we would have caught onto the con by now? If Easterlin was right, economic growth would be a glum proposition. If everybody's income rose equally, people's relative position wouldn't change. If growth benefited some more than others, the increase in happiness among the winners would balance out the loss of happiness among the losers in a zero-sum game. Adaptation proposes a world with even less hope, running pointlessly on our treadmill of happiness, rooted to the same place. The founding fathers of the United States included the pursuit of happiness as one of the inalienable rights they thought its citizens should have. But if we truly adapt to everything, what point is there in striving to be happy?

Some psychologists have even suggested happiness is hardwired, determined not by changes in our environment but by our individual genetic makeup. And there seems to be some evidence that our genes do play a part. The Minnesota Twin Registry has followed thousands of twins born between 1936 and 1955. Researchers have found that changes in happiness are very highly correlated among identical twins, who share all their genetic material. Regardless of whether they grew up together or apart, the happiness of one twin is more closely related to that of the other than to his own level of education or his wealth. By contrast, the correlation disappears for fraternal twins—who come from two different eggs.

But if our happiness is in our genes, we will have to answer a question deeper than Bobby Kennedy's: what is the point of striving for anything if nothing will improve our sense of well-being? That would turn economics on its head. A few years ago, Easterlin wrote an essay titled "Feeding the Illusion of Growth and Happiness" in which he starkly laid out the conclusion of a lifetime of happiness studies: they "undermine the view that a focus on economic growth is in the best interests of society." In fact, the proposition that we are on a treadmill of happiness undermines the belief that society can improve at all.

## THE AMERICAN TRADE-OFF

But we shouldn't despair just yet. The treadmill of happiness is a metaphor too far. And Easterlin overstates his case. The evidence arrayed against the proposition that progress—economic or otherwise—can make us consistently happier is weaker than it appears. Economic progress can still do a lot for humankind.

American happiness remains peculiarly impervious to progress. Between 1946 and 1991 income per capita in the United States rose by a factor of 2.5—ownership of consumer durables from TV sets to cars soared, educational attainment jumped, and life expectancy at birth climbed. Still, Americans' average happiness measured by surveys fell slightly. The United States was one of only four industrialized countries—alongside Hungary, Portugal, and Canada—where life satisfaction fell between 2000 and 2006.

But outside the United States, surveys of life satisfaction find that gains in income almost always led to gains in happiness. Surveys in fifty-two countries over the past quarter century or so found that happiness increased in forty-five and declined in only seven. Among the poorer countries—India, Ireland, Mexico, Puerto Rico, and South Korea—it increased a lot. With the odd exception of Belgium, all nine countries that were members of the European Community in 1973 have reported rising happiness alongside economic growth since then.

These data contradict the proposition that we are stuck, recalibrating our aspirations with every step we take, falling right back to where we were. They suggest that if indeed we do adapt to improvements in income, adaptation does not swallow all our gains. If we get a kick out of staying ahead of the neighbors, we also enjoy the improvements to life that money can buy.

If $100 provides much more happiness in Burundi than in the United States, that reflects the fact that $100 is a much bigger deal when your annual income is less than $400 than when it is more than a hundred times that much. But economic development seems to improve the satisfaction with life in rich countries too. In fact, the lesson to take from Easterlin's research is not that economic growth doesn't provide further happiness past a certain point of development. It does. What happens is that having a bigger income matters less when our income is already big. This dynamic is well understood by economists. It is called diminishing returns. Other scarce endowments, such as free time or an unpolluted environment, are also important for our well-being. As money becomes relatively less important they start to matter more. When we sacrifice some of these endowments to achieve economic prosperity, the net extra happiness must balance the money gained against all that is spent to gain it.

Americans are richer than Europeans. Gross domestic product per head in the United States averages $47,700, more than one-third greater than in France or Germany. Yet the average American recorded a 2.2 happiness level on a scale of one to three, according to the General Social Survey, almost identical to Europe's ranking, according to the Eurobarometer polls, of 2.9 on a scale of one to four.

Several things probably account for Americans' stagnant satisfaction. The first is the lopsided nature of American income growth. From 1972 to 2005, household income grew less than 20 percent for those in the poorer half of the population. It grew 59 percent for the richest fifth. Happiness followed the trend: it increased slightly for the top 40 percent of earners but declined for everybody else. If today the United States has the most unequal distribution of happiness among the richer members of the Organization for Economic Cooperation and Development (OECD), it is likely because it also has the most unequal distribution of income.

But there are other potential explanations. The notion that money doesn't improve our perceived well-being may be due to conceptual confusion about what such improvement means. Using the survey responses of some 450,000 Americans, Daniel Kahneman and Angus Deaton of Princeton found that people's "emotional well-being"—measured by their reporting of recent feelings such as joy or sadness—did in fact stop improving after income hit a threshold of about $75,000 a year. But people's sense of satisfaction with their life increased continuosly with income, with no evidence of satiation at all.

Money makes us feel better about our lives, but so does having free time. Americans have sacrificed enormous amounts of time to achieve their unparalleled economic prosperity. Easterlin's paradoxical finding that Americans' growing wealth hasn't made us any happier is, in reality, proof that the time we spend earning money is erasing the happiness we get out of counting and spending it.

Researchers studying a group of one thousand Texan women who kept detailed diaries about what they were doing with their time and how they felt about it found that the women's happiest activity was sex, followed by socializing after work and relaxing. The most undesirable tasks were commuting and working. Unfortunately for the women, they spent only about three hours and forty minutes doing their favorite things, and nearly nine hours on the unpleasant stuff.

No other workers in the industrial world work as much as Americans. Every country in the OECD except the United States mandates a combination of paid leave and paid public holidays. Portuguese workers get a total of thirty-five days off a year. Even the famously workaholic Japanese get ten. In the United States, by contrast, workers have no mandatory paid days off. And Americans get fewer vacations too. While the time devoted to work has declined in most industrial countries, in the United States it has remained flat over the past thirty years. Full-time American workers toil forty-six weeks a year, on average. That's five more weeks than in Spain. Four decades ago Japanese workers logged 350 more hours at work per year than Americans. By 2006, Americans worked more than the Japanese.

This work has produced a lot of growth. Between 1975 and 1997 the nation's GDP per head grew almost by half. Yet perhaps what went wrong is that all the happiness gained by Americans from the extra income was consumed by the unhappiness of having to work seventy-six more hours a year to get it. Compare this with the situation in France. The French economy has grown a little more slowly. But the

French worked 260 fewer hours in 1997 than in 1975. Comparing the happiness boost provided by money with that provided by free time, researchers estimated that the United States would have had to grow almost three times as fast as it did to compensate Americans for their extra work and provide them as much happiness as the French got.

The trade-off changes as we become richer. The value of our scarce free time increases, while the things money can buy become less important the more we have. That's why people in rich countries usually work less than people in less developed ones. Koreans enjoy about 650 more hours of leisure a year than Mexicans, but about 400 fewer leisure hours than Belgians. But the trade-off itself generates anxiety. Because the more our incomes rise, the more money we forgo when we spend time on nonproductive endeavors. The tension between time and money peaks when we make the most money of all.

The curve of happiness over the life cycle looks like a U, declining steadily until middle age and rising again. American men are unhappiest in their early fifties and Europeans of both sexes in their late forties. Mexicans hit their happiness minimum at about age forty-one. Middle age can be a disappointing inflection point. It's when we finally admit our limitations and shelve the long-held plans to become a pop star, strike it rich, travel the world, and live forever. It is the point in life when we hit the peak of our careers and make the most money. But it is also the point at which we enjoy the least free time. The average middle-aged American man sleeps 8.3 hours a night, down from 9.8 hours in our late teens and early twenties.

Information technologies, portrayed as revolutionary tools to improve our lives, are the shackles of the contemporary economy. At the height of the dot-com bubble of the 1990s, Stephen Roach, the chief economist at investment bank Morgan Stanley Dean Witter, wrote a scathing critique of government statistics that purported to show spectacular increases in the service sector's labor productivity. How could it be, he wondered, that service professionals could expand their output per hour so readily when their output consisted mainly of ideas?

He concluded that the so-called productivity boom brought on by computers was a mirage. What was happening was that technology made it easier for workers to work longer hours. Laptops, cell phones, and other appliances allowed them to take their work with them everywhere they went. "The dirty little secret of the information age is that an increasingly large slice of work goes on outside the official work hours the government recognizes," Roach wrote. The time we now devote to work on our gizmos we used to devote to other activities that were frequently more rewarding. As recently as 1985, Americans spent an average of two hours and twenty-nine minutes a day preparing food, eating it, and cleaning up. By 2003, the time invested in meals had fallen to one hour and fifty minutes.

## LA JOIE DE VIVRE

Americans have not always worked more than everybody else. In the 1970s European workers labored more than their counterparts in the United States. Some economists suggest higher tax rates in Europe discouraged work there. Others point to stronger unions that pushed social democratic governments in Europe to create more leisure time, including mandated holidays and shorter workweeks. In the late 1990s, the French Assembly passed the thirty-five-hour workweek as a strategy to combat unemployment—based on the idea that more people would work if each worker labored fewer hours. While the effort failed to promote job growth, it did give workers more time off.

Olivier Blanchard, the French chief economist of the International Monetary Fund, who spent much of his professional career in the United States, argues that Europe and the United States made different choices as they became richer and more productive. Americans chose to deploy their higher productivity to earn more money and buy more goods and services. Europeans "spent it" on more leisure time and more time working on household chores.

Many economists will understand these choices as rational

manifestations of different preferences. The French chose time and the Americans money because they preferred it. Their choices should make them both happy. But there is another possible reading: Americans chose an unhappier path.

Some of the same studies that show Americans stuck in a happiness rut since the end of World War II suggest that the French have become happier with their lot. The French work 440 hours a year fewer than Americans partly because they take seven weeks' vacation, compared with fewer than four in the United States. They sleep the longest of all citizens of the industrial world. They spend two and a quarter hours a day on meals, an hour more than in the United States. And they devote almost an hour a day more to leisure than Americans do.

French women spend more than twice as much time as Americans on meals and almost 50 percent more on active leisure—like doing sports or going to shows. American women spend about 10 percent more time working and a third more on passive leisure activities like watching TV. As it turns out, Americans like the French life better than their own. Researchers found that if American women were to reorganize their days to spend time as the French do, they wouldn't be quite as happy as the French, but they would be happier than they are with the lives they lead.

The conclusion to be drawn from the American happiness paradox is not that money cannot increase happiness. It can. It simply underscores that money is not the only relevant variable. Happiness can be purchased in other currencies too. It can be bought with love. It can be bought with time. And pursuing growth at all costs can lead us to sacrifice other components of our happiness.

You can trust Mexican soaps. In the 1990s, the Mexican television network Televisa tried to replicate the success of *The Rich Also Weep* with a remake that they titled *María la del Barrio* or *María of the Hood*. Perhaps to address the original's hopeless naïveté, or a new understanding of the world, the writers gave the heroine, now named María Hernández de la Vega, a new line: "I know the rich also weep," she said. "But the poor weep more."

CHAPTER FOUR

# The Price of Women

**I SOMETIMES WONDER** why polygamy has such a bad reputation.
We frown upon it as a barbarous practice of the past, when rich
men would amass harems to produce herds of children and women
could be bought and sold like livestock. Ninety percent of Americans think polygamy is morally wrong, according to a Gallup poll,
more than those opposing cloning humans, abortion, or the death
penalty. In most of the world monogamous marriage is the norm.

But strict monogamy has been historically rare. In fact, polygamy—
when men have more than one wife at the same time, or a wife and several concubines—has been popular across human history. It thrived in
the great empires of the past, among kings and emperors who could
afford many mates. It was common practice among the powerful in
Zoroastrian Iran, the Egypt of the pharaohs, and in the Aztec and Inca

empires. King Solomon had seven hundred wives and three hundred concubines. Yet according to the Bible this troubled God only because many weren't Hebrew but Moabite, Ammonite, Hittite, and so on, and had their own deities. Polygamy was banned from Ashkenazi Judaism only in the synod convoked by Gershom ben Judah around the year 1000 of our era.

From the 1960s to the 1980s the anthropologist George Murdock compiled a so-called Ethnographic Atlas, recording customs and practices in nearly 1,200 societies, both ancient and contemporary. Polygamy was prevalent in 850. Similarly anthropologists surveying 172 western North American Indian societies in the 1960s and 1970s reported that polygamy was only absent or very rare in 28.

Polygamy was legal in Japan until 1880 and in India until 1955, when it was banned for Hindus but not for Muslims. In the United States, the Mormon Church only disavowed the practice around the turn of the twentieth century under intense pressure from the United States Congress, which disincorporated the Church and seized its assets in 1887. Even in the 1980s, scholars estimated that about 10 percent of the world's population lived in polygamous societies. Today, taking more than one wife is still common in parts of the Middle East, in much of Africa—from the Sahel in the north to a band crossing from Senegal in the west to Tanzania in the east—and among Mormon breakaway sects in the American West.

Polygamy is in our genes. Geneticists studying genetic variation in populations in China, France, Africa, and the South Pacific found that females passed down more genetic variety than males to their offspring, suggesting that more females than males managed to breed successfully. That fits a typical marker of polygamy: rich men mate a lot with lots of different women; poor men breed very little or not at all.

In his essay on polygamy and divorce, the eighteenth-century Scottish Enlightenment philosopher David Hume blasted polygamy as unnatural: "This sovereignty of the male is a real usurpation, and destroys that nearness of rank, not to say equality, which nature has established between the sexes." But in 1979, more than two hundred years later, Ayatollah Ruhollah Khomeini told the Italian journalist Oriana Fallaci that Iran's "law of the four wives is a very progressive law, and was written for the good of women since there are more women than men." Polygamy, he concluded, "is better than monogamy."

**IT MIGHT SEEM** odd to bring the invisible hand of the market to bear on the most intimate transactions between men and women. But there is an economic rationale for these mating arrangements. It has to do with the relatively low cost of sperm.

Prices are on prominent display in the most intimate transaction that we know. In the market for mates, prices are attached to different things—husbands and wives rather than diamonds or sound systems. But they perform essentially the same task as they do on the supermarket shelf, allocating resources to maximize an associated benefit. In this particular market the benefit consists mostly of surviving children.

Darwin's theory of sexual selection posits that the first, most important driver of behavior—of humans or animals—is the imperative to pass genes down to future generations. In a world in which males need only invest a dollop of sperm in this endeavor, while females must produce an egg, carry, and nourish the embryo, it is only natural that mates would have asymmetrical reproduction strategies.

In the natural world this means that for males the ideal system would allow them to plant their seed in as many females as possible. Females, whose fertility is constrained by the enormous cost of bearing offspring, would have less use for multiple males. They would choose quality instead, males who could provide resources to help ensure that the next generation survived.

These are not the only considerations shaping the mating arrangement. Female bonobo apes are extraordinarily promiscuous.

They have lots of sex, with whichever male happens to be around. Researchers suggest this behavior evolved as a strategy to avoid infanticide. Males would kill unrelated babies so their mothers would stop breast-feeding and recover their fertility. Indiscriminate sex ensured that a male could never be sure whether the kid was his.

Mating strategies are influenced by all sorts of ecological constraints—ranging from the abundance of food to the density of the population. Many species of birds establish stable monogamous relationships—an arrangement that reduces competition between females and ensures that males collaborate closely in the rearing of their offspring. But bird adultery is common—as males try to wriggle out of their marital strictures to maximize their reproduction potential while females try to find males with better genes than those of their faithful mates.

Still, the asymmetry between male and female investments in reproduction sheds light on many sexual mores. It helps explain, for instance, why cheating husbands usually choose women who are younger than their wives while cheating wives choose men who are more educated than their husbands. Men are most interested in women's curves—a measure of their reproductive abilities—while women are most interested in men's earning power—a measure of their command of resources. The asymmetry also explains why in many societies across the span of human history women have had a price.

**POLYGAMY IS BRED** of inequality. Polygamy is rare in subsistence societies, where resources are scarce, because males cannot sustain multiple females. And if all men are equally poor, women have little cause to choose to be the second wife of one man rather than the first wife of another. Polygamy became prevalent because it allowed economically successful men to extend their success to the market for reproduction, planting their seed in several mates. It also allowed more than one woman to mate with the most resourceful man and share his successful genes. This combination of incentives bred a market in which women sold reproductive services for men to bid for. The most resourceful men could offer more. This often led husbands to pay for their brides.

Roughly two thirds of the societies recorded in Murdock's atlas feature payment for the bride. Among them are the Kipsigis, a polygamous society of herders and farmers in Kenya. The anthropologist Monique Borgerhoff Mulder, who studied the group in the 1980s and 1990s, found that each extra wife added 6.6 children to a man's fertility. This fecundity—added to women's contribution in labor to household income—commanded a price, usually paid by the groom to the bride's family. From the 1960s to the early 1980s the average price for a Kipsigi bride was six cows, six goats, and eight hundred Kenyan shillings. For a man of average wealth, this amounted to one third of his cows, half his goats, and two months' salary.

Yet prices followed the ebb and flow of supply and demand. Borgerhoff Mulder reported that bride prices declined in the 1970s and 1980s as land became scarcer and men had to wait longer to accumulate enough wealth to marry. Since Kipsigi men marry younger women, the wait tilted the ratio of males to females further in men's favor. Moreover, it increased the opportunity for women to have kids out of wedlock, reducing their subsequent bridal price.

Polygamy can be problematic. It can entrench poverty, diverting productive capital into the bridal market. It encourages men to have large numbers of children, reducing the resources available to invest in their education. One study suggested that banning the practice in Africa would lead to a 40 percent drop in fertility, a 70 percent increase in national savings, and a 170 percent increase in economic output per head. But that doesn't mean polygamy is worse for women than, say, monogamy.

Across human history, the world has remained mostly a patriarchal place. Both in polygamous and monogamous societies, sons typically carry the bloodline and inherit the family property. Daughters marry into their husband's family and name. Still, there are important differences. In polygamous societies the male-to-female ratio is tilted in women's favor. So women have a chance of mating above their station. In monogamous cultures, lower-quality women are reduced to mating with lower-quality men. As the American anthropologist Laura Betzig once said, "Which woman would not rather be John Kennedy's third wife than Bozo the Clown's first?"

Bride prices, of course, are rarely paid to the brides; payment is usually made to their parents, who often turn around and use them to purchase brides for their sons. Yet even in the most patriarchal cultures, parents who expect to get cash for their daughters are likely to appreciate them more. Theodore Bergstrom, an economist at the University of California at Santa Barbara, developed an economic model of polygamy that concluded that when families use the money they get from marrying off their daughters to buy brides for their sons, a family with at least one son would gain more grandchildren if its additional children were daughters. This makes women valuable.

In many monogamous societies, daughters often represent nothing but a cost. Bride prices are rare among them. Instead, they feature dowries, payments from the family of the bride to the groom that are virtually unheard of in polygamous cultures. That's probably why many traditional monogamous societies have been prone to female infanticide and feticide.

Polygamy faded over the past two thousand years, first in Europe and then across much of the world, pushed by European colonial expansion. But it doesn't seem to have been due to the opposition of women. The more likely reason is that men turned against it. One theory posits that economic development fostered monogamy because of the way it changed the reproductive goals of rich men. In less developed societies where wealth was mostly inherited, it made no sense to invest in educating one's children. The purpose of mating was to have as many children as possible to improve the odds that a man's genes would survive into the next generation. This suggested maximizing the number of mates regardless of their quality.

As economies developed and work became the main path to wealth, investing in children's human capital started to make sense. In this new richer world more children survived into adulthood, reducing men's need for a harem of wives to sire as many as possible. Instead, it paid off to have a smart wife who could educate them. This change encouraged women's education. In poor, primitive societies it was pointless, let alone potentially destabilizing, to educate women. But once men's purpose shifted from having many children to having a few better-educated kids, educating mothers to rear them became a useful investment. These shifting priorities changed the economics of the mating market too, pushing up the price of higher-quality women and thus making polygamy less affordable.

Perhaps the most compelling hypothesis, however, is that polygamy succumbed to the need for social cohesion in larger, more developed societies, which had a competitive advantage over less organized neighbors. A 1999 study comparing 156 states found that monogamous societies were more populous, less corrupt, less likely to use the death penalty, and richer than polygamous ones.

Polygamy entrenches disparities, allowing the rich to hoard all the women and bumping the poor out of the gene pool. This doesn't make for very harmonious social relations. Throughout much of the 2000s, hundreds of teenage boys were ejected from the Fundamentalist Church of Jesus Christ of Latter-day Saints, a breakaway Mormon settlement straddling the border between Utah and Arizona, to allow its religious leaders to hoard dozens of brides. The argument suggests that for big democratic states to survive, polygamy had to go.

Polygamy was common among the elites in the Homeric world. But classical Greece and Rome, from the tenth century before the Christian era, were monogamous in an important way: citizens were allowed only one wife and were not allowed to cohabit with concubines, but they were allowed to have as much sex as they wanted with their slaves, mostly taken in war against other cultures. Researchers have suggested this arrangement allowed even poor, weak men to have a wife and reproduce, yet also allowed the powerful to plant their seed in many gardens.

From Greece and Rome through the medieval church, monogamy spread across the Judeo-Christian world. In the fifth century of the Christian era, Saint Augustine called monogamy a "Roman custom." One hundred twenty-five years later, the Emperor Justinian said "ancient law" forbade husbands from having both wives and concubines. Christianization spread monogamy across the ancient world. Except for a few outbursts of polygamy—among the Anabaptists in the sixteenth century—monogamy became the established mating institution of the West.

## THE VALUE OF WOMEN'S WORK

The economist Gary Becker won the Nobel Prize in economics for a body of work started in the 1960s about human behaviors and interactions beyond simple market transactions. Paramount among them was his analysis of the family. Becker described it as a little factory in which husband and wife are specialized producers of complementary household goods: women equipped for rearing children trade home production with men, who will specialize in bringing home the bacon from the labor market. Together they profitably provide communal goods and services—among which the most important are kids. The power of Becker's economic formalism explains more than just the nuclear family. It sheds light on an array of institutions governing the entanglement of men and women, tracing them to transactions in markets for mates and family goods.

The economic nature of the marriage bargain explains why most societies have codified special protections to ensure wives' access to resources. In a Darwinian world in which men's optimal strategy is to plant seed in as many women as possible, this ensures that women have the needed resources to successfully carry their off-spring. More than two thousand years before the Christian era, the Sumerian code of Ur-Nammu set a price for divorce. A man had to pay his ex one mina of silver, about enough to purchase three slaves, or only half if she was the widow of a previous marriage. The Babylonian code of Hammurabi demanded that a man who left the mother of his children restore her dowry and provide her sufficient income to ensure their sustenance.

But if laws were deployed to guarantee women's access to men's resources, so they codified strict standards to ensure that men would not rear someone else's child. Harsh penalties for female adultery have historically protected men from women's optimal reproduction strategy: to choose an okay man to marry and provide resources, and have occasional affairs with other mates with superior genes.

Anthropologist Bronislaw Malinowski documented that in the Trobriand Islands of Papua New Guinea, husbands had the right to kill their wives if they committed adultery, while wives were entitled only to leave their adulterous husbands. Sumerian law established that while a willingly adulterous wife should be killed, a philandering male merited death only if he deflowered the virgin wife of another man. If a wife was accused of adultery, she had to prove her innocence by jumping in the Euphrates. If she drowned, she was guilty. If she survived, her accuser had to pay her husband twenty shekels of silver, or about seven ounces.

Vestiges of these institutions remain with us today. Until the 1970s, family law in the United States obligated men to support their wives up to their own standard of living. Today, alimony payments to the spouse with lower earnings are still a standard feature of divorce. But the terms of the marital transaction have changed, and the main driver of the transformation has been the transition of women into paid work.

In *The Theory of Economic Growth*, published in 1955, the development economist W. Arthur Lewis of the Caribbean island of St. Lucia wrote, "It is open to men to debate whether economic progress is good for men or not, but for women to debate the desirability of economic growth is to debate whether women should have a chance to cease to be beasts of burden and to join the human race." The raw Darwinian marketplace values women as wombs, selling reproductive services and household service in exchange for men's sperm and economic resources. But development changed the terms of the transaction. It gave women another function, as producers in the market. It thus increased their value, both in the household and in society at large.

**THROUGHOUT THE TWENTIETH** century, economic growth offered women in industrializing societies new opportunities to produce outside the home, which transformed their contribution to the household and improved their bargaining status. Work changed women's perspectives—offering new careers and lives. Lewis argued that "woman gains freedom from drudgery, is emancipated from the seclusion of the household, and gains at last the chance to be a full human being, exercising her mind and her talents in the same way as men."

But if development opened a new set of options for women, the addition of women to the workforce contributed to shape the path of development. Women brought to the workforce a different set of skills that eased the shift from heavy industry to service-based economies in the rich nations of the West. Of equal importance, as women increased their clout over decisions about household investments and expenditures, they helped usher in vast social and economic changes that profoundly altered Western civilization.

The economic historian Claudia Goldin argues that women's labor supply follows a sort of U-shape as countries develop. In pre-industrial societies, such as colonial America, women worked a lot, from caring for children to making soap and candles, while the men tilled the family plot. Families were little production units. The family economy wasn't productive enough to allow anybody not to contribute. But as economies grew, rising family incomes took pressure off women to contribute to household production, leading them to retreat from the workforce and focus more on child care. Facing a strong cultural bias against taking the dirty "guy jobs" that are typical of early stages of development, women reemerged into the labor force only after countries became rich enough to provide secondary education for women and white-collar clerical jobs that they could do without incurring social stigma.

In West Bengal, India, the first leg of this dynamic occurred during the green revolution in the 1960s and 1970s, when the introduction of high-yielding varieties of wheat, rice, and other crops ushered in a burst of farm productivity that raised household incomes and changed the type of work needed in the fields. Herbicides reduced the demand for weeding, traditionally a female occupation. The increased use of tractors and other farm machinery provided exclusively guy jobs. As a result, households became more specialized. While the men remained in the fields, women moved into the home to take care of the household. Unsurprisingly, West Bengali fertility increased.

The pattern also showed up in the United States of the late eighteenth century. Textile mills offered jobs to unmarried girls, who used their pay to supplement the family income and accumulate a dowry to make them more attractive partners in marriage. But as soon as they married, they left the workforce to care for their families.

American women remained in the home for a long time. By the end of the nineteenth century, only 5 percent of married women in the United States worked outside the home. Indeed, until the late nineteenth century, husbands had legal claims to their wives' earnings and property. States started passing laws granting women property rights only in the final few years of the nineteenth century. Economists suggest this is because women had very few chances to get a paid job or accumulate assets. But as industrialization opened more opportunities for women in the workplace, this arrangement started getting in the way of development, inhibiting women's incentives to work.

The pattern described by Goldin fits the curve of economic development in the world today. In extremely poor countries like Rwanda and Tanzania, nine out of ten women of ages forty-five to fifty-nine work. Women's labor supply declines as countries progress, reaching a low point around the stage of development of Mexico and Brazil, and then bounces back as countries reach the stage of Sweden, Australia, or the United States.

SOCIAL DYNAMICS BEYOND the workplace have evidently contributed to shape the evolving role of women around the world. Between the early 1900s and the 1970s American women gained the right to vote and to decide whether to terminate a pregnancy as part of broad egalitarian movements. Technology helped. From the washing machine to the frozen dinner and the microwave oven, new inventions made it easier for women to seek opportunities outside the home. The mass distribution of the birth-control pill made it cheaper for men to have sex, reducing their incentive to marry. But it also allowed women to take control of their own fertility, delay marriage, and start a career. Women lost a traditional source of material support but gained economic autonomy.

The linchpin of these changes, however, was work. Work increased women's leverage and impelled them to push for gender equality in the workplace, the home, and beyond, driving broader legal and political changes. Institutional changes then encouraged more women to work, producing a positive feedback loop. For instance, women's growing clout contributed to the spread of the no-fault, unilateral divorce in the 1970s. The change, which lowered the cost of ending a marriage, increased women's incentive to work as a form of economic insurance in case it ended.

Women's labor supply grew sharply throughout the twentieth century. In 1920 less than 10 percent of married women aged thirty-five to forty-four were in the workforce. By 1945 the share was around 20 percent. Women's educational attainment also grew by leaps and bounds. Outside the American South, high school graduation rates for women jumped fivefold from 1910 to 1938, to 56 percent. This produced a stream of qualified workers prepared for the new clerical jobs opening up across the economy.

Still, educated women faced an uphill battle to find better jobs. By 1950 a quarter of married women in their prime were in the job market, but the census reported that the top women's jobs were teacher, secretary, and nurse. Former Supreme Court justice Sandra Day O'Connor had a hard time getting a job interview with a law firm after graduating from Stanford Law School in 1952 near the top of her class. When she did, it was for a job as legal secretary. "I was shocked," she reminisced in 2008, two years after retiring from the Court. "It never entered my mind that I would not be able to get a job." She ultimately took one in the public sector: deputy county attorney in San Mateo County, California.

Women's attitudes toward work changed. In 1929 the labor supply of wives typically fell as their husbands' wages grew—suggesting they worked only to supplement the family income. By the early 1960s, however, economist Jacob Mincer found that women were making the decision on whether to work based on their own wages, rather than those of their husbands.

Work even transformed women's bodies. Men tend to like women with big hips and breasts for reproductive reasons. Female hourglass shapes are associated with the onset of fertility—girls have similar shapes to boys, but begin accumulating fat around breasts and bottoms at puberty, when their estrogen levels rise. But these aren't the only determinants of success. As women's opportunities in the job market improved, they embraced a different, slimmer archetype of beauty. The architecture designed for success in the mating game—big breasts and waspish waists—lost ground to a more slender body ideal that was better suited for a workplace still ruled by men who tended to see curvaceous women exclusively as mating opportunities.

Around 1900, the chests of models depicted in *Vogue* magazine were twice as big around as their waists. But as more women took professional jobs, busts in *Vogue* slimmed down until by 1925 they were only about 10 percent bigger. Women's body shape became more curvaceous again in the 1930s and 1940s, perhaps as a consequence of the relative scarcity of men during World War II, and the marriage surge after the end of the war that took many women out of work. But they would slim down again. As a wave of women joined the professional ranks over the next three decades, breast sizes declined progressively relative to waists until by the late 1980s, the breast-to-waist ratio in *Vogue* was back near its trough of 1925.

The dynamic fits patterns found in other cultures. One study across dozens of primitive societies found that plump women are less desirable in societies that value women's labor, suggesting that body fat associated with higher energy storage and reproductive fitness also makes it more difficult to succeed at work.

Education, coupled with increasing demand for women in the labor force, ultimately changed women's expectations for good. In 1960 there were 1.84 men for every woman graduating from a four-year college in the United States. By 2008, the graduation ratio had flipped to 1.34 women for each man. And most of these highly educated women worked. In 2000, women accounted for some 40 percent of first-year graduate students in business, and about half of those in medicine and the law. About 60 percent of American women of working age are in the formal workforce, either holding a job or looking for one. This is still about 11 percentage points below men's labor participation. But it is 15 percentage points above women's share forty years ago.

Differences remain in men's and women's positions in the workplace. In 2009, women's median income had risen to about 80 percent of that of men. But the pay gap has remained stuck there for years. Women's wages are still penalized because they take more time off and are more likely to work part-time than men, mainly because of motherhood. A study of MBA graduates from the University of Chicago's Booth School of Business found that the gender wage gap rose from $15,000 a year on average, right after graduation, to $150,000 nine years out. It also found that nine years after graduation only 69 percent of female graduates were working full-time all year, compared with 93 percent of males. Yet, despite the persistent wage gap, for most women work has become the norm, irrespective of their earnings. It is what they do, just like men. This has changed American society in fundamental ways.

## RENEGOTIATING THE MARRIAGE BARGAIN

One cannot overstate how completely the traditional marriage bargain was overturned by the new dynamic. The standard family deal, in which women exchanged the service of their uterus, child care, and household chores for their husband's wage, was rendered obsolete the moment women arrived home with a paycheck of their own. Women devoted about forty-seven hours a week to household chores at the turn of the twentieth century. By 2005, they had cut back to twenty-nine. Men's work at home quadrupled to seventeen hours a week. Polls in the late 1970s found that a little more than a third of women disagreed with the statement that "it is more important for a wife to help her husband's career than to have one herself." By the late 1990s, four out of five disagreed.

At the same time, men and women discovered that the things family had been designed to provide—dinner, laundry, sex, and kids—could be had without it. By 2007, about 40 percent of births in the United States occurred out of wedlock. In the early 1970s there were eleven marriages for every one thousand Americans. By 2006 there were seven, the lowest in history. Divorce rates shot up. And having lots of kids, the principal purpose of the archetypal family unit, became less popular. The share of women who had four or more children dropped from 36 percent in 1976 to 11 percent in 2006. Over a fifth of women are now childless.

Both men and women had trouble adjusting to the new deal. A few years ago, I wrote an article about a slowdown in the labor supply of women that was showing up in American employment statistics. After four decades of growth, it seemed that women's rate of entry into the workforce had stalled sometime in the mid-1990s. I remember talking to Cathy Watson-Short, a thirty-seven-year-old former executive from Silicon Valley, who pined to go back to work but couldn't figure out how to mesh the job and caring for three young daughters. Most interesting was her shock at not being able to do it all: "Most of us thought we would work and have kids, at least that was what we were brought up thinking we would do—no problem." But her bottom line was that despite all the revolutionary changes unleashed by women's march to work, the relations between the sexes hadn't changed enough. "We got equality at work," she told me. "We really didn't get equality at home."

Surveys in the United States about the use of time confirm that women spend more than twice as much time as men tending the kids; men spend 50 percent more time working outside the home. But men too had a tough time navigating changes in the balance of power between the sexes. Over the past five decades the share of prime-aged women, aged twenty-five to fifty-four, who had jobs rose from under 40 to around 70 percent. Over the same period, the share of men in their prime who were employed dropped from 93 to 81 percent. When unemployment peaked in 2009, the share of men in their prime who lacked a job was at its highest since the end of World War II. That proved devastating in the marriage market too. Having lost their edge in the financial contribution to the household, many men were left with little to offer.

. . .

**RESEARCHING AN ARTICLE** about the decline in marriage rates among American men, I came upon a relatively new market taking shape on the Internet: online marriage brokerages to help frustrated American men find a wife in countries like Colombia and the Ukraine. The men I met were mostly middle-aged; some were well educated and financially successful. Some just wanted quick sex with exotic women abroad. But others were legitimately searching for a lifelong mate. They wanted one who would play by older rules, closer to the 1950s Doris Day template. Sam Smith, a former insurance salesman in Houston who set up the service I Love Latins, told me: "It all started with women's lib. Guys are sick and tired of the North American me, me, me attitude." BarranquillasBest.com, which offered Colombian brides, had tips on how to prevent foreign women becoming Americanized: "Let her have constant contact with her family in Colombia. Phone cards and 2 trips home a year are important."

Sam offered two-day package tours to Barranquilla for $895, including airfare, hotel, and mixers where a group of 17 American men would be introduced to 750 young Colombian women. "The guys think they died and went to heaven," he told me. Sam himself was into his second marriage to a Colombian woman, following a divorce in the United States.

In 2008 more than 42,000 foreign women were brought by Americans into the United States on temporary fiancée or spouse visas. In a way, the bargain they entered into was not unlike that of marriages in the past. The man offered a green card and a crack at a relatively prosperous life; the woman offered youth, beauty, and acquiescence. I spoke with several such couples who declared themselves happy—some after years of marriage.

The danger was that the men often did not realize that the Doris Day model was no longer operative in other countries either. "He wants to be the king of the house and buys into the promotional claim that he can get a more traditional woman in Russia—she will cook dinner and have sex and otherwise shut up," said Randall Miller, a lawyer who has represented foreign women abused by their American fiancés and husbands. "He is taken aback when the woman is outspoken and has opinions and wants to get a job."

Changes in the marital bargain even seeped into politics. They pushed women to the left, as economic vulnerability increased their support for taxes and government benefits. And they nudged men, who typically earn more and usually don't have custody of the kids, to the right. In 1979, American women were 5 percent more likely to say they preferred the left than men, according to election surveys. By 1998 the gap had grown to 13 percent. In the 2008 presidential election, women were 30 percent more likely to vote for President Barack Obama than for his Republican rival, John McCain. Men, by contrast, split their vote almost equally.

To some extent, similar dynamics have been at play around the industrial world. In Canada, New Zealand, and the Nordic countries, even more women work than in the United States. And women's labor supply has soared in traditionally patriarchal countries such as Italy, Spain, and Japan. Between 1994 and 2008 the share of Spanish women at work grew from 32 to 56 percent; in Italy it jumped from 36 to 48 percent.

In these countries too, the traditional family capsized. The marriage rate has fallen to about five marriages per one thousand population a year, on average, across the industrial countries of the Organization for Economic Cooperation and Development, from eight in the early 1970s. Nowhere has divorce reached the heights it did in the United States in the 1980s. Still, it rose everywhere. And fertility declined sharply, as women decided to delay childbirth to pursue careers, and fewer families were formed. Only 5 of 31 countries in the OECD—the United States, Iceland, New Zealand, Mexico, and Turkey—have a fertility rate at or above 2.1 children per woman, the so-called replacement rate that guarantees a stable population. In Spain women have only 1.5 kids, on average, and in Germany 1.3; in Japan they have 1.4. Fertility is so low that the population in some of these countries is starting to shrink. By 2050, Korea's population is forecast to shrink 17 percent.

## THE NEW MATING MARKET

One of the world's demographic mysteries is why, considering the current changes in the structure of the family, Americans still have so many kids.

Religion is one possibility. It is more popular in the United States than in pretty much every other wealthy nation. I heard a story on the radio about a small evangelical movement called the Quiverfull, a name based on Psalm 127 in the Bible, which says, "Like arrows in the hands of a warrior are sons born in one's youth. Blessed is the man whose quiver is full of them." The group frowns on contraception. Apparently, its members believe that if they have enough children, they will be able to take over the Congress in a few generations. "The womb is such a powerful weapon," suggested one of their leaders. "It's a weapon against the enemy."

The reason for America's prolificacy could also be that pensions in the United States are particularly stingy, making kids more useful as old-age insurance. A typical worker in the United States receives as little as 40 percent of his or her last wages from Social Security. European pensions are more generous. In Italy, fertility started rising slowly in 1996 after plummeting for ages. Perhaps not coincidentally, that was the year in which pension reform kicked in, reducing the payments promised to younger workers from 80 percent of their last wage to only 65 percent. Indeed, economists found that the odds of having a kid rose 10 percent for those workers who had their pensions cut, relative to those who hadn't.

But the most convincing explanation seems to be that the United

States has been better at accommodating work and childbearing than other nations. In the United States and some other countries, such as Sweden and Denmark, men have taken over some household tasks, lowering the cost of childbearing for women, allowing them to juggle kids and work outside the home. Some analysts also suggest that the weakening of the marriage bond has had a comparatively mild impact on American fertility because American women chose to have kids on their own. Countries like Italy or Spain, where traditional sexual roles are more entrenched, have had a tougher time overcoming beliefs that tie childbearing to marriage and a more traditional division of labor. Where mothers are expected to rear the young single-handedly, women face a starker choice: either employment or reproduction. As job opportunities have appeared, many have opted to work, dropping out of the mothering business altogether.

The fact that the archetypal marital transaction has been rendered obsolete does not mean modern marriage has nothing to offer. Marriage can yield substantial savings on everything from rent to magazine subscriptions. One study comparing the expenditures of single and married men and women in Canada found that singles living by themselves can spend substantially more than half of what a couple spends to achieve the same standard of living.

Marriage is also a form of insurance. Families with two sources of income are more financially secure than one and are thus more willing to take financial risks. A study of Italian women found that single women invest less in risky assets than married women, suggesting they feel more financially vulnerable. Other researchers found that the legalization of divorce in Ireland in 1996 led to higher savings rates among couples, as they hedged against the higher probability of breaking up and bolstered their finances. Married couples became 10 to 13 percent less likely to be in debt. And savings grew fastest among those who weren't religious and thus were more likely to divorce.

Marriage in the United States is a more symmetrical institution than it has ever been: both parents work; both care for the children. Today, in 57 percent of married couples, both spouses earn money. In a quarter of these the wife makes more than the husband, up from 16 percent two decades ago. Partners are more similar, in age, education, and earnings prospects. Rather than a kid factory, it is now more like a club, where husbands and wives pool the resources they earn from work to buy leisure and other goods—like child care—from the market.

The classic Hollywood formula where the rich executive married his secretary after discovering she was a pretty young woman once she took off her glasses no longer has any purchase on reality. Today, Americans are about four times as likely to marry someone with the same level of education as they are to marry someone who is more or less educated. And if one spouse in a marriage has more education than the other, it is likely to be the wife. As husbands and wives have become less dependent on each other to produce what the family unit needs, marriage, once meant to last until death, has become a more diverse arrangement than it ever was.

**THE CHANGES HAVE** taken a toll. Marriage has become unstable among poorer, less educated Americans. They marry and have children at a younger age, but divorce relatively soon, cohabit, and remarry. Among the least educated—people with no high school degree—marriage has become a rarity, and single mothers abound.

College graduates, by contrast, are marrying more. In the 1960 census 29 percent of women in their sixties with a college degree said they had never been married. By the 2000 census the share of never-married women in their sixties with a college degree was 8 percent. The better educated are marrying later, in their thirties and forties rather than their twenties, but they are much more likely to stay married. Twenty-three percent of white women with a college education who married in 1970 divorced within ten years. By 1990 the share had fallen to 16 percent.

These different experiences of marriage have a clear economic rationale. For the poor and less educated, marriage retained the old rationale of the shared production unit—where women and men trade complementary skills in the workplace and at home. Husbands make money in the workforce and trade it with their wives for child care and domestic labor. Marriage couldn't adapt to the fact that women now often had more stable jobs than men.

For the more educated, the transformation was easier to take in stride. They could allow marriage to be transformed into a partnership built not around production but around consumption. For those who could more easily buy goods, services, and leisure, marriage became more about sharing the fun. Yet the experiences of women like Cathy Watson-Short, the former Silicon Valley executive, suggest that even highly educated American families are still learning to cope with some of the changes. The tension between the workplace and the home seems to be prompting some to reconsider working. The share of prime-aged women in the workforce peaked almost ten years ago, at 77 percent, and has declined modestly since then. The participation rate of married mothers with kids of preschool age in the job market dropped some 4 percentage points from its peak in 1998 to 60 percent in 2005. A 1997 survey by the Pew Research Center found that a third of working mothers said they would ideally work full time. By 2007 the share had declined to about a fifth.

Until the financial crisis of 2008, which put many families under increasing financial strain, fertility rates had been edging up for the first time in many years. Many of the young women who had delayed marriage and childbirth fifteen years earlier to start a professional career had become older professionals considering children for the first time. In the late 1970s only about 10 percent of forty-year-old women reported having a young child at home. By the early years of this century, the share had jumped to 30 percent. Some economists suggested this burst of late childbearing could put a lid on the labor supply of women.

It seems unlikely, however, that this pause means that women have rejected their new identity forged in the workplace. After nearly a century of women marching into work, I don't see any signs suggesting a wholesale retreat back into the home.

## THE CHEAPEST WOMEN

On a visit to India several years ago, I fell into the habit of doodling with a new pastime while I sipped my morning coffee, trying to decipher the matrimonial ads in the *Times of India*. The ads were mystifying and fascinating. One suitor described himself as a "boy 27/171/4-LPA B.E. Sr S/W Engr in IBM," which I decoded as a twenty-seven-year-old boy who was 171 centimeters tall, earned four somethings, had a degree in engineering, and worked for IBM.

Another beckoned "handsome Hindu Mair Rajput Swarnkar boy M.Sc. Mtech PhD (IIT) 32/170/23000 pm. Central Government Class 1 Officer," which probably means the prospective groom was a civil servant and had gotten a Ph.D. from the Indian Institute of Technology.

Beyond the economy of words and the similarity in cadence with American real estate classified advertisements, the section underscored just how different mating is in India from, say, New York City or London. I was struck by the chastity of the advertisements, a far cry from the latex-clad suggestiveness of similar entreaties in the lonely-hearts section on Craigslist, and by the narrow segmentation of love. Ads were segregated not merely into main social classes, like Brahmin, Kshatriya, or Vayshia, but divided into dozens of castes, regional ethnic groups, and languages, nested one within the other like Russian dolls.

In India, 70 percent of marriages occur within the same caste, and the Indian public disapproves of intercaste marriage. Among middle-class families in Kolkata, the capital of West Bengal, women will consider a husband with no education from the same caste over one with a master's degree if he comes from another. A survey of Indian men found that marrying within their caste had twice the value of marrying a "very beautiful" woman over a "decent-looking" one.

But the most notable quality of the matrimonial classifieds was their blunt businesslike tone. Matrimony, the ads made clear, is a family business, negotiated by the parents of the bride and groom, designed to ensure the passage of the bloodline to the next generation and beyond.

Marriage has changed around the world as a growing number of employed and increasingly assertive women have subverted the archetypal mating transaction. But despite the power women have attained in places like Paris, Berlin, or even Mexico City, in others, age-old marital patterns have resisted change. These happen to be the places where women are cheapest.

In India, many matrimonial ads offer boys. But despite appearances, this isn't about empowering women. India is not the flip side of polygamous societies in which men go shopping for girls. Brides in India are very nearly powerless. Their parents may still usually pay a dowry to the groom, but brides are still the groom's property.

Dowries are onerous. Research among a subcaste of potters in Karnataka found the average dowry to be equivalent to six years' worth of the bride's family income. In Goa, on the west coast, average dowries rose from about 2,000 rupees in 1920 to between 500,000 and 1 million rupees in 1980.

They are rising. One study estimated that dowries across India rose by 15 percent a year between 1921 and 1981. Some suggest it is due to economic development and rising income inequality, which has allowed richer lower-caste women to bid up the prices for higher-caste grooms. Others suggest that fast population growth since the 1920s tilted the male-to-female ratio in favor of men. That's because women marry at a younger age than men. As the population grew, there were more young brides available for each successive cohort of older grooms. Indeed, among the Karnataka potters, one woman complained that her fifteen-year-old daughter was among thirteen girls competing for six men.

Yet the high prices brides' families pay to the grooms do not afford women much security in marriage. Even upper-class women are reportedly threatened, beaten, and even killed by husbands and their families demanding higher dowry payments after marriage. India's National Crime Bureau reports some 6,000 "dowry murders" a year, in which the husband's family burns the wife alive. Another study put the figure at 25,000 deaths.

The payment of a dowry is relatively rare compared to bride prices, but it is not exclusively an Indian dynamic. In the Chapainawabganj, Chittagong, and Sherpur regions of Bangladesh, researchers in 2001 reported dowries ranging up to 160,000 taka, which is almost four times Bangladesh's gross domestic product per capita. The researchers also reported extreme violence against women. Lower dowries usually led to higher levels of domestic abuse. Yet women who paid no dowry reported similar low levels of domestic abuse to those who paid the highest dowries of all. Perhaps this is because they had another source of power.

This naturally leads to the question of why would brides pay to be beaten? Why do dowries exist at all? Mostly, it's not up to the brides. Their parents cut the marriage deal. India is a patrilineal, patrilocal culture. Men carry on the family line, stay in the parental household, care for their parents, and inherit their estate. Daughters, by contrast, are a liability. Parents expect them to leave their parents' house to live with their husbands. Parents pay whatever it takes to marry them off.

For poor Indian families this can be costly, however. That's why they often cull female fetuses to get rid of the problem before they reach the age of marriage.

## KILLING GIRLS

Consider the Punjab and Haryana in northwestern India. According to India's 1981 census, there were about 108 boys aged six or less for every 100 girls, already a lopsided ratio. Then ultrasound technology spread through the country, allowing parents to determine early the gender of their expected baby. Selective abortions surged. By 2001, the census reported that for each batch of 100 young girls there were 124 young boys.

Dowries no doubt are an important reason why women are such a burden to their families. But they are not the only reason families in South and East Asia try to unburden themselves of their daughters. In South Korea, marrying off a son is often much more expensive than marrying a daughter. Still, in South Korea, the 2000 census reported a ratio of 110 boys for every 100 girls four years old and younger, a ratio that suggests systematic culling of females—either just before birth or quickly afterward. According to one study, there were 61 to 94 girls "missing" in China for every 1,000 born in 1989–90, and 70 missing girls in South Korea in 1992.

It might all be about supply and demand. In polygamous cultures—for example, among Kenya's Kipsigis—available women are scarce commodities because rich men hoard them, making them valuable. In India, they do not have the benefit of scarcity.

Monica Das Gupta, a demographer at the World Bank, believes bride prices were common in northwestern India at the turn of the twentieth century. Dowries emerged as declining child mortality boosted population growth and tipped the mating balance in favor of men—who marry older. Today, she told me, the trend is reversing as declining population growth and prenatal culling of female fetuses have reduced the number of young girls for older men to marry. Parents in the Punjab these days scour other Indian regions offering money for brides to marry their sons.

Demand for women is also lower in patriarchal cultures in which male descendants are meant to carry the family line. The killing of girls in South and East Asia has increased not only because of advanced ultrasound technology but also because falling fertility has reduced the size of families and families still want at least one son.

Researchers argue that girls are cheap in the patriarchal systems of South and East Asia because they are excised from their birth families, transplanted forever to those of their husbands. They are useless to pass the lineage down and provide no economic support to their parents. Women are not part of the clan. Men make up the social order; women are brought in to help men reproduce. They must bear a son. Otherwise they have no point.

Some of these biases were codified in law. South Korea's Family Law of 1958 said inheritance should go down the male line, men must marry outside their lineage, and wives must be transferred to their husband's family register. The kids, of course, belonged to the father's line. Only in 2005 did the Supreme Court mandate that women could remain on the register of their parents after marriage. In 2008 parents were allowed to register the children under the mother's family name.

These practices survive even outside their social and economic context. A study of the 2000 census in the United States found similar lopsided sex ratios in the children of Chinese, Indian, and South Korean parents. Among third children, sons outnumbered daughters by 50 percent if the family already had two girls.

But even in South and East Asia, there is hope that demographic and economic changes could raise the value of women. Industrial development in South Korea has reduced the importance of the family at the center of social and economic life. Living in cities and earning pensions, parents have become less dependent on their sons, who have been able to pursue more independent lives. Having a son has become less urgent. Daughters, meanwhile, have acquired value outside of marriage, gaining an education and joining the labor force.

Unlike India, where sex ratios of children have become steadily more imbalanced over the past half century or more, in Korea, between 1995 and 2000 the number of young boys recorded in the census for each 100 girls fell from 115 to 110.

## MISSING BRIDES

Jiang Jin, a thirty-one-year-old mother of three, has decided to live an undercover life in Beijing—babysitting her sister's children for a thousand yuan per month—rather than return to her hometown in Jiangxi and face the penalties for having had three children in violation of China's one-child law. Enforcement of the law is looser in China's countryside. Families are often allowed two children. Still, authorities in Jiangxi would fine her perhaps up to five thousand yuan, she says, to register her illicit kids and send them to school. "If you don't pay the fine," she said, "they take your house; they sterilize you."

Jiang Jin's predicament is not unusual. Like many other Chinese, she wanted a boy, and kept having children until one came. Other Chinese have resorted to more radical solutions. When Deng Xiaoping instituted China's one-child policy in 1979, his intention was to limit the size of the population so that it would peak at 1.2 billion before shrinking to 700 million by the middle of this century. But he didn't foresee one of its most notorious consequences. The systematic killing of girls, as families who had a baby girl got rid of her to make space for the boy they needed to take the bloodline to the next generation. While families in some rural areas were allowed to have two children, it still forced parents with one girl to ponder abortion if they happened to expect another. In 2010, China's Academy of Social Sciences reported that 119 boys were born for every 100 girls.

This, paradoxically, means that girls in China will eventually become very expensive. Today, China is "missing" tens of millions of women. This poses a different demographic challenge: what to do with millions of Chinese men who will fail to marry—what the Chinese call *guang gun,* or "bare branches." Economists at Harvard estimated that by 2020 there will be 135 men of marriage age— twenty-two to thirty-two—for every 100 potential brides, aged twenty to thirty. The Chinese Academy of Social Sciences estimated that by 2020 there would be 24 million men of marriage age without a spouse. The chance that a man over age forty in the countryside would find a spouse would be virtually zero.

This bodes ill for China's development. The lopsided sex ratios are likely to result in higher crime rates, increasing the number of frustrated and unmoored young men prowling the streets. It will increase the incidence of prostitution, and thus probably of HIV, and increase economic uncertainty for millions of men who will likely reach old age without heirs to care for them. The imbalance will also deepen regional disparities as women from the poorer regions in inland China are drawn to the wealthier coast to find both jobs and better pickings in the marriage market.

Researchers have even suggested the sex imbalance pushed Chinese households into a race to save more, so their sons would have money to compete in the increasingly tight marriage market. This enormous savings rate has contributed to China's accumulation of some $2.5 trillion in foreign exchange reserves at the end of 2009. If one can believe Alan Greenspan, the former Fed chairman, China's gender imbalance helped inflate the global housing bubble, as the mass of Chinese savings sloshing through the world's financial system kept interest rates low and fueled the boom in housing prices all over the world.

Beyond marriage imbalances, China's disregard for women is squandering a valuable resource. Women accounted for more than half of China's internal migrants aged between fifteen and twenty-nine, according to the 2000 census. Most of the migrant workers fueling China's economic boom were young women, who trekked from rural China to the vast assembly lines along the coast.

Studies across the developing world have found that women make more productive decisions than men about the allocation of household resources. In particular, they invest considerably more in their children's welfare. One study among female tea pickers in rural China found that the survival rates of baby girls increased when tea prices rose. The educational attainment of girls and boys improved noticeably too. This was because rising tea prices boosted women's wages, ensuring more investment in their children's health and education.

When Chiang Kai-shek and the Chinese Nationalist Army fled to Taiwan in 1949 after being defeated by Mao Zedong's People's Liberation Army, sex ratios in Taiwan tilted abruptly in girls' favor, as the island was suddenly flooded with young single men. This enhanced women's bargaining power in the mating market. As a result, the survival rates of baby girls increased, fertility fell, and investments in children's education grew.

Realizing its predicament, the Chinese government has now set about formulating policies to increase the value of women in their parents' eyes through programs like the "Care for Girls" initiative, which offered free public education for females and other incentives. And it has even begun to selectively loosen the one-child policy. Three decades after its inception, Shanghai authorities are even offering financial incentives to families who want to have a second child.

If nothing else, the gender imbalance has opened some new

business opportunities for women in the marriage market. Payments to the bride's family, a common institution in rural China known as *cai li*, have surged since the early 2000s, reaching tens of thousands of yuan as rural families become increasingly desperate about finding wives for their sons at any price. The *Wall Street Journal* reported that in Hanzhong, in Shaanxi, central China, eleven newly minted brides had fled from their husbands in a matter of two months—and taken their bride price with them.

CHAPTER   FIVE

---

# The Price of Work

**THE INTERNATIONAL LABOUR ORGANIZATION** estimates that, excluding sex workers, 8.1 million people around the world are co-erced into doing their jobs. That's not very many, if one considers the popularity of coerced labor through human history.

Slavery and forced labor were prevalent from the Aztec and the Islamic empires to Rome and ancient Greece, from feudal Europe to the antebellum American South. By some standards one might think today's labor markets are well suited to coercion: it would help employers save real money. These days workers draw almost 65 percent of the nation's income in wages and benefits—about ten percentage points more than they did eighty years ago, when the government started measuring the statistic consistently. That kind of money seems like a fairly potent incentive for their employers to enslave them. So why don't they?

Perhaps we've learned to be repulsed by slavery. But the historical record suggests that societies' choice of working conditions has less to do with values and morality, and more with the profitability of how labor is organized. From sixteenth-century Russia to the European colonies in the New World, the decision of whether to employ indentured or free workers has hinged on whether it is cheaper to pay a wage or to feed, clothe, and house slaves while paying for security to keep them enslaved.

Throughout history, slavery was rare in subsistence economies, such as early hunter-gatherer societies where people produced just enough to stay alive. In early horticulturalist cultures, land was not productive enough to generate a surplus that would justify enslaving additional workers. But as advances in food production generated surpluses that could feed larger populations and justify employing additional workers, landowners resorted to coercion as a way to get around the rising cost of labor. Only when population rose to a point where there were many laborers competing for jobs on scarce land did wages become a more attractive proposition for landowners than slavery.

Data from George Murdock's *Ethnographic Atlas* shows that in advanced horticultural societies, which supported populations of about forty people per square mile, some 80 percent of landowners were found to employ slaves. Yet as the plow increased agricultural productivity and population densities rose past one hundred people per square mile, more than half of landlords paid their workers a wage rather than coerce them to work.

Slavery could quickly reestablish itself, however, if something were to change the ratio between land and labor. The Black Death, which wiped out half the population in fourteenth-century Europe and returned periodically for three hundred years, provided one such change. Serfdom was unknown in Russia before the sixteenth century. But the population shock from the plague led the landed gentry to lobby the czar to restrict the mobility of tenant peasants, keeping them attached to the land through debt servitude and laws allowing landlords to recover fugitive peasants.

In Western Europe, where serfdom had been popular for four hundred years, the Black Death paradoxically seems to have hastened its demise. Though landowners had the same incentive to shackle peasants to the land, powerful Western urban elites that were nonexistent in the East also wanted the labor and opposed these efforts.

The evolution of serfdom provides a clue as to why slavery is not more popular today. The massive loss of population following the Black Death failed to entrench serfdom across Western Europe because big cities offered workers opportunities outside agriculture. While there were attempts to reintroduce serfdom, the lack of strong central authorities made it difficult to limit peasants' movements. The emergence of competing economic interests among the powerful urban bourgeoisie prevented landowners from imposing their will.

That didn't mean Western Europeans renounced coercion, however. The discovery of vast, scarcely populated lands in the Americas led Western Europeans to embrace slavery where labor was scarce on the other side of the Atlantic Ocean.

Slaves accounted for about 90 percent of the population of the West Indies in the eighteenth century. About 2 million slaves were shipped from Africa to the Caribbean isles between 1600 and 1800. And three quarters of the 290,000 European migrants were indentured servants. Slavery was a particularly effective institution when the land supported large-scale farming. On these plots a few gang bosses could monitor large groups of slaves, keeping the costs of enslavement down. That made the lucrative Caribbean crops of sugar and tobacco particularly attractive to slave owners.

**MANY DYNAMICS CONTRIBUTED** to the decline of labor coercion. Employers who could increase production by adding more inexpensive slaves had little incentive to invest in laborsaving technologies. Coerced workers had no incentive to become more productive—because they would just be handing a higher surplus to the boss. Both these effects hindered economic progress.

In the Americas, slavery led to slower subsequent economic growth. New World colonies in which slave labor was common in the 1830s, such as Jamaica and Guyana, are today much poorer than colonies in which slavery was rare, such as Barbados or Trinidad. In the United States, states where slave labor was widespread in the mid-nineteenth century, such as Mississippi, South Carolina, and Louisiana, are much poorer today than free states such as Connecticut, Massachusetts, and New Jersey.

An examination of the prices of slaves underscores how the institution slowed productivity growth. The price of a slave in South Carolina rose from about $110.37 in 1720 to about $307.54 in 1800. But that increase barely matched the rate of inflation. In real terms, slave prices remained flat. But, as economists point out, the price of slaves should represent the stream of profits that farmers expected from their labor. Price stability thus suggests that this expected stream did not grow very much.

Substitute illegal immigrants for slaves, and similar patterns emerge in the United States today. For decades American farmers have relied on cheap immigrant labor to tend their crops. In 1986, they pressed to pass the Immigration Reform and Control Act, which legalized nearly 3 million illegal immigrants. After that, their investments in laborsaving technology froze. By 1999, capital investments had fallen 46.7 percent from their peak in 1980.

Indeed, the institution of immigrant work in the United States may provide an answer to the question about the seeming unpopularity of slavery: it is not as unpopular as it may seem; it has just taken on a different, subtle form. Illegal immigrant workers look not too unlike indentured servants. Hiding from the cops, unable to stand up for their rights in the workplace, illegal immigrants are beholden to their employers like no other workers. Some legal immigrant laborers are formally tied to their jobs through visa requirements that forbid them to seek alternative employment.

But perhaps the most compelling answer is that, on average, workers are too cheap to make slavery worthwhile. Some workers draw high wages—bankers and other professionals with sought-after, lucrative skill sets. But the federal minimum wage is lower than it was thirty years ago. What's more, globalization has provided manufacturers with an enormous supply of cheap workers. In March 2010, the Vietnamese government raised the monthly minimum wage to 730,000 dong—less than $40. Slaves might not be any cheaper.

## WHAT'S FAIR PAY?

The price of work is probably the most important price in people's lives. The labor market is where we trade our skills for our keep—the rent, the food. Our wage will go a long way in determining the sort of life we will lead.

It has improved since slavery gave way to a free market for work. In developed industrial economies, wages soared in the past century alone. In 1918 a dozen eggs cost the typical American manufacturing worker the equivalent of a little more than an hour of work at the prevailing wage. Today she can afford them in less than five minutes. The Montgomery Ward catalog, launched in the late nineteenth century to bring big-city goods to small-town America, in 1895 offered a one-speed bicycle for $65—about six and a half weeks of work for a typical worker. Today the online Ward catalog lists multispeed models for about $350, which the average worker at the prevailing wage can pay for in fewer than nineteen hours of work.

But though the pay may be better, the market for labor is in some respects no less ruthless than it ever was, and in some regards perhaps more so. Two things drive wages: productivity—how valuable the job is to the employer—and the supply and demand for workers of a given skill. Rising pay has nothing to do with justice. Today, a worker can produce in less than ten minutes what it took a worker in 1890 an hour to make. That's why wages rose.

Some patterns of compensation are fairly easy to understand. Highly educated workers tend to earn more than those with less schooling. In India, men who are fluent in English earn 34 percent more than those who don't speak the language, even if they otherwise have the same level of education. Other patterns are less so. The tall make 10 percent more for every four inches in extra height. American men who are six feet two inches tall are 3 percent more likely to be executives than those who are only five feet ten inches. And the ugly earn less than the pretty—regardless of whether beauty has anything to do with the job. A study based on job interviews in the United States and Canada concluded that workers who were identified by the interviewer as of below-average beauty made about 7 percent less than the average, while those of above-average looks made 5 percent more. Men suffered a 9 percent ugliness penalty; ugly women were paid 5 percent less.

These pay gaps are probably due in part to discrimination. But much of the difference in pay has to do with how physical traits signal productivity improvements. Studies in Sweden found that taller people are smarter and stronger and have better social skills because they were healthier and better nourished as children. Being taller, they had higher self-esteem. The short are simply less productive. And productivity is what bosses go to the labor market to buy.

Then there is competition among workers for work. Those given to nostalgia like to reminisce about a kinder, gentler labor market, where wages weren't so precisely calibrated to skills and employers cared that their workers had a decent standard of living. Early in the twentieth century, firms like Sears and Eastman Kodak created mini–welfare states for their workers in an attempt to foster labor stability and keep unions out of their plants and stores.

The Eastman Kodak Company was famous for taking photography from the professional studio to the corner drugstore. (Its slogan—"You press the button. We do the rest"). But founder George Eastman was also an innovator in industrial relations. Kodak offered a performance bonus to workers as far back as 1899. By 1929, six years before Roosevelt signed Social Security and the National Labor Relations Act into law, it had profit sharing, a fund to compensate injured workers, retirement bonuses and a pension plan, accident insurance, and sickness benefits. After Eastman committed suicide in 1932 by shooting himself in the heart, the obituary in the *New York Times* applauded his "advanced ideas in the field of personal industrial relations."

Other pioneers tried to deploy pay as an incentive. Facing low worker morale and high turnover on the production line, in January 1914 Henry Ford raised wages to five dollars a day, doubling at a stroke most workers' pay. It worked, apparently. Job seekers formed a line around Ford's shop. The journalist O. J. Abell wrote at the time that after the pay hike Ford was churning out 15 percent more cars a day with 14 percent fewer workers. Henry Ford later observed: "The payment of five dollars a day for an eight-hour day was one of the finest cost-cutting moves we ever made." Gradually, the rest of the car industry followed. By 1928, wages in the auto industry were already about 40 percent higher than at other manufacturers. And this was before the United Auto Workers union had placed its stamp on the industry.

But the soft, paternalistic corporations of a century ago are not that different from their descendants. The critical difference today is that companies have cheaper options. And they can no longer afford the generosity of the corporate leviathans of the early twentieth century, which relied on a unique feature of American capitalism of the time: monopoly profits. As a dominant company in a new industry with high barriers to entry, Eastman Kodak had a near monopoly over photographic film. Ford also enjoyed fat profits unheard of in the cutthroat competitive environment of today. Today, multinational companies scour the globe seeking cheap labor and low taxes, abundant raw materials, and proximity to consumers. And competition is ruthless.

Princeton economists Alan Blinder, a former vice chairman of the Federal Reserve, and Alan Krueger, deputy Treasury secretary in the Obama administration, estimated that about a quarter of the jobs performed in the United States are "offshorable"—meaning they could be done by cheaper workers overseas taking advantage of new information technology and telecommunications networks. Computers have also replaced workers in a range of tasks, in the corporate suite or on the factory floor. Technology has enabled new players to tap markets once thought impenetrable. The steel mills along America's rust belt suffered not just because of cheap imported steel. The minimills in the South that made steel from scrap metal contributed at least as much to the demise of the nation's integrated mills as foreign rivals.

These economic forces have brought prosperity to many workers around the world. China's gross domestic product per person tripled over the last decade, to $7,200, as manufacturers have relocated production there to take advantage of its cheaper workforce. Since 1990, the share of the Chinese population living on less than a dollar a day dropped from 60 percent to 16 percent. But in the United States, this intense competition upended many of the agreements and institutions that governed the labor market through much of the twentieth century. Eastman Kodak is going through a wrenching transformation as film gives way to digital imaging. In 2009 it discontinued Kodachrome, which had been around for seventy-four years. And it lost $232 million. Its workforce has dwindled to fewer than twenty thousand, less than a third of its staffing at its peak.

Unions, once tools to obtain higher wages from employers, have lost power. Private-sector workers represented by unions make about 21 percent more than those who are not, a premium that is worth about $148 per week. Union contracts remain useful in recessions—when employers look for easy places to cut costs. But unions are dying off as unionized firms shrink or go out of business while new arrivals resist them tooth and nail. Over the past thirty years, the share of workers in the private sector covered by collective labor agreements plummeted from almost 21 percent to 7 percent.

Until the 1970s, Detroit's Big Three carmakers made nine out of ten cars and light trucks sold in the United States. General Motors was known as Generous Motors. By 2009, the Big Three's share of the American market was about 45 percent. General Motors and Chrysler went bankrupt, rescued by a government bailout. The United States still has an auto industry, but most of it grows in non-union shops outside Michigan. In 1999, about 38 percent of the nation's autoworkers were covered by union contracts. In 2008 only 25 percent were. This emergent auto industry is unlikely to provide the generous pay and benefit packages that union shops once did.

## PAYING SUPERMAN

The American labor market is about as ruthless as it gets for a rich industrial nation. Western European social democracies have many rules mandating minimum holidays and maximum working hours. Higher minimum wages and tax rates on high incomes favor more homogeneous wages. The American workplace, by contrast, is mostly about free competition—unblemished by government interference. The job market is structured with one objective in mind: to reward success. It has led to an enormous pay gap between the best and the rest.

In 1989, the San Francisco Giants, the most expensive team in Major League Baseball, paid a median salary of $535,000, more than five times the median wage at the Baltimore Orioles, the cheapest club at the time. Big as it seems, the gap is small by current standards. In 2009, the New York Yankees paid a median wage of $5.2 million, nearly twelve times more than the Oakland Athletics at the bottom.

A similar dynamic is on display in the corporate suite. In 1977, an elite chief executive working at one of America's top one hundred companies cost about 50 times the wage of its average worker. Three decades later, the nation's best-paid CEOs made about 1,100 times the pay of an average worker on the production line. This change has separated the megarich from the simply very rich. A study of pay in the 1970s found that executives in the top 10 percent made about twice as much as those in the middle of the pack. By the early 2000s, the top suits made more than 4 times the pay of the executives in the middle.

An elegant economic proposition takes a stab at explaining this phenomenon. In 1981 the University of Chicago economist Sherwin Rosen published an article titled "The Economics of Superstars." In a nutshell, Rosen argued that technological progress would allow the best performers in a given field to serve a bigger market and thus reap a greater share of its revenues. But it would also reduce the spoils available to the less gifted in the business.

The reasoning fits smoothly with the income dynamics of pop stars. The music industry has been shaken by several technological disruptions since the 1980s. First MTV put music on television. Then Napster took it to the Internet. Apple allowed fans to buy single songs and take them with them. Each of these breakthroughs allowed the very top acts to reach a larger fan base, and thus take a bigger share of consumers' music budget and attention. In 1982, the top 1 percent of pop stars took 26 percent of concert ticket revenue. By 2003 they were raking in 56 percent of the concert pie.

Superstar effects go a long way to explain the pay of Tom Cruise, which grew from $75,000 in *Risky Business* to somewhere between $75 million and $92 million for *Mission: Impossible II*. They apply to European soccer, where the top twenty teams reaped revenues of €3.9 billion in 2009, more than 25 percent of the combined revenues of all European soccer leagues. Brazil's Pelé, the greatest soccer player of all time, made his World Cup debut in Sweden in 1958 when he was only seventeen. He became an instant star, coveted by every team on the planet. By 1960, his team, Santos, reportedly paid him $150,000 a year—about $1.1 million in today's money. These days that would amount to middling pay. The top-paid player of the 2009–2010 season, Portuguese forward Cristiano Ronaldo, made €13 million playing for the Spanish team Real Madrid. Including sponsorships, the highest-earning player today is David Beckham, the brilliant English midfielder who made $33 million from endorsements in 2009, on top of $7 million in salary from the Los Angeles Galaxy and AC Milan.

Pelé was not held back by the quality of his game, but by his small revenue base. He might be the greatest of all time, but few people could pay to experience his greatness. In 1958 there were about 350,000 TV sets in Brazil, for a population of about 70 million. The first television satellite, Telstar I, wasn't launched until July of 1962, too late for Pelé's World Cup debut. By contrast, the 2010 FIFA World Cup in South Africa, in which Cristiano Ronaldo played for Portugal, was broadcast in more than two hundred countries. Adding up the audiences of each game around the world, tens of billions of pairs of eyes watched the tournament—more than the world population. Cristiano Ronaldo is not better then Pelé. He makes more money because his talent is broadcast to more people.

Rosen's logic has been invoked to explain executive pay too. As American companies, banks, and mutual funds have grown in size, it has become crucial for them to put at the helm the "best" possible executive or banker or fund manager. This has set off an enormous competition in the market for managerial talent, pushing the prices of top executives way above the wages of anybody else. Xavier Gabaix and Augustin Landier of New York University published a study in 2006 estimating that the sixfold rise in the pay of chief executive officers in the United States between 1980 and 2003 was due entirely to the sixfold rise in the market size of large American companies.

The pattern follows the same Darwinian logic of elephant-seal sex. Elephant-seal cows consistently favor big bulls that can wallop rivals into submission. This happens despite the fact that the heavier they become the easier it is for sharks and orcas to eat them. Corporations deploy pay packages to attract talent as elephant seals deploy fat to attract mates. And yet humongous compensation plans are unlikely to produce benefits to shareholders. Fat paychecks have been found to encourage fraud—tempting executives loaded with stock options to do anything to increase the price of their companies' shares. They have also been found to encourage excessive risk taking.

And it is doubtful that this strategy benefits society at large. Over the past fifteen years, the top 1 percent of American families raked in half the entire increase in the nation's income. In 1980, they took home about a tenth of it. Today, they get to take home almost a quarter. That amounts to very few elephant seals eating all the fish.

## FARMERS AND FINANCIERS

The biggest seals work for banks. Banks pay enormous bonuses to draw the brightest MBAs or quantum physicists. These bright financiers, in turn, invent the fancy new products that make banking one of the most profitable endeavors in the world.

Remember the eighties? Gordon Gekko sashayed across the silver screen. Ivan Boesky was jailed for insider trading. Michael Milken peddled junk bonds. In 1987 financial firms amassed a little less than a fifth of the profits of all American corporations. Wall Street bonuses totaled $2.6 billion—about $15,600 for each man and woman working there. Today, this looks like a piddling sum. By 2007 finance accounted for a full third of the profits of the nation's private sector. In 2007 Wall Street bonuses hit a record $32.9 billion, $177,000 per worker.

It goes without saying that this type of pay is not the norm across industries. In America's rural economy, far from the steroid-laced streets of Lower Manhattan, remuneration is less about incentives than about keeping workers alive. In the spring of 2009, the average wage of fieldworkers on American farms was $9.99 an hour.

Among other tactics to ensure cheap labor, farmers regularly lobby Uncle Sam. They asked the government to open the door to farmworkers from Mexico as far back as World War I. They did it again in the 1940s, when the Bracero program was launched to replace the American men who had been shipped off to World War II. The program survived until 1964, a tribute to the lobbying power of growers. But when it ended and farmworkers' wages started to rise, farmers replaced them with something cheaper.

Farmers today estimate that about 70 percent of the million or so hired workers tilling fields and picking crops are illegal immigrants. In 2006, as the United States Congress debated an overhaul of immigration law, I met Faylene Whitaker, a farmer who grew tobacco, tomatoes, and other crops in the Piedmont area of North Carolina. Whitaker was concerned about the high cost of employing immigrant workers through the prevailing legal channels and wanted a better deal. "We would rather use legal workers," she said. But "if we don't get a reasonable guest worker program, we are going to hire illegals." The visa set a minimum wage by comparison with other farm wages in the area. At the time it was about to rise to about $8.51 an hour from $8.24. Illegal workers, by contrast, could be had for less than $6.50.

ILLEGAL IMMIGRANTS, OF course, want the $6.50-an-hour jobs. That's why they risk life and limb to come across the border to get them, evading Border Patrol agents, criminal gangs, and snakes. These are the best jobs many poor Mexicans can aspire to. They are a path to relative prosperity, compared with the deep poverty of their villages and neighborhoods. Migrants' comparative good fortune— loudly displayed each time they return home with spare dollars in their pockets—spurs their younger brothers, sisters, and cousins to make the voyage as soon as they come of age. They want to be rich like them.

This is exactly what is supposed to happen. Like differences in other prices, pay disparities steer resources—in this case people—to where they would be most productively employed. Some of the hardest-working Mexicans are drawn by the relative prosperity they can achieve north of the border. Similar drives motivate the 11 million immigrants living in Germany, 7 million in Saudi Arabia, and about 6.5 million each in France, Britain, and Spain.

The inequality that has spurred such vast movements of people is an inevitable and, indeed, necessary feature of a capitalist economy. In poor economies, fast economic growth increases inequality as some workers profit from new opportunities and others do not. The share of national income accruing to the top 1 percent of the Chinese population more than doubled between 1986 and 2003, to almost 6 percent. Inequality, in turn, can spur economic growth, drawing people to accumulate human capital and become more productive. It draws the best and brightest to the most lucrative lines of work, where the most profitable companies hire them.

But for all its incentive power, is the vast income gap between financiers and farmworkers useful in any way? The United States grew rapidly over the past three decades. Gross domestic product per person increased about 69 percent since 1980, as inequality soared to levels not seen since the 1920s. Yet it also grew fast—83 percent—between 1951 and 1980, when inequality measured as the share of national income going to the very top of the population declined.

One study concluded that each percentage-point increase in the share of national income channeled to the top 10 percent of Americans since 1960 led to an increase of 0.12 percentage points in the annual rate of economic growth. But even at this higher rate, it took thirteen years for the bottom 90 percent of Americans to recover the share of income they had sacrificed to speed up the economy.

The United States remains the rich country with the most skewed income distribution. According to the OECD, earnings of the richest 10 percent of Americans are 6 times those of the 10 percent at the bottom of the pile. That compares with a ratio of 4.2 in Britain and 2.8 in Sweden.

Still, Americans are less economically mobile than the citizens of many other countries. There is a 42 percent chance that the son of an American man in the bottom fifth of the income distribution will be stuck in the same economic slot. The equivalent odds for a British man are 30 percent, and 25 percent for a Swede.

Even if inequality were an undoubted motor of economic growth, we might invoke other reasons to put some limit to the concentration of riches at the top. Intense inequality breeds mistrust, envy, and hostility across income groups. Equity fosters a sense of solidarity and shared purpose that makes for good social glue.

Rising income disparities push less fortunate families out of desirable neighborhoods as the rich snap up the real estate. In cities like Manhattan, central Boston, or San Francisco, the only people on moderate incomes are those who clean the homes, cook the food, and care for the kids of the rich before going home at night to a cheaper location.

Between 1970 and 2000, house prices in central San Francisco rose 1 percent to 1.5 percent a year faster than in the rest of the country, and it became a city of the rich. The share of families that made more than $136,000 a year, in today's money, rose from 10 percent to 31 percent, more than double the national rate of increase. People of middle income were elbowed out. In 1970, some 70 percent of families in San Francisco made less than $90,000, in current dollars. In 2000, the share was about half.

Geographic segregation fosters educational segregation. School finances depend on property taxes, which in turn depend on property prices. Given that people's wages are closely dependent on the quantity and quality of their education, families that are forced into areas with inferior schools will lag further behind.

Ultimately, inequality's power as a goad for growth depends on its being perceived as fair, or at least not entirely illegitimate. Today, many Americans doubt the rich "deserve" their pay. This is especially true of bankers, who somehow managed to cause a catastrophe like we had not seen in decades and still made off with an enormous bonus.

## THE VANISHING MIDDLE

There was a time when the United States offered workers a shot at prosperity. My father's parents were not highly educated. My grandfather grew up on a farm in Winnipeg and may not have finished elementary school. As a young man, he worked in Chicago's slaughterhouses. But he moved to Phoenix, got a union job at the Salt River Project power plant, and trained as an electrician. In the 1970s, when I spent summers with my American grandparents, they lived in a house with a front yard, a backyard, a den with an eight-track system, central air-conditioning, a car, a pickup truck, and a trailer. In Mexico, where I lived at the time, electricians did not have that life.

Incomes per person in the United States soared almost sixfold over the twentieth century, driven by a burst of technological progress. But the most remarkable feature of this growth was that through most of the century it was widely shared. In 1928, the top 1 percent of American families hoarded nearly a quarter of the nation's income. By the 1950s their share had fallen to 10 percent.

Economists have ventured several hypotheses for this dynamic. Some suggest the playing field was leveled by the institutions that emanated from the New Deal—including the minimum wage, labor protections, and government programs like Social Security, coupled with high tax rates and strict regulations constraining the profits of industries like banking. The rise of organized labor played a part, as unions negotiated better pay for their members.

Yet another factor stands out: education. Throughout the century, businesses demanded increasingly educated workers to keep pace with technological progress, offering higher wages to laborers with more schooling. And workers responded by going to school.

From the generation born in 1870 to that born in 1950, each cohort of Americans received more education than their parents. By the 1950s, 60 percent of seventeen-year-olds had graduated from high school; roughly six times the share in the United Kingdom. Then the GI Bill kicked in, offering to finance college for veterans returning from World War II. In 1915, the average American worker had 7.6 years of education. In 1980, he had 12.5.

One consequence of this investment in human capital is that the income of most American families grew 2 to 3 percent per year in the quarter century after the end of World War II, more or less evenly across the income scale. These families built the American middle class.

SOMETIME IN THE 1980s the dynamic broke down. Since then bankers, lawyers, and engineers, those with a college education or more, have seen wages rise substantially. Workers at the bottom—janitors and nursing-home staffers, housekeepers and nannies—have also benefited from slightly improving pay. But workers in the middle, like union workers in steel plants and car companies, have suffered as their pay stalled and declined.

It all comes down to the question of who is easiest to replace. It's tough to mechanize a nanny. It's also difficult to replace lawyers and bond traders. But jobs that can be reduced to a mechanical routine, like spray-painting a car, have disappeared or gone somewhere else. In 2008, the *Orange County Register* in California hired an Indian company, Mindworks Global Media, to take over some editing functions. In 2007, Reuters opened a bureau in Bangalore, India, to cover American financial news.

The education premium is bigger than ever. In 1973, men who

had at least a college degree made 55 percent more than those who had only completed high school. In 2010, they made 84 percent more. Yet perhaps due to the hollowing out of the labor market, this premium is no longer working well as an incentive. The educational attainment of the average American worker grew only one year from 1980 to 2005.

These days the American Dream is a pretty misleading reverie. The hourly wage of the average shop-floor worker was lower in 2009 than it was in 1972, after accounting for inflation. The typical American family—two earners, a couple of kids—made less than it did a decade before. It's been forty years since the last time the average worker could afford to pay the bills of the average household on a forty-hour workweek at the average wage. At the end of the first decade of the new millennium, the prosperity boom experienced by many workers in the twentieth century looks like a flash in the pan.

## A BANKER'S PARADISE

This reconfiguration of prosperity is not simply about changes in the way we pay for work. The entire set of rules governing American capitalism changed. Those that emerged over the past three decades hammered the middle class.

Trade barriers fell during this period, and capital controls were done away with. Welfare payments were redesigned to force the unemployed to look for work. Large swaths of regulation were cast aside as misguided hindrances to business. The shift lifted many of the protections that had shielded American workers from some of the harshest economic forces. And it provided enormous opportunities to those able to seize them.

Take banking. Finance today is one of the most lucrative industries for bright college graduates. But it wasn't always this richly paid. Financiers had a great time in the early decades of the twentieth century. From 1909 to the mid-1930s they made about 50 percent to 60 percent more than workers in other industries. But the stock-market collapse of 1929 and the Great Depression changed all that. In 1934, corporate profits in the financial sector shrank to $236 million, one eighth what they were five years earlier. Wages followed. From 1950 through about 1980, bankers and insurers made only 10 percent more than workers outside of finance.

To a large extent this mirrors the ebb and flow of restrictions governing finance. A century ago there were virtually no regulations to restrain banks' creativity and speculative urges. They could invest where they wanted, deploy depositors' money as they saw fit. After the Great Depression, President Roosevelt set up a plethora of restrictions to avoid a repeat of the financial bubble that crashed in 1929.

Interstate banking had been limited since 1927. In 1933, the Glass-Steagall Act forbade commercial banks and investment banks from getting into each other's business—separating deposit taking and lending from playing the markets. Interest-rate ceilings were also imposed that year. The move to regulate bankers continued in 1959 under President Eisenhower, who forbade mixing banks with insurance companies. Barred from applying the full extent of their wits toward maximizing their incomes, many of the nation's best and brightest who had flocked to make money in banking left for other industries.

Then, in the 1980s, the Reagan administration unleashed an unstoppable surge of deregulation that continued for thirty years. By 1999, the Glass-Steagall Act lay repealed. Banks could commingle with insurance companies at will. Ceilings on interest rates had vanished. Banks could open branches anywhere. Unsurprisingly, the most highly educated returned to finance to make money. By 2005, the share of workers in the finance industry with a college education exceeded that of other industries by nearly 20 percent. These smart financiers turned their creativity on, inventing junk bonds in the 1980s and moving on, in the last few years, to residential mortgage-backed securities and credit default swaps. By 2006, pay in the financial sector was again 70 percent higher than wages elsewhere in the private sector. Then the financial industry blew up.

Since the end of 2008, when the demise of the investment bank Lehman Brothers sent financial markets into a tailspin around the world, bankers have argued insistently against regulatory efforts to limit their remuneration packages, observing that curtailing financial activity will hamstring their ability to hire the best of the best. That's perhaps true. The new financial regulations passed by Congress in 2010 may reduce the financial sector's profitability. Bonuses might suffer.

Still, this is probably a good thing. Only 5 percent of the men who graduated from Harvard in 1970 would end up working in finance fifteen years later. By the 1990 class it was 15 percent. Meanwhile, the percentage of male graduates going into law and medicine fell from 39 percent to 30 percent. Of the 2009 Princeton graduates who got jobs after graduation, 33.4 percent went into finance; 6.3 percent took jobs in government. From our current vantage point, this looks like a misallocation of resources. For the good of the rest of the economy, bankers should earn less.

# CHAPTER SIX

# The Price of Free

**TO THOSE WHO** believe the Internet will change everything, October 10, 2007, marks a minor watershed. On that day, the British alternative band Radiohead offered fans the chance to pay whatever they chose to download its new album *In Rainbows*. If they wanted, they could get it for free. About a million fans downloaded the album in the first month, according to comScore, a market research firm, of whom more than six in ten paid nothing. Several million more downloaded the album from peer-to-peer services that offer fans the ability to share their music online, rather than from Radiohead's free Web site.

To economists, whose understanding of civilization starts with the assumption that people are hardwired to seek value for money, what was perplexing was that 38 percent of those who downloaded

*In Rainbows,* by comScore's estimate, chose to pay even though they didn't have to. Could these fans have been overwhelmed by some altruistic urge to give money to rock stars, rich though they are? Maybe they believed it was unjust to pay nothing for something they coveted, made by people they loved. Maybe they appreciated the novelty of the experiment.

ComScore estimated that the band made $2.26 per download; a decent sum considering the audio file available for download was of fairly low quality. Moreover, the band didn't have to share any of the money with a record label. And there was more money to be made. Fans rushed to buy a higher-quality version of the album when it went on sale a few months later—pushing it to the top of the American and British charts. In the United States it remained on the charts for fifty-two weeks, longer than any other Radiohead album. By October of 2008, *In Rainbows* had sold more than 3 million copies, according to the band's publisher, including 100,000 of a special boxed set that retailed for about $80. This surpassed the sales of the previous two albums, *Hail to the Thief* and *Amnesiac.* Pumped by the enormous publicity surrounding the album's release, the subsequent concert tour was a smashing hit.

To believers in the transformational potential of the Internet, Radiohead's experiment suggested that the information economy could revolutionize capitalism by allowing creators to make a living while giving away their creations for free. This new economy might require people to radically change their approach to property. But *In Rainbows* demonstrated that if creators would free themselves of the capitalistic shackles represented by record labels, Hollywood studios, and other representatives of corporate greed that siphoned off a big slice of their revenues, this new paradigm could work out for everybody.

No longer would it be necessary for creators to hide behind the walls of copyright erected to protect "intellectual property." The production of information goods would be supported by consumers' altruism, much like philanthropy or tipping. Artists could stoke consumers' sense of fairness and reciprocity by giving away the product of their toil to anybody who wanted it for free.

Yet despite the utopian feel of Radiohead's implicit proposition, *In Rainbows* was less a product of communitarian idealism than of stark, urgent necessity. The nexus between creativity and commerce that has powered capitalism for hundreds of years is under increasing threat. Computers and the Internet have made it so easy to copy and share information around the world that its creators have lost their ability to charge for it. Radiohead was looking for alternatives to survive in a world in which, like it or not, its fans could listen to its music at will, free of charge.

Music is the tip of the iceberg. Over the past decade or so, most young people have come to believe that news is a free commodity too, readily available online. Google scanned millions of out-of-print books and, if the courts accede, hopes to create a vast free library online. Movies are available gratis to those with a broadband connection and a modicum of computer chops. VoIP technology allows anyone with an Internet connection to make free phone calls around the world. And corporate software giants now must routinely compete with the "freeware" designed by thousands of engineers, contributing their labor to a collective enterprise.

The information revolution has even undermined the old economy's paragon of free media: broadcast TV. An hour-long show on most television networks typically involves forty-two minutes' worth of programming and eighteen minutes of ads, which are supposed to pay for the show. In 2009, for instance, advertisers reportedly paid about $230,000 for a thirty-second spot on ABC's *Desperate Housewives*. At that rate, each of the 10.6 million households watching *Desperate Housewives* was worth about seventy-nine cents to the network.

Digital video recorders like TiVo that allow viewers to skip commercials threaten to deprive the networks of this money and allow fans to watch shows at no cost in money or time. "Your contract with the network when you get the show is you're going to watch the spots. Otherwise you couldn't get the show on an ad-supported basis," said a frustrated Jamie Kellner, chairman and chief executive of Turner Broadcasting, in a 2002 interview. "Any time you skip a commercial or watch the button you're actually stealing the programming." Viewers, of course, have no legal obligation to watch anything. Still, Mr. Kellner accurately articulated the implicit economic trade-off that has sustained broadcast TV. If that falls apart, it will need to fund itself another way.

## THE ALLURE OF THE FREE

We can't have a functioning economy based on free stuff. It would violate an ironclad law of the universe known as "There's No Such Thing as a Free Lunch." The term apparently originated in the United States of the mid-twentieth century, when some perspicacious observer noted that the free food offered to patrons at bars and saloons was not really free, but incorporated into the price of drinks. It has found a place in astrophysics, where it means that in a closed universe, as most believe ours to be, you can't conjure up new matter or energy out of nothing. But it is most important to economics, distilling the very essence of the discipline. The saying means that in a world of scarcity all decisions entail a trade-off. You usually can't get something without giving up something in return. You might not always recognize the price, but even hidden prices can be high.

Free is precisely the kind of concept that can make us part with our money without noticing that we are doing so. Businesses have long used the device to lure customers to spend. Tricks include the standard "buy one, get one free" and the typical late-night cable-TV pitch, which asks viewers to "call now and get" some free knickknack on top of the advertised product.

Receiving something gratis conjures a sense of indebtedness and incites deep-seated feelings of reciprocity that can be stroked for profit. Sales representatives of the direct sales giant Amway have been known to leave potential clients with a free sample basket of toiletries and other household goodies and return a few days later to make the sale, harnessing the customer's feeling of obligation. In the 1970s, members of the Hare Krishna Society would give a flower or a small trinket to passersby before hitting them for money. It worked so well that airports where Hare Krishnas operated posted signs and made public announcements to forewarn people about what they were up to with their "gifts."

Getting something for free adds to its intrinsic value. In an experiment at the Massachusetts Institute of Technology, two thirds of students who were offered a ten-dollar Amazon gift card for one dollar or a twenty-dollar card for eight dollars chose the latter because it provided them with a higher profit. But when the prices of both cards were dropped by one dollar, everybody switched to take the ten-dollar card because they would get it for free, even if choosing the alternative would have netted them thirteen dollars.

The mirage of free is so tempting that governments spend a lot of effort protecting us from its allure. In 1925 the Federal Trade Commission tried and failed to stop the John C. Winston Co. from providing "free" encyclopedias that came with costly supplements attached. The appeals court decided a customer would have to be "very stupid" to think the free offer was really free. But in 1937 the Supreme Court supported the FTC's action to stop the Standard Education Society from pulling a similar gimmick. Justice Hugo Black pointed out: "There is no duty resting upon a citizen to suspect the honesty of those with whom he transacts business." And in 1953 the consumer regulator forced the Book-of-the-Month Club to stop using the big ads with enormous print offering a free book, only to warn customers in the smallest of print that they had to buy four more books a year from the catalog as part of the deal.

**THE CONFLICT BETWEEN** makers and consumers of information is of paramount importance to our era. The American historian Adrian Johns argues that just as the key industry of the nineteenth century was manufacturing and the central industry of the twentieth was energy, power in the twenty-first century will gravitate toward those who are better at producing and managing knowledge and information.

Those extolling the social benefits of free online information see themselves as countercultural revolutionaries willing to liberate the era from the oppressive shackles of capitalism, lift it from under the thumb of profit-seeking corporations, and take us all back to our supposedly communitarian roots. But free lunches aren't easy to find among precapitalist societies either.

Gifts play a big role in many societies. There's the potlatch among the natives of the American Northwest and the *kula* among Melanesians of the Trobriand Islands, cycles of ritual gift giving among neighboring tribes. Bronislaw Malinowski, the anthropologist who studied natives of the Trobriand Islands off Papua New Guinea in the 1910s, witnessed farmers take mounds of yams and taro root to the fishermen's village. Then he saw the fishermen reciprocate, taking mounds of fish to the farmers' village.

But these gifts aren't free. The French sociologist Marcel Mauss argued that such acts of conspicuous giving are designed to foster a sense of indebtedness in the receiving group, creating social pressure for it to reciprocate with a gift at least equal in value. This tends to act as a social bond. When Malinowski thought to have found a definitive gift with no strings attached—small presents husbands regularly gave their wives—Mauss objected that these presents, called *buwana* or *sebuwana*, were "a remuneration-cum-gift for the service rendered by the wife when she lends what the Koran still calls 'the field.'"

The price of any commodity in a market transaction is the point at which both the buyer and the seller find the transaction to be profitable, leaving them both better off. Free things, even if only a mirage, can short-circuit society by introducing two distortions. They encourage consumers to consume much more than they otherwise would, and they discourage producers from producing enough to satisfy consumer demand.

Take spam. It amounts to around 90 percent of worldwide e-mail traffic. That's because it's virtually free to send. In 2008 researchers estimated that spammers' costs for domain registrations, hosting fees, e-mail lists, and so forth amounted to next to nothing: $80 per million messages. So spammers send tons, and recipients pay the price. A study at a German university concluded that each one of its employees spent about twenty hours a year detecting and deleting spam. Considering the average wage in Germany amounted to about €20 an hour, spam was costing the university some €400 per employee. Across eight thousand employees it added up to €3.2 million.

If spam were costly to send, it would be less abundant. On April 1, 2002, the Korean Internet portal Daum started charging bulk e-mail senders a fee of up to ten won (about 0.8 cents) per message, depending on the volume sent. Inbound bulk e-mail fell 54 percent in the first three months of the fee.

Just as costless spam encourages its overproduction, free information inhibits its creation. Those who believe information online should be available at no cost like to see it as the light from a lighthouse. Any ship passing through the bay at night will benefit from its light, yet this use will not reduce the supply of light for other ships in the vicinity. The analogy is apt. Downloading a copy of the latest Batman movie doesn't make it less available to others. The cost of making one more copy is so close to zero that we can't tell the difference. So the supply of Batman never ends.

But the analogy also highlights creators' existential problem: somebody has to pay for the lighthouse's light. The light and the movie won't happen unless shipowners and Batman fans can be made to pay for them. Lighthouses—like clean air and national defense—are known because of their peculiar nature as "public goods." The fact that consumers can use them without paying has a name too: the "free rider problem." It is a problem because private companies cannot earn enough money from selling public goods to give them a reason to produce them. So left to the private sector, they won't be produced. Transported to the Internet era, the argument suggests that if information becomes truly free, we will stop producing any.

## NAPSTERING THE WORLD

Technology brought us to the edge of free. The price of computers fell 99 percent between 1980 and 2009, after accounting for inflation. A computer in 1980 cost seventy-nine times what it does today. As the price of storing, copying, and transmitting information in digital form fell, the producers of songs, movies, and other digital media lost their ability to stop consumers from copying their products endlessly and distributing them as widely as they wanted. In June of 1999, Shawn Fanning, a teenager from Brockton, Massachusetts, known to his friends as the Napster, launched a system that allowed people to share over the Internet the music files stored on their hard drives. By July of the following year, one in four adults who used the Internet said they had downloaded music for free.

Stewart Brand, a countercultural prankster of the acid-laced sixties who evolved into a revolutionary futurist, told the nation's first hackers' conference near San Francisco a quarter of a century ago that "information wants to be free." In the 1990s, Apple advertised its new iMacs equipped with a writable CD drive as the tool to "Rip. Mix. Burn." Today, creators have lost control of their creations. The minute they become a digital file they "belong" to everybody, so nobody owns them.

In *Free: The Future of a Radical Price,* Chris Anderson, the editor of *Wired,* argued that people can no longer own things made out of ideas because anybody can get them for nothing. Since most of what advanced economies produce is made of information, this could mean that much of the product of modern economic activity would inevitably become gratis.

The dictum seems to be true. Retail sales of music in the United

States—from CDs to ring tones—declined by about a fifth in 2008 to $8.5 billion, as consumers stopped buying music and turned to peer-to-peer networks, where it is available for free. Globally, wholesale shipments of recorded music fell by nearly a tenth, to $18.4 billion. This changed the very meaning of success. The biggest album of 2008, Lil Wayne's *Tha Carter III*, sold 2.87 million copies in the United States, according to Nielsen SoundScan. Nine years earlier the top album was *Millennium* by the Backstreet Boys. It sold 9.45 million copies.

**IT IS HARDLY** surprising that whoever owned the rights to these songs and movies would resist their liberation. Record labels and Hollywood studios deployed battalions of lawyers to turn back the tide of free. They devised so-called Digital Rights Management technologies—known as DRM—to bar users from copying their products.

In 2000, A&M Records and other labels sued Napster, forcing it to shut down the following year. In April 2009, a Swedish court convicted the three founders and the financial backer of The Pirate Bay, one of the largest file-sharing services in the world, for breach of copyright law, sentencing each to a year in jail plus fines totaling some $3.6 million. In August of that year, a jury in Boston decided that Joel Tenenbaum, a twenty-five-year-old graduate student of physics at Boston College, was guilty of illegally downloading and sharing thirty songs—which could have been bought for less than $30 from iTunes—and fined him $675,000. The amount was cut to $67,500 on appeal.

Yet the music industry's victories so far have been pyrrhic. Napster lost. But file sharing exploded. In May of 2010, a New York judge ordered Mark Gorton, the founder of the LimeWire, a file-sharing service that allowed people to share their songs and movies online, to pay up to $450 million to record labels for copyright infringement. Still, that same month the LimeWire software was among the top ten computer programs downloaded from download.com.

In 2008, a survey by the Pew Project on the Internet and American

Life found that 15 percent of adults who regularly went online admitted to downloading or sharing files. The International Federation of the Phonographic Industry estimated 40 billion illicit downloads in that year alone, accounting for 95 percent of total music downloads worldwide. And the decision against The Pirate Bay so angered young Swedes that they elected a member of the Pirate Party to the European Parliament in Strasbourg, giving it 7.1 percent of the votes in the election of June 2009.

The record labels seem ready to change strategy. After some thirty-five thousand lawsuits in the United States over five years, in 2009 the Recording Industry Association of America abandoned its campaign of taking alleged file sharers to court. In early 2009, Apple chairman Steve Jobs made a deal with the labels to strip away the DRM locks on songs sold through its iTunes online music store, which would allow users to copy the songs and listen to them on as many devices as they wanted.

**FREE IS SPREADING** to other industries of the information era. Within days of its publication, more than 100,000 copies of Dan Brown's bestseller *The Lost Symbol* had been downloaded from file-sharing sites in e-book or audiobook format, according to file-sharing tracker TorrentFreak.com. Movie studios seem to be going the way of record labels as well. In 2005, a report commissioned by the Motion Picture Association of America found that piracy cost the movie industry worldwide $18.2 billion a year and online theft accounted for 39 percent of the total. These days, more people copy movies than go see them in theaters. In May of 2008 the French bought 12.2 million tickets to see films but downloaded 13.7 million free copies of movies online through peer-to-peer networks.

In the summer of 2008 Warner Bros. made an impressive display of security to launch the hit Batman movie *The Dark Knight*, using technology that allowed it to track each and every copy of the film. A few months later I sat in Bryant Park, behind the New

York Public Library with a lanky, twenty-four-year-old philosophy major from the State University of New York. He opened his Mac iBook and took me to a Web site where at the click of the mouse, he could download a high-definition copy of *The Dark Knight* for free. According to the tracking service BigChampagne, by the end of the year 7 million copies of the movie had been downloaded illegally around the world.

The news media, the industry that employs me, has been eviscerated. Rather than raise the drawbridge as movie studios and record labels tried to do, the news embraced the Internet as the most promising new proposition in a generation. After all, most of the news media's money came from advertising. Consumers only paid a small fraction of the cost it took to produce the news. Newspapers thought the Internet represented a godsend—a cheap and effective platform to distribute the news more widely and reap vast new sources of advertising online.

Imagine their surprise when instead the Web became the most cutthroat competitor they had ever encountered. As the cost of serving information to the public approached zero, the flood of news online destroyed media companies' centuries-old monopoly over people's attention, which had been protected by the high costs of producing and distributing physical newspapers. Newspapers and magazines hemorrhaged print subscribers, who chose to read them online instead. And print advertising went up in smoke.

When Michael Jackson died on June 25 of 2009, his page on Wikipedia received 1.8 million visits. According to a study by the Associated Press, Google News and Wikipedia became the most popular sources of information about the pop star, respectively capturing 7.1 percent and 6.8 percent of all "Michael Jackson" searches in the four weeks to July 4. YouTube followed in third place. The only traditional media company that made the top ten was the Web site for CNN, in tenth place.

To compound the pain, the tide of online advertising that media companies had hoped for when they put themselves up on the Web for free turned out to be a trickle. Traditional media companies lost ad dollars to aggregators and, most important, search engines, which made billions selling ads alongside pages of search results that amounted to a list of links to articles in the traditional news media.

The information revolution didn't make information free. What it did was transfer the money from the producers of information to the owners of the technologies that deliver it to their audience. The Pirate Bay, one of the world's largest file-sharing Web sites, makes its money through advertisements. By forcing record labels to accept the low price of ninety-nine cents a song on its iTunes music store, Apple transferred much of listeners' music budget from buying music to buying Apple iPods. And Google has absorbed a large share of advertising budgets that used to be dedicated to newspapers and magazines. In 2009, the total advertising revenue of the entire American newspaper industry added up to $27.6 billion, the lowest level in twenty-three years, 44 percent down from its peak in 2005. Google's advertising revenues, meanwhile, jumped almost fourfold over four years, hitting $22.9 billion in 2009.

## PROFITING FROM IDEAS

Ever since people first turned ideas into profit, they have clamored for protection from those who would copy these ideas without paying for them. In 1421, the Florentine architect Filippo Brunelleschi told the town notables in the Signoria that he had designed an enormous barge with hoisting gear that could carry marble up the Arno River. *Il Badalone*, as it was called, could satisfy Florence's hunger for raw materials to build the Renaissance. But Brunelleschi only agreed to build it after the Signoria agreed to some conditions:

"No person alive, wherever born and of whatever status, dignity, quality, and grade, shall dare or presume, within three years next following from the day when the present provision has been approved in the Council of Florence, to commit any of the following acts on the river Arno, any other river, stagnant water, swamp, or water running or existing in the territory of Florence: to have, hold, or use in any manner, be it newly invented or made new in form, a machine or ship or other instrument designed to import or ship or transport on water any merchandise or any things or goods." Any such new or newly shaped machine "shall be burned."

Patents today are not quite as generous to inventors. An inventor who wants one needs to provide somewhat more detailed information about the invention. Well-designed patents aim to protect only the inventor's specific new contribution—not bar others from making anything that might serve a similar purpose. But the logic of patents is not unlike that inspiring Brunelleschi six hundred years ago. They are meant to ensure that an inventor can reap the rewards from his invention so he will have an incentive to invent. They do this by awarding inventors monopoly rights to exploit their creations.

Patents are decidedly a second-best solution. In economists' utopia, access to a good or service should be available to every person whose marginal benefit from using it exceeded its marginal cost of production. By granting inventors a monopoly, patents allow them to sell their inventions at a price way above their marginal cost—keeping them beyond the reach of many consumers. They are nonetheless necessary. The marginal cost of an invention—the cost of producing one more cholesterol management pill—will never capture the cost of inventing it. If the price were no more than the marginal cost, it would be impossible for the producer to recoup its investments.

Prescription drugs embody the good and the bad of the patent system. The research and development that goes into developing a new drug and shepherding it successfully through the regulatory process in the United States costs the pharmaceutical industry ten to twelve years and about $1.27 billion. Yet after all that is done, the cost of making the pills often falls to a few pennies apiece. So new drugs are granted twenty-year patents—from the day they are registered—to stop generics' makers from selling cheap knockoffs and undercutting their creators.

But patents have a dark side. By keeping drug prices high, they bar many sick people from access to potentially lifesaving medicines—setting the interests of inventors against the public-health imperative of saving lives. Brazil, Argentina, India, and other developing countries that were not in the business of inventing drugs refused until recently to grant patent protection for pharmaceuticals. India's patent law of 1970 made it easy for domestic generic manufacturers to get around multinational companies' patents on medicines. This fostered the growth of a large generic drug industry—which could sell pills for much less than the pharmaceutical companies that invented them.

Fifteen years ago, many developing countries accepted granting drugs twenty-year patents as part of global negotiations that led to the creation of the World Trade Organization in 1995. Since then, however, many poor countries battling the scourge of AIDS—like Zimbabwe, Indonesia, and Brazil—have taken advantage of escape clauses in the agreement to break patents in order to get needed drugs for less. In 2008 the Brazilian health ministry estimated that Indian generics manufacturers could supply the antiretroviral drug tenofovir for $170 per patient per year, a small fraction of the $1,387 charged by Gilead, who owned the patent.

On the other hand, inventors of drugs would not survive in business without patents. And without the inventors the drugs would not come into being. Granting patents for a limited period seems a reasonable trade-off. The time must be long enough to allow those who invented the drug to recoup their costs and make a profit, but no longer—to ensure that competition with generics will bring its price down and make it broadly accessible across the population.

In the United States, the period of patent protection starts ticking the moment a pharmaceutical company requests it. On average,

THE PRICE OF EVERYTHING

new drugs have about twelve years of protection left after they finally arrive on pharmacy shelves. Once generics enter the fray prices plunge. They capture about 60 percent of the market by volume within nine years. In twelve years they take 80 percent. By then, the price of drugs has fallen by half.

Patents have been drivers of innovation. They have encouraged inventors to create and have diffused their creations—encouraging owners to license their intellectual property. For instance, a survey of 133 multinationals by a British consulting firm found that 102 had licensed technology from others and 82 had licensed technology to others. The market for technological licenses is worth about $25 billion in North America alone, according to one study. In 2000 approximately 20 percent of IBM's profit derived from the sale of licenses. And in the United States, new firms and investment groups have appeared in recent years to buy, sell, broker, license, and auction patents, drawing venture capital into the field.

This transfer of ideas would be unlikely to happen if information were free. Chances are nobody would have bothered to think it up. Or inventors would keep their inventions under lock and key until they could figure out how to profit from them.

## THE CASE FOR BOOKANEERING

Artists and pharmaceutical companies have a lot in common. However much we like to think of pop stars and other artists as interested only in the deeper meaning of their art, they like to make money too. As Paul McCartney once said, "John and I literally used to sit down and say, 'Now, let's write a swimming pool.' " If they can't earn the pool through what they create, most will stop creating.

Yet the ownership of raw ideas—a poem or a melody—was always a more controversial concept than ownership of things made of ideas, like drugs. Books were protected in seventeenth-century Britain through a monopoly over printing granted to the Stationers' Company, which kept a registry of all titles in a vellum-bound volume in London's Stationers' Hall.

But the first copyright law was only passed by the English Parliament in 1709, after the Stationers' Company lost its 140-year monopoly in 1694, unleashing cutthroat competition in the printing business. After independence, the United States Congress followed the English lead, passing a copyright act in 1790 that granted publishers protection for fourteen years, with the chance of a fourteen-year extension. It had one novel twist, however. It covered only American authors—freeing American printers to copy foreigners' work at will. Foreign information was free; domestic information was not.

American printers rushed to snatch up and republish English bestsellers, sending their prices tumbling. According to one report, in 1843 Charles Dickens's *A Christmas Carol*, which in England cost the equivalent of $2.50, cost merely six cents in the United States. Americans' refusal to protect foreign works lasted until 1891, by which time a domestic literary scene had emerged and American writers had started to clamor for protection from the cheap imports. Even as Congress extended the protection to foreign works, it threw a bone to domestic printers by limiting copyright only to works from overseas that were typeset in the United States.

This provision remained in place in various forms until 1986, leading to vociferous complaints of American piracy, or "bookaneering," as some English writers called it. The famed British composer Sir Arthur Sullivan even paid American musicians to sign their names to some of his scores, like that of *The Mikado* of 1885, and transfer the rights back to him. That way he could gain copyright protection otherwise unavailable to a foreigner.

"The present American copyright regulations tend to keep all English and Continental authors in a state of irritation with something American," wrote Ezra Pound in 1918. "There is a continuous and needless bother about the prevention of literary piracy, a need for agents, and agents' vigilance, and the whole matter produces annoyance, and ultimately tends to fester public opinion."

Many of the arguments articulated by the current crop of Internet rebels were first made many years ago by the pirates of generations past. In the eighteenth century, members of Congress claimed that withholding copyright protection for popular imported works would serve a virtuous purpose: providing cheap books to an increasingly literate population. Complaints by English writers were, by comparison, minor irritants. Today's warriors of the online revolution argue that file sharing enables an unprecedented access to music, a self-evident good. They hold the music labels and the Hollywood studios in the same sort of disregard as Congress held eighteenth-century British writers.

**RADIOHEAD'S EXPERIMENT SUPPORTS** an additional point with which contemporary pirates want to clinch the argument. Giving away intellectual property for free would allow its creators to make more money than if they were to keep it under locks. If in the past artists toured to promote their latest album, today the latest album would promote concert tours. A band that gave away songs for free online would allow fans to sample its offerings and persuade them to buy more of its music, T-shirts, key rings, and more.

Some artists have been converted to the creed. Paulo Coelho, the bestselling author of *The Alchemist*, claims file sharing boosted sales of his books in Russia by several orders of magnitude. He started a Web site, dubbed "Pirate Coelho," where he put copies of his work to download for free. "A person who doesn't share is not only selfish but bitter and alone," he wrote.

Still, the economic case mustered by the supporters of online theft is slim. Indeed, the evidence so far is fairly unequivocal: offering stuff for free means not making money from it. One analysis of undergraduate students at the University of Pennsylvania concluded that downloading free music reduced students' annual expenditures on hit albums from $126 to $100, on average. In 2002, other researchers found that peer-to-peer music sharing cut music sales in Europe by 7.8 percent, reducing the chance that somebody would buy music by 30 percent. Yet others concluded that from 1998 to 2002 downloading could have reduced worldwide music sales by a fifth.

The experience of *In Rainbows* is held as a prime example of what art can do once it is free from the poisonous embrace of copyright, to be shared around the world. Yet these tactics only seem to work for a select group of bands that are already famous.

In 2003, when the RIAA started taking people to court for downloading as little as a handful of songs from a peer-to-peer site, they offered researchers a window into the impact of piracy. Tracking the impact of the decision on music sales, a group of researchers uncovered an interesting pattern of behavior. As expected, file sharing plummeted in the months following the announcement of the labels' legal campaign, as teenagers freaked that they could wind up in jail.

The interesting finding, however, was that while curtailing piracy had no discernible impact on the sales of top-ranked artists, it provided a significant boost to lesser acts. For albums that debuted on the *Billboard* charts below the twentieth position, the labels' legal threat boosted their survival time on the charts from 2.9 weeks to 4.7 weeks. The sales suggested that piracy was particularly harmful to the sales of lesser artists.

From 1996 to 2003, when free file sharing started to decimate music sales, the price of tickets to top rock-and-roll concerts jumped at about five times the rate of inflation—substantially faster than tickets to the theater or sports events. But the evidence suggests touring is not the solution for smaller bands.

The "free" strategy works for Trent Reznor, of the American postindustrial rock project Nine Inch Nails. When he launched *Ghosts I–IV* in March of 2008, Reznor offered a series of formats, from a $5 digital download to a $300 ultra-deluxe package bundled up with a DVD and other merchandise. He also offered *Ghost I,* the first part of the album, for free online—putting it up on The Pirate Bay and other file-sharing services. And he licensed the album under a so-called Creative Commons license, an alternative to regular copyright offered by a nonprofit organization in San Francisco that allows creators to reserve some property rights but waive others, granting free access to many users on a noncommercial basis. In the first week, Nine Inch Nails made $1.6 million. And *Ghosts I–IV* was the bestselling MP3 album sold on Amazon in 2008.

Reznor's experience, however, also underscores the limits of the strategy for those below the first echelon of pop stardom. On November 1 of 2007, three weeks after the noisy release of *In Rainbows,* Reznor's friend Saul Williams tried a similar stunt. He released his album *The Inevitable Rise and Liberation of Niggy Tardust!,* which Reznor produced and helped bankroll, offering listeners a choice between a free version and a higher-quality one for five dollars. Over the next two months, 154,449 people downloaded the album. But only 28,322, fewer than one in five, paid. A true believer in the transformative power of the Internet, Reznor was dismayed that most of Williams's fans interpreted free as meaning they didn't have to pay anything:

"Saul and I went at this thing with the right intentions," Reznor said later. "We wanted to put out the music that we believe in. We want to do it as unencumbered and as un-revenue-ad-generated and un-corporate-affiliated as possible. We wanted it without a string attached, without the hassle, without the bait and switch, or the 'Now you can buy the s**** version if you buy . . .' No, no, we said: 'Here it is. At the same time, it'd be nice if we can cover the costs and perhaps make a living doing it.'" For Williams, the "pay what you wish" model allowed 126,177 people—more than four out of five of those who downloaded his music—to pay nothing at all. It is very difficult to make a living against odds like that.

## STEALING SNEAKERS

In 1979, the Canadian government asked Stan Liebowitz, an American economist who studied copyright, to look into the impact that photocopying and retransmitting TV broadcasts on cable channels would have on publishers and broadcasters. Liebowitz observed that publishers were able to increase the price of the works they published because users valued the fact that they could make copies. To the chagrin of the networks and publishers, he concluded that copying wouldn't necessarily hurt them. "I appear to be the first economist to suggest that illicit copying might actually benefit copyright owners," Liebowitz wrote, years later. "But in those days there was not an army of copyright critics to embrace my work and make me a hero, as there is now."

Yet by now he's changed his mind. Three decades since his seminal photocopying study, Stan Liebowitz too doubts there is money to be made from giving music away for free. In a recent study he concluded that the entire decline in the sales of albums in a sample of ninety-nine American cities between 1998 and 2003 was due to rampant online file sharing. Interestingly, sales of jazz and classical music increased—perhaps a testament to the average age of their typical listeners. But sales of hard rock, rap, and R&B fell by double digits.

It's a little bit like stealing sneakers, he observed. It is not impossible that a street gang that steals a shipment of sneakers might ultimately boost sales of the footwear if it happens to be a trendsetting paragon of coolness in the neighborhood. A kid who shoplifts steak might mean more business for the butcher over the long term if the theft induces in the thief a lifelong taste for prime beef. Still, Liebowitz pointed out, "I have never seen these types of argument put forward in a serious way to suggest that society might be better off if the prohibition on theft were overturned."

On the Internet, the thief is trying to convince the butcher it is in his best interest to hand the steak over to influence his dietary habits. When Google needed illustrations with which to garland its new browser, Chrome, it suggested to illustrators that providing the art for free would be in their best interest. "[W]e believe these projects provide a unique and exciting opportunity for artists to display their work in front of millions of people," Google said. Melinda Beck, an illustrator in Brooklyn, sent Google an e-mail in response to the offer. She noted that she had worked for high-profile clients like Target and Nickelodeon, which had given her work lots of exposure. Still, she pointed out, "Both clients still paid me."

The Google spirit is catching, though, as could be seen in an ad in the fall of 2009 for a law firm in Menlo Park, California, on the free classifieds service Craigslist. "The current economic climate has made it difficult for young lawyers to find paid positions," it read. "Good experience with a top notch firm is what we offer. If you can realistically make a six to twelve month commitment and can get by without compensation (other than billable travel, mileage, parking and related expenses), this is an excellent opportunity." Comments to the ad, picked up on a legal blog, were not very nice. One read: "The guys soliciting this should be rewarded with the quality of work they're paying for and I hope they end up committing and are successfully sued for malpractice."

**THERE APPEAR TO** be two broad classes of potential solutions for information industries. One is to find more effective barriers—technological and legal—to keep content behind a paid gate. Having dropped its lawsuits against individual downloaders, the RIAA has put its sights on Internet service providers—hoping they could become the enforcers of legality online—curtailing and maybe even disconnecting the service of those who download material illegally.

ISPs could even become the collectors of user fees for legal downloads or streams, like a toll at the on-ramp to the freeway. They have become the focus of a flurry of legal activity. In September of 2009 the French Parliament passed a law that would allow ISPs to disconnect clients who were caught downloading material illegally three times. A new copyright law in Sweden forces ISPs to reveal information about unauthorized file sharers to copyright holders, paving the way for legal action. In April of 2010 Britain passed a law that would not only force ISPs to slow or stop the Internet connections of those who repeatedly downloaded pirated material, but would allow the government to demand that ISPs block Web sites that hosted substantial amounts of pirated material.

This might not work. Time and again hackers have bested even the best software locks. And creating effective legal walls would require international cooperation on copyright that might prove difficult to achieve. "Copyright is becoming obsolete," Hal Varian, the chief economist of Google, told me. "Even as the law has become more and more restrictive, the practice is getting looser and looser." Varian doesn't think companies can protect themselves with gadgetry either: "There is no real technological solution."

If this is so, the only thing providers of content can do is try to reconfigure the way their content is offered to consumers, to persuade them to voluntarily pay for at least some of it. Conceptualizing the CD as an ad for the concert would fit in this category, as would the new attempt by music companies to sell subscriptions to legal music streams on mobile phones. For the news media, Varian suggests "versioning"—offering a no-frills version of the news for those who want it for free and premium offerings for those willing to pay. The point "is to get the consumers to sort themselves into different groups according to their willingness to pay," Varian suggested. "The producer chooses the versions so as to induce the consumers to self-select into appropriate categories."

Hopefully some of this will work. If it doesn't, it might force information off-line altogether. The *Newport Daily News* in Rhode Island, which faces virtually no competition from other newspapers, tried to drive readers back to the printed page. In June of 2009 it started to charge $345 a year for an online-only subscription and $100 for a print-plus-online combo. Within three months, Web site traffic was down 30 percent and single-copy sales were up 8 percent.

## WHERE INFORMATION GOES TO DIE

Ultimately, I fear free information will result in less creation of information products. In France there were 8 percent fewer albums released in the first half of 2008, and music releases by new artists fell 16 percent. More than a dozen newspaper companies in the United States have filed for bankruptcy protection since the end of 2008. This includes the Tribune Company, which owns the *Los Angeles Times* and the *Chicago Tribune*, the *Philadelphia Inquirer*, and Freedom Communications, which owns the *Orange County Register* and thirty-two other dailies. The *Rocky Mountain News* of Denver, Colorado, which had been around since 1859, published its last newspaper on February 27, 2009.

In July of 1999, 425,000 people worked for newspaper publishers in the United States. Ten years later employment in the industry had fallen by 150,000. Employment in other periodicals fell by 45,000 since its peak in 2000, and radio and television broadcasters too lost many jobs over the period. Yet for all the high hopes that dot-coms could replace crusty old-school media companies delivering the news, Internet publishing and broadcasting and Web search portals added only 15,000 jobs since their nadir in 2004. In July 2009 their total employment added up to 82,000—30,000 fewer jobs than at the peak of the dot-com bubble a decade ago.

The raiders of the Internet seem pretty sure of the power of their cause. Among the cognoscenti surveyed in December 2008 by the Pew Project on the Internet and American Life, fewer than one in three thought creators and their lawyers would find a legal way to reclaim control over their creations anytime soon. "Copying data is the natural state of computers," said Brad Templeton, chairman of the Electronic Frontier Foundation, an advocacy group for civil liberties on the Internet. Giulio Prisco, a former scientist at CERN who founded Metafuturing Second Life, an Internet services company, added: "You cannot stop a tide with a spoon."

Perhaps not. The media companies that rose in the twentieth century might be irrevocably doomed. Record labels might disappear. But I doubt that free information will ever be the natural state of affairs in a capitalist economy. In fact, I would wager that whatever the information economy looks like ten years from now, information in it will not be free.

The last battle over free might serve as an illustrative precedent. Music piracy didn't exist until the late eighteenth century because property rights didn't cover music compositions. Agents from opera companies would attend the opening nights of their rivals to "steal" the best melodies and reuse them in their own dramas. Only in the nineteenth century, when Romanticism propagated the idea of author as genius, did composers complain. Hector Berlioz called bootleggers thieves and assassins.

Technology changed the game. The popularity of the player piano in late-nineteenth-century Britain spawned the first recorded music industry for the masses, sheet music. By 1900 Britain had one piano for every ten Britons. Music publishers were minting money, selling sheets—known as dots—at one shilling and four pence apiece. Puccini and Handel were written for player piano, as well as more popular acts. Inevitably, the pirates came, using the new technique of photolithography to copy tunes flawlessly and sell them for only two pence.

Then, like now, much of public opinion sided with the pirates. The British Parliament passed the Musical Copyright Act of 1902, which allowed for the summary seizure of pirated music. Still, music publishers floundered, confiscating hundreds of thousands of pirate sheets only to see more appear on the market. But in December of that year the police caught the "king of the pirates," James Frederick Willetts, who ran the People's Musical Publishing Company.

Willetts made a strong defense of piracy in court. He argued that artists should not be given a free hold over their works because their talent was a God-given gift that should be used for the public benefit. He argued that piracy allowed the fruits of this talent to reach consumers who couldn't afford the extortionate prices charged by the labels. But Willetts lost and was jailed. And the bootleggers were cowed out of existence. Information became expensive again.

Ultimately, information cannot be free. It only looks that way sometimes. The quote by Stewart Brand that became the slogan of online freedom fighters has a prelude that acknowledges that information also "wants to be expensive" because of its enormous value to recipients. This is a reasonable proposition. Still, it leaves no space for the producer of information. Information can't exist without her.

# CHAPTER SEVEN

# The Price of Culture

**DEMOCRACY SEEMS TO** have taken over the world. By one account, at the end of the twentieth century 63 percent of the world's population lived in democratic regimes, up from 12 percent at the end of the nineteenth. Democratic rule—giving citizens a choice in electing their political representatives—can mean different things in different places, however. It is an umbrella term used equally in the United States, where transfers of power between opposing parties are routine, and Zimbabwe, where the opposition is still regularly clubbed into submission.

Still, a couple of variables can help us determine the quality of democratic governance around the world. The first is the quantity of resources—Kuwaiti oil, Congolese diamonds—at the disposal of rulers to purchase the acquiescence of the ruled. The other is the going price of voters, the value they give to their vote. This provides a precise measure of the legitimacy of the political system. The most corrupt countries are those in which voters are cheapest.

The price of a vote is typically a function of a voter's income. Poorer ones demand less because they deem their vote to be worth little compared with direly needed cash. In the 1996 Thai general elections, voters were offered an average of 678 baht apiece, but those in Bangkok were likely to receive twice as much as those in rural areas, who were poorer. In São Tomé and Príncipe, a poor former Portuguese colony on two tiny islands off the coast of West Africa, a survey of voters in the 2006 election found that the median price for a vote in the election to the national assembly was $7.10, but the average reached about $37 in the capital district.

Price is also determined by what is at stake in the election. In São Tomé and Príncipe, vote buying took off only after oil reserves were discovered offshore in the late 1990s in the Gulf of Guinea—offering the prospect of a windfall. Not all races were worth the same. A vote for a president, whose power is mostly limited to the domains of defense and foreign affairs, cost merely $4.20. The real money was in the election to the national assembly—which wields most executive and legislative power.

While the direct purchase of votes might seem a perversion of democracy, it has a long-standing tradition with substantial pedigree. In Britain, elections were bought at least as far back as the seventeenth century. The practice grew as moneyed members from Britain's colonies and its new commercial class tried to break into the landed gentry's monopoly of political power. In 1812, George Venables-Vernon, the second Baron Vernon, left his son-in-law, Edward Harbord, third Baron Suffield, "one sum not exceeding £5,000 towards the purchase of a seat in Parliament." Such commerce prevailed until the Corrupt and Illegal Practices Prevention Act of 1883 imposed harsh penalties on those who gave or received bribes and established tight limits to campaign spending.

Across the Atlantic, newspapers in nineteenth-century New York would quote the price of votes just like that of hogs. The *Elizabeth-town Post* quoted a vote in Ulster County, at twenty-five dollars. Voters played the system so well they would wait to be paid before voting for the candidate they preferred anyway. On November 13, 1879, the *Watkins Express* in Schuyler County printed a harangue by Congregationalist minister Thomas K. Beecher extolling the virtue of political free markets: "When a good man for a good purpose buys the vote of a fellow man, the voter—being a principal and a sovereign—is free to do as he chooses; the act is right. The buyer is no briber in the court of conscience, not at the bar of God, except he have an intent to pervert the judgment. And the humble-minded voter who accepts the gift and guidance of the good man aforesaid is obeying motives manlier and more nearly safe than those which ordinarily sway our more active and enthusiastic voters."

Direct vote buying died in the United States when the introduction of the secret ballot made it impossible for politicians to check whether voters were delivering their vote as promised. Still, the practice of purchasing political power has stayed with us forever. Buying votes was first replaced by the equally dubious tactic of paying voters who supported the opposing party to stay home on Election Day. More recent techniques are more sophisticated. The objective of the transaction is, however, not unlike that in São Tomé and Príncipe. The key distinction from the small African archipelago is the higher price of American voters.

Mark Hanna, the nineteenth-century Republican kingmaker and senator from Ohio, famously said: "There are two things that are important in politics. The first is money, and I can't remember what the second one is." More than a century later, despite many laws passed to reduce the influence of money in politics, in 2008, the campaign of Barack Obama spent a record $730 million—mostly in campaign ads—to win the presidency. That amounts to almost $10.50 for each of the voters who supported him at the polls.

And Republican John McCain spent only about $5.60 for each one of his.

This might not seem too different from the price of voters in rural São Tomé and Príncipe. But the direct comparison is misleading. Many of Obama's voters would have voted for him for free. The cost of convincing the uncommitted was much higher. A study of elections to the House of Representatives from 1972 through 1990 found that an additional $100,000 worth of campaign spending, in 1990 dollars, increased an incumbent's share of the vote by only a tenth of a percentage point, on average. Challengers, who were less known and benefited more from campaign exposure, could buy 0.3 percent of the total vote for this amount. Correcting for inflation, this would mean that in the 2008 House election, the price of gaining an additional vote was about $212 for a challenger and $640 for an incumbent.

**SUPPORTERS OF PRIVATE** financing of political campaigns claim the purchase of political influence in the United States is very different from buying votes. Politicians use money to provide voters with information needed to reach a decision. TV ads are meant to convince voters that a candidate is the best and most viable—or that her rival is unworthy. If it looks as if the candidate with the most money always wins, it's because good candidates are good at drawing campaign contributions. And if politicians vote the way their financial donors would want them to, it's because they agree with them anyway.

This defense doesn't fit reality, unfortunately. American campaign strategists deploy sophisticated marketing techniques rather than cold cash. They stroke voters' biases rather than pay them. They seduce rather than buy. But their objective too is to get as many voters as possible to ignore their self-interest and vote for them. I admit that governance in the United States is better than in São Tomé and Príncipe. There are more institutional checks on power. Despite occasional bursts of antigovernment vitriol, government is still considered mostly a legitimate institution.

By contrast, vote buying in São Tomé and Príncipe delegitimizes democracy in the eyes of voters. Politicians who pay for a vote won't feel constrained by policy commitments. Voters who took politicians' cash won't waste time keeping an eye on the quality of governance. Social scientists who have studied political institutions in the developing world argue that the ability of the rich to buy the votes of the poor contributes to poor countries' unshakable poverty, hindering redistributive policies. São Tomé and Príncipe has had already two coups since its first free elections in 1991. It is in 111th place out of 180 in Transparency International's corruption perceptions index—alongside kleptocracies such as Egypt and Indonesia.

But both political cultures rely on the purchasing of power. The key differences are the way power is bought and its price. In the United States votes are much more expensive. In a way, the difference between the forms of payment for elections in the United States and São Tomé and Príncipe and replicates the difference between corruption and its rich cousin, lobbying. Big firms in rich countries prefer lobbying—the use of money to persuade politicians to change the law—because it has more permanent effects. But it is too expensive for smaller firms in poor countries, which instead turn to corruption: using money to sway bureaucrats to ignore the law.

The United States may rank ninety-two rungs above São Tomé and Príncipe on Transparency International's corruption perception index. But it is unlikely those surveyed by the corruption watchdog took into account the $3.5 billion spent by industries in 2009 to lobby Congress and the White House to tailor laws more to their liking. They probably rarely think about the 1,447 former federal government employees—including 73 ex-members of Congress— hired by financial institutions to lobby Congress and influence the debate over the reform of financial regulation in 2009 and 2010. The finance, insurance, and real estate industry alone spent $467 million lobbying in 2009. Banks were lavishing so much money on Congress that House leaders started putting vulnerable freshmen on the Financial Services Committee so they could raise enough money to defeat their challengers.

The difference between the tactics used to wield political influence in São Tomé and Príncipe and in the United States has little to do with virtue and much to do with strategy. Indeed, economists have proposed that countries evolved from bribery to lobbying as growing firms reacted to increasing demands for bribes from a growing number of bureaucrats by switching to lobbying, which was more cost-effective because it could be used to change laws rather than just sway those who enforced them.

Businesses practice both, depending on where they are. In 2010 German carmaker Daimler AG was caught spending tens of millions bribing government officials in at least twenty-two countries, including China, Russia, Thailand, and Greece, to win government contracts over the course of a decade. In Turkmenistan, it gave a government official a $300,000 armored Mercedes-Benz S-Class as a birthday present. In the rich world, Daimler behaves differently. From 2001 to 2009 it spent more than €4 million in campaign donations in Germany. In the United States, where until 2007 it owned Chrysler, its Political Action Committee has spent almost $1 million in each of the past few election cycles. In 2007, when it sold Chrysler, it spent $7 million lobbying members of Congress.

Though a politician who demands a bribe is breaking a law while one demanding a campaign contribution is not, to the layman the difference can appear subtle. In fact, campaign contributions can be just as valuable to a politician as cold cash under the table. A study of how members of Congress reacted to campaign-finance legislation in 1989, which barred them from pocketing their leftover campaign funds when they retired, concluded that lawmakers valued their seat at anything from $300,000 to $20 million, depending on their outside wealth, age, tenure, and seniority in Congress.

Reform left 159 lawmakers with a stark choice: to retire before the 1992 election and keep their stash or to run for reelection. Comparing the campaign funds of those who decided to run against those who quit, economists concluded that a fifty-three-year-old lawmaker with $50,000 in the bank would relinquish his or her seat for $800,000. A representative of the same age with savings of $2 million would not give it up for less than $11.8 million.

The object of this comparison is not merely to underscore that political power can be bought and sold in the richest nation on earth just as it can in one of the poorest. The broader point is that the political cultures in rich and poor nations, different as they may be, are the product of similar evolutionary dynamics. The political norms and institutions codify how each society "resolved" the challenge of how to distribute power in the market for influence. The resulting set of written and unwritten rules came out of evaluations of their political efficiency. If a behavior became entrenched in a nation's political culture, it is because it was deemed to be worth the price.

In Britain, vote buying emerged as a necessary tool for a new moneyed merchant class to challenge the political power of the landed aristocracy. In São Tomé and Príncipe it was a response to the discovery of oil, which increased the profitability of political power. Daimler chooses its tools to fit the environment. The Daimler executives in charge must have deemed a $300,000 Mercedes to be a reasonable price for whatever they wanted in Turkmenistan. Evidently, so did the Turkmen government official. And though it probably wasn't a good deal for Turkmenistan, it was consistent with its political culture.

In the United States, by contrast, it would not be a good trade. In fact, Daimler had to pay $185 million in fines and disgorgement of profits to the Justice Department and the Securities and

Exchange Commission for violating the Foreign Corrupt Practices Act. Yet had Daimler chosen a more subtle technique to influence Turkmenistan's politics, chances are they would have gotten away with it.

## WHAT CULTURE DOES

"Culture"—as in political culture—is a broad concept, deployed to describe all sorts of customs, conventions, and collective behaviors that operate within societies. It includes modes of dress, dancing styles, and music. It includes the stories we use to shape our collective identities. There are the beliefs and the rituals—religious or otherwise. There are the rules—the institutions and the taboos. Culture includes a pierced twentysomething with purple hair banging a guitar onstage. And it includes the norms and institutions that determine how power is exercised and transferred.

A common, and in my view accurate, critique of economists' worldview is that it often ignores how culture affects our choices—positing people as calculating, self-involved creatures oblivious to any notion of "social good." *Homo economicus* is expected to approach life as a string of cost-benefit analyses, evaluating the prices involved in each decision to maximize his individual well-being. Margaret Thatcher, the former British prime minister known for a fondness for the market that led her to battle labor unions, privatize state-run companies, and slash public spending on social programs, articulated this view succinctly: "There is no such thing as society," she said. "There are individual men and women, and there are families."

Thatcher was wrong, of course. Humans are about as social as animals come. We depend on society—on others—for our very survival. For society to emerge we had to subsume some of our self-interest into the collective interests of the tribe. Culture helps us with that. It codifies acceptable forms of behavior. It determines the price lists of penalties and rewards to fit the patterns of conduct sanctioned by the clan. Culture sets our personal cost-benefit analysis within the collective price system of society.

Culture affects the price of parking in front of a fire hydrant, the value of prayer, the risks of tax evasion, and the rewards of corruption. Voting, in a democracy, makes little sense to the individual voter. It costs time and effort and yields nothing, personally. The likelihood of a single vote determining a big election is so small that the act is about as sensible as tipping a taxicab driver one will never see again. It's the equivalent of throwing money away. Still, we do it. It is a cultural artifact.

In the United States, the daughters of immigrants from more "liberal" countries have been found to be more likely to work than the daughters of immigrants from more "conservative" countries where women stay at home to care for husband and kids. This is regardless of how much they can earn or how much they might need the money.

Collective notions of propriety often determine individual calculations about the price of any given choice. Fines are supposed to be effective deterrents. Who likes losing money? But an experiment at a handful of day-care centers in Israel found that imposing a small fine on parents who picked up their kids late actually worsened tardiness. Before, tardy parents had borne the burden of shame, knowing they had broken the rules. When the day-care center replaced this burden with a small fine, being late became much more affordable.

Cultural preferences affect many prices. Prices in Japan are still about 40 percent higher than the average across the industrial nations of the Organization for Economic Cooperation and Development, after accounting for exchange-rate fluctuations. This reflects economic constraints, to some extent. Japan is a small, mountainous country with lots of people, little energy, and scarce arable land. But culture too has a hand in its prices. The high price of food in Japan, for instance, can be attributed mostly to political norms rooted in Japan's rural past.

In Japan, legislative districts in the countryside are much more sparsely populated than those in cities—giving rural voters more clout. It can take three times as many votes to win a seat in the legislature from an urban district as from one in the countryside. The political might of rural Japanese puts a premium on protecting farmers with tariff barriers against competition from imported agricultural products. The cost is that city dwellers have to pay top yen for their food.

But though economists are wrong to ignore the influence of culture on the prices that steer us this way and that, they are right that this very culture is more of an economic artifact than those who criticize economics' narrow assumptions would have us believe. Sociologists and anthropologists like to portray culture as an ad hoc complement to our economic motivations. Something that comes from somewhere else, beyond the dimension of costs and benefits. But this representation does little to help understand human behavior. Why does culture exist?

Culture divides the world into two spheres. Outside the boundaries, our inner economic man can run rampant, focusing exclusively on our individual benefit. Inside, within the domain of the clan, we are expected to sacrifice individual urges to a collective need for cohesion. Within the group, taboos and cultural conventions reconfigure the price system, steering individuals' choices to build trust and solidarity. The dances and ritual songs, the purple hair and the pants at half-mast—these are culture's borders. They are totems around which to build common purpose, separating the inside from out.

Cultural institutions do not descend fully formed upon societies. They are shaped by the transactions within each and its interactions with the outside environment. Culture's institutions are determined by the choices the group has taken over the course of its existence.

Culture embodies the prices that have determined the communal choices. It is society's collective price system.

---

## WHERE CULTURE COMES FROM

Trust, for instance, is essential to economic transactions. It encourages trade, and is related to investment in physical and human capital. Researchers have found that trusting people are more optimistic and take lots of risks. Though they are cheated more often, they are essential for economic growth. Untrusting people take fewer risks and miss opportunities for profit. Trusting societies tend to be more stable and prosperous. Sixty-eight percent of Swedes and 59 percent of Finns say that most people can be trusted. In Rwanda and Turkey, only 5 percent agree.

Trust could not have developed in a world exclusively populated by the selfish. It could only emerge within boundaries where norms tempered self-interest in favor of the common good. The boundaries needed to be clear to all.

In the late 1990s I lived in São Paulo, Brazil, where I edited a business magazine. My apartment in the neighborhood of Jardins was near an Orthodox synagogue. Every now and then I would see Orthodox Jewish families out for a stroll. I recall my bewilderment as they walked down the street in the summer heat, decked out in long black overcoats and enormous fur hats that would have served a more useful purpose during a Polish winter.

Only later did I understand the purpose of such incongruous dress: it was a sacrifice. The hot winter coat signaled to every other Hasidic Jew that the wearer was one of them—a member of a tight-knit group that provided spiritual and material comfort to its members. The coat helped bond São Paulo's Orthodox Jews into a community. The discomfort, whether acknowledged or not, represented the sacrifice demanded by the group on its members, a necessary barrier to keep interlopers out and thus protect the group from external forces of change.

**AS IT SETS** the boundaries, culture codifies the price system that operates inside them. The Mursi, nomadic herders in southern Ethiopia, disfigure the lower lips of fifteen-year-old girls, cutting them and inserting progressively larger clay plates that stretch out the lip. Anthropologists describe the plates as markers of adulthood and reproductive potential. This provides no clue as to why such a painful marker was chosen. Economics suggests disfigurement may have arisen as a strategy to make Mursi women less attractive to slave traders. The practice persisted after the slave trade died out because parents tend to pass what they are taught on to their children, providing norms with momentum. But it was originally viewed as a trade-off: big lips were the price of freedom.

The supposedly universal human propensity to fairness has different modalities around the world—depending on individual societies' calculations of costs and benefits. They can be measured using an experiment called the Ultimatum Game.

In this game, player A is given money and instructed to share it however she wants with player B. If B refuses, they both walk away empty-handed. If A behaved according to the dicta of economics, she would offer as little as possible and B would accept, on the grounds that it's better than nothing. Both would end up better off. But people rarely exhibit this kind of behavior. In a series of experiments performed around the world, a group of social scientists encountered a wide array of strategies, reflecting different cultural attributes that seemed shaped to mesh with their specific societies.

In the tropical forests of southern Perú, Machiguenga villagers playing the Ultimatum Game offered only 26 percent of their money, on average. But the Paraguayan Aché sometimes went to the extreme of offering all their money. And the vast majority of Lamalera whalers from Indonesia offered at least half. The researchers suggested that specific strategies used by each group fit each group's social dynamics. In groups that trade little outside the family unit, like the Machiguenga, people are likely to feel little social pressure to share—so it's cheaper to be selfish. The Lamalera in Indonesia, by contrast, hunt collectively. They have elaborate rules to share entire whales. Social stigma is more costly.

Culture not only sets collective prices, it surrounds them in a ritual, narrative envelope. In the winter of 1984–1985, very few caribou returned to the hunting grounds of the Chisasibi Cree of James Bay in northern Quebec. The hunt had been heavy the year before. Many caribou had been killed. The village elders told the young hunters a tale: in the 1910s, there was a gruesome hunt. Indians newly armed with repeating rifles butchered thousands of caribou. Food was wasted. The river was polluted with rotten carcasses. For many years after that, the caribou stayed away.

The point of the story was that the caribou would return to the Chisasibi's hunting grounds only if hunters behaved responsibly. It was effective. In the winter of 1985–1986 each of the approximately four hundred Chisasibi families took only about two caribou apiece. The imperative of resource management—the price of overhunting—was conveyed by invoking the caribou's presumed will.

The different beliefs that we take to be markers of deep cultural distinctions arise as adaptations to different environments. Nigerians and Ugandans are much more likely to agree on values than Nigerians and Japanese. Egyptians and Jordanians agree more readily than Danes and Pakistanis. A Dane disagrees with a Swede 33.8 percent of the time but disagrees with a Tanzanian 56.3 percent of the time. This is not merely about race or geography. The more two countries trade with each other, the smaller the gap between their values.

In the former Soviet satellites of Eastern Europe, four decades of government control over all production and distribution instilled a worldview that is quite different from opinions common in the West. East Germans are more likely to say that success is the product of external social circumstances, while West Germans attribute it to individual effort. In 1997, nearly a decade after the fall of the Berlin Wall, "Ossies" were much more likely than "Wessies" to say government should provide for people's financial security. But views are changing along with economic realities. Researchers suggest that the differences in preferences between East and West are likely to disappear entirely within the next twenty years.

## WHO CAN AFFORD ANIMAL RIGHTS?

We choose cultural traits we can afford. Large families are the so-called cultural norm in countries where many kids die before the age of five and those who survive are needed for their labor. Richer countries where child mortality is lower and children don't work have fostered a culture in which fewer kids are the norm and parents invest more in each of them.

Cultural mores about sex in the West are all about setting prices. Sexual permissiveness was enabled by access to contraception and abortion, which reduced the cost of becoming sexually entangled. More than two thirds of all criminal cases in New Haven, Connecticut, between 1710 and 1750 were for premarital sex. In 1900 still only 6 percent of American women under the age of nineteen had engaged in premarital sex. Today, women rarely marry before nineteen, yet three out of four women have had sex by then, and the stigma has faded away.

People in industrial nations are more promiscuous than those in the developing world, indulging in more sexual partners and having more sex. In rich countries, about 70 percent of unmarried women told pollsters they had had sex in the last month, according to one survey. By comparison, in East and South Africa just over 25 percent of unmarried women reported having sexual relations in that time. Men reported similar patterns. The findings came as a surprise to many observers who assumed Africans' high rates of infection with HIV meant they had more sex. But this was a misreading of reality. In poorer countries with shoddier health care and higher rates of deadly sexually transmitted diseases, the price of having sex is higher. It is natural that people would have less.

Consider English cooking. It is surely one of the world's most perplexing cultural artifacts, alongside yodeling, Bhutan's Langthab, and the binding of baby girls' feet. I still remember my encounter with steak-and-kidney pie, though it happened a long time ago. When I went to college in London in the 1980s, I couldn't fathom why the only way one could eat cod was deep-fried.

There may be an explanation. Paul Krugman, the Nobel Prize–winning economist, once suggested that English food was so awful because early industrialization moved the English off the land and into cities, far from natural ingredients, before there were good technologies to mass-produce fresh food cheaply, store it, and transport it over long distances. Victorian London had more than a million people, yet got its food by horse-drawn barge. So Londoners had to rely on food that would keep for long periods of time: preserved vegetables and meats, or roots that didn't require refrigeration. By the time technology allowed Londoners to be decently fed with fresher foods, they had become used to their Victorian diet. So bad food became an integral part of English culture.

**THE PRICE OF** subsistence offers an unvarnished perspective on how cultural mores follow the uneven path of economic progress and opportunity around the world. A family in Azerbaijan must spend almost three quarters of its total budget on food. In Brazil it must devote a little over a fifth. At the top of the heap, an American family spends less than a tenth of its income on eating.

The fact that food occupies a smaller place in the budget of the typical American household also means the typical American cares less about its price. The United States Department of Agriculture estimates that if the price of meat were to rise 10 percent, an American family would eat 0.9 percent less. A Mexican family, by contrast, would slash its meat consumption by over 5 percent.

That alone can explain why animal welfare movements are much more popular in the United States than in places like the Congo or Mexico. It is more expensive to kill a steer in a humane sort of way. More Americans can afford that. A 2005 study by economists at Utah State University and Appalachian State University found consumers in the United States would be willing to pay 9 percent more to ensure the beef in their sandwich came from humanely treated animals.

In Mexico, this decision would change people's diets: this range of price increases would lead families to cut their meat consumption by almost 5 percent. The price an American would pay to ensure the burgers hewed to the moral code would lead the typical Congolese family to eat 6 percent less meat. So perhaps one shouldn't be surprised that Americans are more likely than Mexicans or Congolese to belong to an animal rights organization.


CULTURAL PREFERENCES ALTER prices, which alter cultural preferences. Restaurants and hairdressers are more common in New York than in Stockholm. Maids and nannies are a fairly common sight across Lisbon. In Oslo they are rare. The household-help sector in Portugal is about three times the size of Norway's, as a share of the economy. Scandinavia is one of the more expensive corners of the world.

All these differences can be traced to one price: that of work. In Portugal, maids and nannies are much cheaper than in Norway, relative to workers in other occupations. In New York, the service industry relies on an army of cheap workers that is not to be found in Sweden. Danish laundry workers are more expensive than Canadian, compared with people in other jobs.

A study in the mid-1990s found that Swedish workers in the bottom tenth of income distribution made three quarters of the median wage, while in the United States they made only 37 percent. So though income per head was 25 percent higher in the United States than in Sweden, on average, the cheapest Swede worker was paid 60 percent more than the cheapest American. These prices are the product of different cultural choices.

The United States and Europe share more in terms of attitudes and beliefs than Europeans or Americans like to admit. Still, the transatlantic cultural gap provides a telling illustration of how self-interested economic motivations intertwine with ideology.

Europeans are a jaundiced bunch. They believe in the luck of the draw as a defining characteristic of life, and are skeptical of the proposition that the rich deserve their riches. They are unlikely to attribute success to effort—ascribing it instead to serendipity and external social conditions. Believers in the world's unfairness, they prefer high taxes and aggressive income redistribution to impose justice on an unjust society.

Europeans' belief in the unfairness of the distribution of income and opportunity is likely rooted in Europe's feudal past—when prosperity had nothing to do with effort and much to do with having the right parentage. Americans tend to live on the other end of the spectrum of outlooks. They believe crime doesn't pay and honest, hard work is the key to prosperity, sure that the American Dream is available to all. Ten times as many Americans say hard work will lead to a better life as believe success is a matter of luck and connections. In Western European countries, the ratio is rarely above two to one. More than a quarter of Germans think taxing the rich to give to the poor is an essential task of democracy. Less than 7 percent of Americans do.

Each of these sets of beliefs has created its economic reality.

Skepticism about the justice of the market led Europeans to build norms that favor redistribution and discourage inequality—including higher taxes, more spending on social insurance, and tighter labor-market regulations. In the United States, belief that the world is essentially just motivates people to work, to take risks and invest. It prompts them to educate their children to scale the economic ladder. It also provides the ideological underpinning for Americans' preference for low taxes and a minimalist government. And it promotes the view that the poor are guilty of their poverty—too lazy to reap the rewards of honest toil.

This view is further bolstered, social scientists suggest, by American racial diversity. In 1996, the American sociologist William Julius Wilson wrote that American whites rebelled against welfare in the 1970s because they saw it as using their hard-earned taxes to give blacks "medical and legal services that many of them could not afford to purchase for their own families." They didn't think it was fair.

In the United States, an optimistic belief in a just market economy is a useful worldview to have—encouraging the investments that are most likely to lead to success. In France—where taxes on high incomes are higher and social supports for those with low income are more generous—these beliefs would be less profitable.

**CULTURAL NORMS OFTEN** lead to what many economists would consider blatantly crazy behavior. Have you ever considered why you tip? To a classically trained economist tips are insane. They amount to paying something for nothing, giving money away. Tipping your regular barber might save you from getting an ear lopped off the next time around. But what's the point of tipping a cabdriver you will never see again? Tips are not, by any means, universal. They are rare in Europe and Asia. I recall a waiter at a restaurant in Tokyo chasing me onto the street to return a few thousand yen I left on the table. Presumably, he thought the absentminded *gaijin* had forgotten his change.

In the United States, however, tipping is at the root of elaborate rituals. Even one-shot diners who will never return to a given restaurant insist on tipping the customary 15 percent. Waiters deploy friendliness to increase their rewards. Studies have found waiters and waitresses who introduce themselves by name, repeat customers' words when taking their order, touch customers slightly on the arm, or draw a smiley face on the back of the check tend to get bigger tips.

These differences are, in part, adaptations to different labor markets. In the United States waiters earn little. As the minimum wage has risen to $7.25, for waiters it has been stuck at $2.13 since 1991, on the grounds that they can supplement it with tips. But the labor-market pricing differences are themselves rooted in different approaches to economic justice. Europeans believe such wages are unfair, and have thus imposed compulsory service charges to add to the bill instead.

## THE PRICE OF REPUGNANCE

There is ample evidence that culture can distort prices. Witness the betting at any international soccer match. No self-respecting fan will vote against the national team. National pride invariably leads fans to overestimate their team's odds of victory. Bookies appreciate the biases. But cultural preferences can subvert economic logic entirely, impeding transactions at any price.

At Le Cheval du Roy, a butchery in Caen, France, in 2009 one could buy horse fillet—a choice cut—for €30 per kilo. In parts of the United States, trying to carve up such a cut might land a butcher in jail. A law in Illinois banning such butchery forced the last American horse slaughterhouse to close in 2007. For the past few years, Democrats and Republicans in Congress have been trying to pass a bill to ban the possession, transportation, purchase, sale, delivery, import, or export of horse meat or horses if they are intended for human consumption. Serving horse meat to humans has been illegal in California since 1998, when state residents voted a ban into law.

This has little to do with the welfare of horses. It is perfectly legal to kill them for export, to feed zoo lions, and, less often, mince them into pet food. What's definitely not acceptable is serving them to people. The ban is a straightforward product of repugnance. It is culture arbitrarily short-circuiting a potentially sensible economic transaction, no matter the price.

Discomfort with transactions can take byzantine shapes. People seem comfortable with paying for sperm, for instance, but get all queasy about eggs. A high-quality egg donor, like a Harvard coed with good scores on her SAT college entrance exams, could net $35,000. Still, some critics have charged that paying for eggs devalues life by treating them as commodities. The guidelines of the American Society for Reproductive Medicine allow paying donors up to $10,000 only because donating is physically costly—requiring screenings and about fifty hours in hospital. Many donations agencies offer more. In the United Kingdom paying for eggs is illegal. Donors can only recover out-of-pocket costs plus "reasonable expenses" of up to £55.19 per day—to a maximum of £250—to cover their forgone earnings.

It makes a difference what the eggs will be used for. In California it is legal for a woman to sell her eggs for fertilization but not for research. If she wants to provide them for research, she must offer them for free. In New York, by contrast, the Empire State Stem Cell Board authorizes using state research funds to pay up to $10,000 to egg donors.

Many transactions that are perfectly normal in one part of the world or at one point in time are considered repugnant in another.

Indentured servitude, once a common way for Europeans to buy passage to America, today is banned across the world. Usury, an old sin of the Catholic Church, is today called credit.

Dwarf tossing, which used to be an everyday bar sport, was banned in France in the 1990s despite opposition from a dwarf, who took his case all the way to the United Nations, accusing the French government of discriminating against him by denying his right to employment. The job, he said, "does not constitute an affront to human dignity since dignity consists in having a job." He lost.

In Seoul, South Korea, a dish of dog stew costs around ten dollars—about twice as much as the beef equivalent. Yet when the country hosted the 1988 Olympics, the city government banned the popular dish lest it nauseate its foreign visitors. When Korea co-hosted the soccer World Cup in 2002 with Japan, the French actress and animal lover Brigitte Bardot tried to move the Korean government to ban the entire industry. "Cows are grown to be eaten, dogs are not," she told an interviewer on Korean radio. "I accept that many people eat beef, but a cultured country does not allow its people to eat dogs."

REVULSION HAS MEANINGFUL consequences. In 2009 there were about eighty thousand Americans on the official waiting list for a kidney transplant, almost five times as many as twenty years ago. But there are only about sixteen thousand transplants done each year. The waiting list keeps growing every year. In 2005, some ten Americans died each day while on the waiting list.

Allowing people to sell a kidney would increase the supply. Economists Gary Becker and Julio Jorge Elías calculated the price of an organ based on the value that government agencies put on Americans' lives and health when they evaluate the benefits of public investments in their safety.

They plugged in certain estimates into the calculation: a 0.1 percent risk of dying during the operation and a 1 percent chance of suffering a nonfatal injury. They assumed such an injury would reduce a donor's quality of life by 15 percent, which is a little worse than the deterioration of quality from blindness. They also assumed the median donor would make about $35,000 a year and would need four weeks in recovery. Plugging in the forgone wages and assuming the statistical value of life to be $5 million, they estimated that a donated kidney should go for about $15,200. At this price, allowing kidneys to be bought or sold would increase their supply by some 44 percent.

In Israel, people who have donor cards are "paid" with priority treatment if they ever need a transplant. The Islamic Republic of Iran legalized payments for kidneys in 1988. Donors get a flat fee of about $1,200 and often negotiate extra compensation with the recipient. Iranian officials argue that the practice has reduced the average waiting time for a transplant to a few months.

But buying a kidney is illegal in most of the world. Kidney donors live just as long and are just as healthy as those with two, according to recent research. But many people—including those at the World Health Organization—oppose renal commerce. In an address to transplant surgeons in Rome in 2000, Pope John Paul II argued that "to use the body as an 'object' is to violate the dignity of the human person."

Some critics fear that desperately poor people would sell a part of themselves to obtain money. They note that an illicit market in human flesh is emerging—with customers hailing from wealthy nations like Saudi Arabia and Taiwan, and sellers from poorer places, like China, Pakistan, and the Philippines. In the United States in 1983, Representative Al Gore of Tennessee, who would go on to become vice president, sponsored legislation to ban the practice, prohibiting donors from gaining anything of "valuable consideration" in exchange, including proper medical care. It became law in 1984.

Proponents of kidney sales note pointedly that those outraged by the idea that the poor could sell bits of their bodies are not so squeamish when it comes to allowing the poor to enlist in the armed forces, where they vastly increase their odds of a violent death in exchange for a wage. But the culture allows for a professional army—perhaps because the individual soldier puts his life at risk for the tribe. Kidney sales, by contrast, are between individuals. So the culture banned them.

## DARWIN'S PRICE SYSTEM

Some people say culture is all about sex. The boy with the nose stud and the purple hair jumping up and down onstage is simply advertising his genetic material, a bit like the peacock with his huge tail. It is an instrument of courtship. This kind of socially sanctioned behavior survived across evolutionary time because it was successful at encouraging reproduction.

I would add that culture also allowed society to happen, helping humankind transcend its self-centered nature. Establishing borders of community, and setting the prices within it, culture helped pro-social attitudes emerge and evolve, improving groups' ability to survive in competition over resources with others.

Some intrinsic notion of fairness and reciprocity must have been essential to survival among the earliest groups of hunter-gatherers 3 million years ago, when there were few legal institutions to enforce contracts. These early humans might have simply killed each other to get at one another's food. Instead, they hunted collectively and traded. Culture helped groups become more cohesive, and thus more effective killers of the people on the other side of the cultural fence. There was one price system inside the enclosure in which stigma carried a cost and there were rewards to selflessness. Reciprocity—trading favors at "just" prices—prevailed.

These dynamics predate humanity. Chimpanzees groom each other and share food. Traveling through the forest, the able slow down to wait for the sick and injured. Wolves collaborate to bring down big prey. Capuchin monkeys have a keen sense of justice. Ordinarily, they are willing to work in exchange for little bits of cucumber. But just offer something nicer, like a grape, to the monkey in the next cage over and they will stop cooperating. The formerly desirable cucumber suddenly becomes unacceptable. The monkeys go on strike. It is costly for capuchin monkeys to reject the food, but by doing so they can ensure they're not given a raw deal again.

And modern humans exhibit different behaviors on each side of the cultural fence. Outside the group—the race, the faith, or the village—we may be the most ruthless bargain hunters. But inside the perimeter of our culture we can afford to be generous. Here we won't always bargain ruthlessly to get the best possible deal at the lowest possible price.

# CHAPTER EIGHT

# The Price of Faith

**WHAT WOULD YOU** stake for a shot at eternity in heaven? Indecorous as it may sound, the proposition has excellent pedigree. It dates back at least to the seventeenth century, when the French mathematician, philosopher, and gambler Blaise Pascal jotted down a series of musings that came to be known as Pascal's wager. An attempt to persuade people to believe in God, Pascal's reasoning offered an interesting innovation over previous arguments for belief: it did not rely on proof of God's existence. He proposed, rather, that it would make sense to believe even if it were impossible to determine whether God existed or not. The payoff of belief if He did was just too good to pass up. Were God not to exist, Pascal offered, one would lose little or nothing by believing in Him. Yet if He did happen to be, belief would lead to eternal bliss, while nonbelief would lead straight to hell. "Let us weigh the gain and the loss in wagering that God is," Pascal proposed. "If you gain, you gain all; if you lose, you lose nothing. Wager, then, without hesitation that He is."

In fact, belief does impose costs on believers, including dietary and sexual restrictions as well as many other sacrifices and prohibitions. Still, in Pascal's view believing was the sensible choice. As long as there is a finite chance that God exists, even if only tiny, faith makes sense because heaven's infinite rewards in the future would outweigh any finite costs today.

Pascal was a fervent Catholic. But he also was a man of logic and reason. He despaired of the byzantine attempts that had been made over the centuries to prove God's existence. Thomas Aquinas, for instance, argued that there had to be an ultimate unmovable mover of all things that move. René Descartes pushed the so-called ontological argument, which stated that because Descartes could conceive of God, God had to exist. "Reason can decide nothing here," Pascal wrote. "We do not know if He is."

**PASCAL'S GAMBLING ARGUMENT** is not watertight. It omits that believing only to claim a future reward would likely be construed as corrupt. God might not be too pleased by such a pragmatic approach to faith. He could condemn mercenary believers to roast in hell anyway. The reasoning glosses over the fact that there are many religions, some of which have gods that punish believers in the other ones. The wager does not contemplate the risks of choosing the wrong faith. And Pascal's logic would lose its power if the rewards of heaven were finite rather than everlasting. Perhaps most important, if you believe that God has no chance of existing whatsoever, the wager makes no sense at all.

But despite holes in the argument, Pascal's reasoning amounted to a big leap for religious thinking. His wager pitched religion not as humanity's only possible response to an omnipotent deity whose existence should not be in doubt. He proposed it as a tool for civilization to cope with an uncertain world. What's more, he argued that faith's rewards were valuable. Pascal probably didn't think of it in quite this way when he proposed his wager in the seventeenth century, but he was setting up religion as a service for which we should, naturally, be willing to pay a price.

This is religion as catastrophic insurance: if it happens that God exists, faith would assure us a place in heaven rather than hell. The premiums are paid partly in money: charity, tithing, and the like. But the most onerous costs are the stringent rules believers must hew to, from fasting and prayer to avoiding sex out of wedlock. Such strictures constitute the main currency of belief. They are the price we pay for God's grace.

We've come a long way since the seventeenth century. But scholars seeking to understand how religion managed to survive as an institution across the ages have arrived at an analogous conclusion. Religion may be portrayed as the ultimate nonmarket institution, built upon unquestioned moral imperatives descended from the heavens. But it is in fact composed of a set of transactions in which believers assess the costs of the faith against its benefits.

Perhaps the biggest difference between Pascal's wager and current analysis of religion is that the seventeenth-century philosopher argued that the rewards for belief would occur in the afterlife. Contemporary scholars, by contrast, have concluded there is payback on this side of death. Be they economists seeking to understand why individuals invest in faith or biologists puzzling over how religion survived the pressures of evolution, most analysts have concluded that faith provides value for money. This is regardless of whether God exists or not.

## THE BENEFITS OF BELIEF

The most tangible benefit religions provide to the faithful is a mixture of insurance and social services. In Israel, tight-knit groups of ultra-Orthodox Jews ensure that the sick receive visitors and the single are matched up with spousal candidates. Rabbis in the Bayit Vegan neighborhood of Jerusalem regularly put out flyers to request donations of time and money. The flyers also list offers of frozen meals for the sick, advice for childbearing mothers, playpens and wedding gowns, all provided for free by other members of the community. Orthodox communities can raise money quickly, providing interest-free loans of thousands of dollars to members in need. And trust is guaranteed: everything is insured by the word of the rabbi.

These sorts of mutual assistance agreements are typical in many religions, including Christianity, Hinduism, Buddhism, and Islam. Gallup polls in 145 countries have found that people who attend religious services donate more to charity and perform more voluntary service than those who do not. When crises drive people into the arms of God, they embrace Him for the insurance as well as the spiritual solace. When the Asian financial crisis struck Indonesia in 1997, the rupiah lost 85 percent of its value, the price of food nearly tripled, real wages plummeted by almost half, and the study of the Koran soared.

Indonesian Muslims study the Koran in communal events called "Pengajian," in which a teacher lectures and leads the recitation of the religious text. At these gatherings substantial social pressure is brought upon believers to make charitable contributions for the needy. After the crisis, participation in the Pengajian jumped to 71 percent of Indonesian villagers, from 61 percent before the crisis, according to one survey.

Indonesian Muslims might have been in need of divine reassurance. But their faith was also driven by physical necessity. In the months after the crisis, the average village family had to cut their budget for everything but food by about two thirds—some $4.70 a month. Every dollar cut from the budget raised the odds that a family would participate in Pengajian by 2 percent. Those most hurt by the crisis—such as government workers on a fixed salary—were more likely to step up their Pengajian attendance than rice farmers, who benefited from soaring prices for rice and were thus less affected by the economic troubles. Indonesians who had access to credit from banks or microlending units did not change their religious participation much. They didn't need the Pengajian for money. But the mosque-based insurance was effective. Three months after it peaked, those who increased their Pengajian participation were much less likely to need alms or credit than those who didn't.

Yet religion isn't just a mutual insurance scheme. Faith offers more than help in time of need. It also promotes specific sets of behaviors, discouraging self-destructive choices because God and his community are watching. Religious people trust others more, trust the government and the legal system more, and are less willing to break the law. In one experiment, people who were made to read sets of words including evocative terms like "spirit" or "sacred" donated more than twice as much to a stranger as those who didn't receive the cues.

Sixty-nine percent of respondents to a recent American poll said more religion was the best tool to strengthen family values and improve moral behavior, 85 percent said it would help parents better educate their kids, 79 percent opined it would cut crime. Regardless of the plausibility of these beliefs, churchgoers in the United States smoke less, drink less, and are less likely to be overweight. They are more likely to be married and they report having more active social lives. They are also happier for it.

The happiness gap between those who go to church every week and those who never go is about the same magnitude as that between the richest 20 percent of Americans and the poorest living among the bottom fifth. All this happiness tends to be good for people. Over a period of eight years, a group of sociologists and demographers tracked the mortality of thousands of people who participated in a national health survey in 1987. They found that going to church once a week added seven years to life expectancy at age twenty: twenty-year-olds who went to church were expected to live until age eighty-two. Those who didn't were only expected to make it to seventy-five.

One can even price the benefits: the extra happiness reported by more religious Americans over their less devout fellow citizens is similar to the happiness premium experienced by people who make more money. Americans pray on average 8.1 times a week. The happiness boost from praying one more time a week is equivalent to that of making roughly an extra $12,500 a year, in current dollars.

JUST AS A car is more valuable in a sparsely populated suburb than to somebody in a dense city with a vast subway network, the proclivity of believers to comply with religious rules will depend on their options outside the faith. Women are consistently more religious than men. Since they typically earn less at work, religious investments require less sacrifice of them in terms of forgone income. From the 1950s onward, church attendance declined after states repealed so-called blue laws that forced retailers to close on Sundays. Churchgoers had more options to spend their time, so they went to church less often. Consumption of alcohol and illegal drugs rose sharply.

People can pay for afterlife benefits with their time—in church, praying, etc.—or with their money. The rich, who have lots of money, yet little time, donate more; the poor, who have more time on their hands, go to church more often. This is not unlike shopping—the poor spend more time at it and typically find more bargains than the rich, who can't bother to go bargain hunting.

And taxes that change the relative value of time and money can alter the composition of religious investment. In the United States, when the government increased tax breaks for charitable contributions, people reacted by increasing their donations but going less often to church. Each 1 percent increase in religious charity was accompanied by an average decline of 0.92 percent in church attendance, as people who contributed more money felt less of an urge to spend their Sundays on a hard wooden pew.

People select their very flavor of faith through cost-benefit calculations of the most mercenary kind. People with more opportunities in the secular world, those with higher wages and a higher cost of time, will choose less demanding faiths as they will have more to lose from strict moral codes. In the United States, France, and Britain, highly educated people go more often to church than those with less education. But they tend to disbelieve the more extreme religious propositions, such as the reality of miracles.

In the United States, educated Christians choose relatively mild mainstream Protestant denominations, like Presbyterianism. Jews, the best-educated believers, are the least likely to buy the literal truth of the Bible. They go to the synagogue for the social rewards.

By contrast, the most fervent and strict religions tend to be popular among the least educated, which have fewer options elsewhere and are thus most willing to invest the time, energy, and commitment. Evangelicals, Mormons, and Baptists, the Christian denominations with highest church attendance in the United States, are also those whose congregations are the least educated and are the most likely to believe in the devil and heaven.

## WHAT DOES IT COST?

The individual process of acquiring a religion evidently depends on many factors. Believers are often unaware of the trade-offs of their faith. Parents tend to make the choice for their kids. Most people conform to the religious beliefs of the communities into which they were born. Religious benefits do not come for free, though. Insurance costs money. The benefits of religious organizations depend on their members' contributions of time, money, and effort. Churches—which can exert substantial moral pressure on their donors—are particularly good at extracting dues.

But money isn't the most important of religion's levies. The most significant costs of faith are the sacrifices it imposes on believers and the constraints with which it shackles their lives. From Judaism to Hinduism, religion carries an additional price in the form of a set of rules on dress, diet, grooming, sexual conduct, and even entertainment and social interactions. These rules are not incidental. They are essential to the survival of the faith. Onerous moral strictures weed out the uncommitted and guarantee a minimum level of solidarity and trust within the group.

Herein resides the core proposition of religion. The benefits of belonging depend on the zeal and intensity of every one of its believers, who donate time and money, buttress behavioral rules, provide moral support, and reinforce the mythical narratives that organize their world. The tougher the rules of admittance, the more committed members will be. This zeal is what gives value to membership in a religion for those who believe.

Rules banning secular activities serve to make sure that the faithful commit time and effort to the faith, spending little time enjoying themselves outside the fold. But sacrifices and behavioral constraints also discourage free riders—the nonbelievers and soft-core sympathizers who are unwilling to commit themselves entirely and whose presence would dilute the benefits for all.

This approach explains why radical religious groups are more proficient at terrorism than their secular peers—engaging in more extreme actions up to and including suicide. The sacrifices required to belong to the faith select those most likely to be good terrorists, naturally screening out the weaker members who would be most prone to defect and endanger the group. Suicide bombing is a service: it signals the intensity of the commitment to the faith and strengthens bonds inside the group. This is on top of any political agenda it may have.

In religious communities, dietary restrictions, tattoos, clipped foreskins, and other rules of behavior help the committed recognize one another, assist one another, and isolate themselves from the rest. Anybody who has ever belonged to a street gang that resorts to hazing rituals and demands a conspicuous patchwork of tattoos will understand how clubs set rules and demand sacrifices to segregate members from those outside. Muslims are expected to pray five times a day, donate a chunk of their income to charity, avoid eating food that is not halal, and participate in dozens of other rituals. Anybody who will subject him or herself to the full ritual treatment is unlikely to be faking it, and can thus be trusted as loyal and committed.

The twelfth-century Jewish philosopher Moses Maimonides wrote that circumcision is not only mandated by God "to limit sexual intercourse, and to weaken the organ of generation as far as possible, and thus cause man to be moderate." It is also supposed to give "to all members of the same faith, i.e., to all believers in the Unity of God, a common bodily sign, so that it is impossible for any one that is a stranger, to say that he belongs to them. For sometimes people say so for the purpose of obtaining some advantage."

The precise content of religious rules is incidental. They just have to be costly to obey. In the sixth century before the Christian era, the philosopher Pythagoras founded a mystic religion heavily influenced by mathematics that proposed the transmutation of souls. Its prohibitions included eating beans, picking up what was fallen, touching a white cock, stepping over a crossbar, stirring a fire with iron, eating from a whole loaf, plucking a garland, sitting on a quart measure, eating the heart, walking on highways, letting swallows share one's roof, and looking in a mirror beside a light.

The strength of the social glue confectioned from the strictures of faith helps explain why religion has proved so resilient over the millennia, surviving the rise of science, which has undercut many of its most deeply held dogmas, offering an entirely different explanation of how the world works.

Communes were popular across America in the nineteenth century, a time of great social experimentation. Hundreds were founded around all sorts of ideas, from the beliefs of the French utopian socialist Charles Fourier and the Scottish Robert Owen, father of the cooperative movement, to anarchist groups and dozens of religious sects. Very few survived more than a couple dozen years, driven asunder by the difficulty of ensuring cooperation and avoiding disputes over the allocation of resources, rights, and responsibilities. What is notable is that religious communes were two to four times as likely to survive in any given year as secular groups. The reason seems to be that they imposed hefty requirements on their members—including celibacy and restrictions on communicating with outsiders—that strengthened the bonds.

New Harmony, the commune established by Owen in Indiana in 1825, lasted only four years before falling apart among acrimonious disputes. The Oneida community in New York, by contrast, whose members believed that Christ had returned in the year AD 70 so they could establish His millennial kingdom on earth, lasted for thirty-three years before dissolving in 1881. That's because their ties were reinforced by restrictive rules—including male continence so as not to waste semen, the collective ownership of children, and group criticism designed to eradicate undesirable character traits. And among the communes set up by religious groups, those with the most costly requirements outlasted those with less stringent bans and rules. In essence, religions that imposed the heftiest prices on the faithful were the best at ensuring communities'—and their own—survival.

## WHEN BELIEF IS CHEAP

Religion encourages segregation by design. In Brooklyn, Orthodox Jews strain to remain apart from secular society and even other
Jews. Marriages between Mormons and non-Mormons are three
times more likely to end in divorce than Mormon-Mormon pair-
ings. Religion is a finely tuned instrument to segregate societies—
encouraging the faithful to fold in upon themselves, to trust one
another, help one another, and nurture one another. This naturally
entails keeping outsiders out and even going to war with them. The
most successful religions in history have been those best equipped
to separate the inside from the outside. They were the ones with the
strictest rules.

That's why religions' most deep-seated fear is that opportunities
in the outside world will weaken believers' fervor. Since fervor ultimately determines the strength of the church and the quality of
the religious goods it provides, its erosion amounts to an existential
threat. So when faith is assaulted by secular temptation, churches'
first reaction is often to batten down the hatches and raise high the
walls, demanding that believers sacrifice more to prove the purity
of their belief. Some of the faithful might leave the fold as faith
becomes more costly to bear. But for those who stay, the rewards will
be correspondingly higher.

The pattern is apparent in the paradoxical emergence of ultra-
Orthodox Judaism in the eighteenth century, just as the Enlightenment swept through Europe offering more economic opportunity
to European Jews. Most Jews responded as standard economics
would suggest. As external opportunities blossomed, their options
in the labor market increased, and the value of their time rose,
they cut back on religious participation, giving rise to more relaxed
forms of Reform and Conservative Judaism. But the ultra-Orthodox
sects, like the Hasidim who emerged in Poland and their opponents

the Misnagdim, who arose in Lithuania, chose the opposite path—rejecting modernity and demanding even more sacrifice from believers. In 1865, for instance, ultra-Orthodox leaders in Hungary passed a pronouncement called the "Pesach Din," forbidding their followers from entering a synagogue that had adopted innovations like speaking German during the service, having a structure resembling a steeple, or employing a male choir.

To this day, the ultra-Orthodox maintain the clothes, eating habits, and lifestyle prevalent in the shtetls of Central and Eastern Europe. They reject modernity as corrupt and shun more moderate Jews. In Israel, they have lobbied the government to restrict retailing and traveling on the Sabbath. And despite entrenched poverty, men remain out of the job market into their forties, choosing instead to stay in the yeshiva studying the holy texts. From 1980 to 1996 the share of prime-aged ultra-Orthodox men in yeshiva who did not participate in the labor force increased from 40 percent to 60 percent.

The most successful religions at building enthusiastic flocks are usually the most extreme in their beliefs, like evangelical Christians in the United States or radical Islamists in Central Asia and the Middle East. Even in the face of increasing opportunities in the secular world outside, these churches have developed a growing following of truly fervent believers by closing down their options. They select their members among people with the fewest opportunities outside and erect higher barriers to keep them in. It is a strange strategy: raising prices to keep your customers. But it works.

The experience of the Catholic Church over the past few decades underscores the risk to religion of following the opposite path and trying to accommodate a rising secular world. Over the centuries, the Catholic Church has managed a large and complex list of rules, restrictions, and sacrifices, by pruning, tweaking, and fine-tuning them in order to survive the rise of science and maintain its relevance despite the spread of economic progress around the world.

But with a flock of about 1.15 billion, the modern Catholic Church has avoided radical strategies to build fervor by toughening up the rules. Perhaps it feared it could lose too many believers. Instead, it has sought to navigate narrow straits between tight strictures, which could turn off marginal believers sitting on the fence between the Church and the secular world, and openness, which would weaken the appeal of the Church for the more committed. By the standards of any secular corporation, the strategy has been wildly successful: Catholicism remains the largest religious institution in the world. Still, its efforts to soften the rules to accommodate modernity have cost it many true believers—who have decamped to the more strict and fervent denominations of evangelical Christianity.

In the 1960s, the Catholic Church struggled to adapt to a world that seemed intent on deviating from the straight and narrow. Wedded to a rigid biblical literalism, the Church seemed increasingly out of touch in this period of enormous social ferment. On April 8, 1966, *Time* magazine even splashed on its cover the question "Is God Dead?" in bloodred letters against a black background—and achieved its biggest newsstand sales in twenty years. "Secularization, science, urbanization—all have made it comparatively easy for the modern man to ask where God is and hard for the man of faith to give a convincing answer, even to himself," wrote John T. Elson, the magazine's religion editor.

The Church responded with a fateful decision to modernize. During the Second Vatican Council, which ended in 1965, the Church proclaimed religious freedom, embraced people of other Christian faiths, and even acknowledged truth in other religions. To make it easier on members in the pews, it relaxed the rules governing mass, encouraging use of vernacular languages rather than Latin so the faithful could understand what was going on. It even allowed incorporating elements from local customs into the liturgy.

For conservative Catholics the changes amounted to betrayal. Not only did the erosion of believers continue. It may have intensified. After peaking at 74 percent in 1958, by the end of the Council in 1965 weekly mass attendance among American Catholics had declined to 67 percent. Over the next four decades it plummeted to 45 percent. "Religions are in the unusual situation in which it pays to make gratuitously costly demands," economist of religion Larry Iannaccone once told me. "When they weaken the demands they make on members, they undermine their credibility." The Church has suffered similarly across the world. In Italy, its stronghold, only 27 percent of Italians say religion is very important to them. In Spain, the share of Catholics who go to mass every week declined from 44 percent in 1980 to 19 percent today.

It is unclear whether there is anything the Church can do to stop the bloodletting, as modernity puts pressure on religious dogma across the board. The current pope, Benedict XVI, has been working to undo some of the Second Vatican Council's reforms. He reintroduced the Latin mass. And he brought back the plenary indulgence, an innovation introduced during the First Crusade in the eleventh century that consisted in a blanket pardon for repentant sinners to skip purgatory in exchange for good works and acts of contrition.

While the Second Vatican Council was all about adapting the teachings and rituals of the Church to a changing world, Pope Benedict focused on reimposing the primacy of the Church over reality. In an interview with the *New York Times,* the Reverend Tom Reese, a former editor of the Catholic magazine *America,* said: "The church wants the idea of personal sin back in the equation." It felt the need to raise its prices to drive more loyal customers in.

## WHAT THE CHURCH WANTS

There's nothing in the most basic tenets of faith that necessitates an institutional church. But churches abound—recording its dogmas, classifying its rituals, and managing its taboos.

To those who share it, the fundamental appeal of faith derives from the community it creates. If that were religion's only purpose, churches might not be so ubiquitous. But civilization gave faith another purpose: legitimization of power. For this, churches are indispensable. From pharaonic Egypt to medieval Europe and from Meiji Japan to contemporary Iran, rulers have derived their authority from the divine. Churches harness the beliefs in a spiritual world in the service of earthly power. They set themselves up as the ultimate arbiters of behavior, fitting rewards to virtue and punishments to crime.

During the high Middle Ages the Catholic Church offered a binary option: salvation or hell. To obtain forgiveness sinners had to submit to extremely difficult trials. But around the eleventh and twelfth century, at the peak of its power in Europe, the Church started relaxing its rules and broadening its offerings. It introduced the concept of purgatory, a halfway house where repentant sinners had to spend time after death before being allowed into heaven. It divided sins into the mortal and the venial, so it could introduce more fine-grained pricing of forgiveness and absolution. A key reform was allowing confession in secret before a priest, rather than in public before the whole town. And it began selling indulgences for money. These innovations reduced the average price of sin. Secret confessions allowed priests to use price discrimination—evaluating the wealth of individual sinners and adjusting monetary punishments according to sinners' ability to pay. It did wonders for the Church's finances.

**THE CATHOLIC CHURCH** ultimately paid a price for these tweaks, as it battled to keep control over the market of medieval faith. It got greedy—collecting levies associated with a widening array of rules to fund a lavish existence. In 1501, during the reign of Henry VII, a papal bull established a price list of indulgences whereby the English could purchase absolution of all sins. Landed lay individuals with income exceeding £2,000 a year had to pay £3 plus 6 sovereigns and 8 dinars. At the other end of the income scale, people making between £20 and £40 a year only had to pay 16 dinars. People could pay to have the souls of relatives extricated from purgatory. Bishops regularly had to pay for their office. And royalty paid to get married.

The Church frowned on intermarriage within families as far back as the fourth century. The policy stemmed, in part, from concerns over interbreeding within families, which posed risks of having children with genetic malformations. But it had other objectives: nobles favored marriage between relatives because it worked to maintain property within the family. The Church feared this would lead to powerful dynasties that could rival its power. Moreover, a ban on intermarriage allowed it to charge rich families for "dispensations" from the rule.

The bans got progressively tighter. In the fourth century the Church banned marriage between first cousins. In the sixth century it extended the prohibition to fifth cousins and in the ninth century to sixth cousins. The bans were lucrative. In the eleventh century, the Duke of Normandy, who would come to be known as William the Conqueror, had to build two churches in Caen—the Abbaye aux Hommes and the Abbaye aux Dames—so Pope Leo IX would undo his excommunication after William married a distant cousin, Mathilda of Flanders, against the will of the Church.

**THE CHURCH'S MANAGEMENT** of the behavioral price list might have sowed the seeds of its demise. There are several competing explanations of the Protestant Reformation that swept Europe in the sixteenth century. Martin Luther, the priest who led the attack, accused the Church of becoming corrupt and morally weak. Historians have argued that the Church allied itself with the losing side in the many wars that raged in Northern Europe. But to me the most compelling hypothesis is that believers were no longer getting value for money. The prices charged by the Church—which by the logic of faith are designed to tighten the bonds among the faithful—had lost their purpose.

The Church stopped working to inspire the faithful and focused instead on collecting rents. By adding sophisticated new ways to raise money from its followers, the Church became too expensive for believers and provided too little of its core services in return. This encouraged the entry of a rival into the market: Protestant Christianity, which came to offer believers direct access to God at a better price. It eliminated the rents and recovered the traditional link between costly sacrifice and religious rewards that had characterized faith since its earliest times.

This approach proved particularly fitting for the emergent capitalist economies that were beginning to develop in Northern European cities, where wealth was inherently less stable than among the landed feudal aristocracy. The Church never established the same alliances with entrepreneurs that it had developed with European nobility. Rather, entrepreneurs resisted its rent seeking and opposed its meddling in economic enterprise. So they chose the competing product.

## SIN VS. THE SECULAR WORLD

Belief in a divine origin of the world has suffered a battering over the past few centuries. In the West, science has gradually replaced God in the schema of the physical world since Nicolaus Copernicus proved the earth was not at the center of everything in the sixteenth century, raising the question of why an omnipresent, omniscient God of everything would care so much about events on a little planet in some corner of the universe.

Since then the Big Bang proposed an alternative to God for the origin of the universe and Darwin's theory of natural selection proposed an alternative explanation to the Bible's for the origin of man. Neuroscience cut the soul out of the picture by equating mind and brain, and modern psychology even challenged religion as a path to happiness.

European sociologists from the eighteenth century onward, from Karl Marx to Émile Durkheim and Max Weber, argued that secular progress killed faith off. It undermined religion's main precepts by providing believers with an alternative explanation of the world that didn't rely on angels. And the edifice of costly rules and sacrifices that defined religious communities, providing them with a collective purpose that helped them succeed over the course of human evolution, was taken over by a secular framework of law. Democratic procedure has replaced religion's menu of norms and taboos, encouraging solidarity through other means.

Secular states gradually took over the provision of education, medical care, and other elements of social insurance like pensions and support for the unemployed. As people became richer, more educated, more socially tolerant, and more politically free, religion lost its purpose. Belief in God declined during the second half of the twentieth century in virtually every Western European country, Japan, and even India. The percentage of Irish who go to church at least once a week fell from 82 percent in 1981 to 65 percent two decades later. In the Netherlands it fell from 26 percent to 14 percent.

**STILL, THERE IS A** gaping hole in the secularization trend in the industrial world: the United States. Americans remain hooked on God despite spectacular economic progress over the past hundred years. In 2001, 46 percent of Americans attended religious services at least once a week, three percentage points more than two decades earlier. And more than three quarters of Americans reported believing in life after death, 12 percent more than did so in 1947. Religious enthusiasm in the United States is closer to that in less developed countries. Fifty-nine percent of Americans said religion was very important in their lives, according to a poll by the Pew Global Attitudes Project in 2002. This was at least twice the share of other developed nations but comparable to rates in Turkey, Mexico, and Venezuela.

The pattern has led a group of American economists and sociologists to posit that the secularization thesis is wrong. If faith declined in other rich countries, it was not due to less demand for religious services but to shoddy supply. Support for religion waned in Western Europe because the Catholic Church was a state-supported monopoly that grew lazy and allowed believers to drift away. Its services became too cheap to matter. By contrast, religion in the United States thrived because of a vibrant diversity that flowered when independence led to the strict separation of church and state. Dozens of churches sprang up to serve the disenchanted market of mainstream Christianity offering high prices and high cohesion. About one in eight American Protestants pray several times a week, compared to about one in thirty Catholics, according to surveys. Protestants are more likely than Catholics to believe in hell and they are more likely to belong to church-related social groups. Twenty-nine percent of Protestants say they try to proselytize strangers at least once a month. Only 11 percent of Catholics do that.

This hypothesis—known as the supply-side or free-market theory of faith—posits that religion survived scientific progress and its alternative narrative of the world because as a club it still offers the real-life benefits to like-minded members willing to sacrifice for their beliefs.

Sociologists Roger Finke and Rodney Stark noted that in 1776 only 17 percent of Americans adhered to a church. But the rate doubled to 34 percent in 1850 and 56 percent in 1926, as scrappy new denominations vied for souls. The most strict and vehement sects, they suggest, like Mormons or Jehovah's Witnesses, are growing fastest not only because they are aggressive about recruiting new members, but because they are much stricter than the Catholic and mainline Protestant churches from which they are taking market share.

There is irony to how the religious pecking order changed in the United States. In the 1960s, the message from secular society to religion seemed to be "modernize." The choice was between opening up to the secular world, adapting to the discoveries of science, or fading into irrelevance. Around the world, the Catholic Church tried just that and it didn't work. The churches that did well were those that took the opposite path. The orders that thrived were the fundamentalists, who preached the literal interpretation of the Bible, and the Pentecostal denominations that engaged in exorcisms and other cathartic rituals—those who stepped back and recovered the traditional proposition of faith as a wall to enclose a community by demanding a very high price for membership.

## WILL GOD BOUNCE BACK?

It's a compelling thesis. A few years ago, I wrote an article about evangelical Protestants trying to expand among Hispanics in the United States, peeling believers from the Catholic Church. I accompanied a group of Southern Baptists on an evangelizing mission in a supermarket in a predominantly Latino neighborhood of Ontario, California. Their zeal and purpose was a sight to see. About a dozen people deployed across the supermarket parking lot, reassuring harried shoppers about the benefits of the Christian life. When the woman pushing her overstuffed cart to her car stopped to glance at the leaflet pressed into her hand, a flock of evangelizers descended upon her like a flock of geese. They never tired. In the course of a week's reporting, I was invited to come to God a good half-dozen times. Contrasted against the tedious, soporific masses I experienced growing up in Mexico, the Baptists offered the energy of a rock concert. And they offered specific promises about how faith would improve people's wayward lives.

There are other potential explanations of the unique strength of Americans' attachment to God, though. I suspect it has to do with the fact that, for a rich country, the United States has lots of poor people. Sociologists suggest that demand for religious services as insurance against potential hazards declines as countries climb the ladder of development.

Development makes people more secure. It provides income, better health services, and education. It reduces the risk of political prosecution and ethnic strife. But it doesn't do this across the board. There are large pockets of misery even in highly developed countries. In these impoverished corners religious belief will thrive, offering a shot at security and ultimate happiness. Here God can play His role as the ultimate form of insurance. In the United States—which suffers the most acute income inequality in the developed world—these pockets abound.

Seen this way, it becomes obvious why religion is growing in some parts of the world even as secularization advances in others: in poor religious countries, people have more babies than in rich, secular states. Across the world, development has reduced fertility rates. Families in rich countries have chosen to have fewer children and invest more resources in each of them. The fervent poor, by contrast, have hung on to traditions that frown on contraception and mandate big families.

The ultra-Orthodox in Israel earn less than half what non-Orthodox families do. In the mid-1990s, their fertility rate was 7.6 children per woman. By contrast, the fertility rate of other Jews in Israel is about 2.3. In the United States, the most religious states tend to be the most fertile and the poorest. New Hampshire is probably the least God-fearing state in the Union: 21.4 percent of its population report being atheist or having no religious belief. It is relatively rich, with a median income per capita of $74,625 in 2007. And it had only forty-two births per one thousand women in 2006. In Mississippi, by contrast, there were sixty-two births per thousand. Mississippi is poor: its median family income was $44,769. And only 5.8 percent of Mississippians report no religion.

Despite the wave of secularization experienced over the past hundred years, I suspect the world might be about to become more religious, not less. Since the Industrial Revolution, growth has been humanity's solution to virtually every problem. As technological progress enabled more efficient and intense use of resources, it ushered in a period of prosperity unlike anything the world had seen.

That period, however, might be coming to a close. Global warming suggests we are running against rigid resource limits in our pursuit of economic prosperity. As we deplete them, economic growth will become more difficult to achieve. Two centuries after the Reverend Thomas Robert Malthus claimed that "the power of population is indefinitely greater than the power of the earth to produce subsistence for man," the Malthusian trap appears like a plausible future.

Were we to hit the limit of our resources, God would likely come back in demand. Halting economic growth wouldn't just boost poverty. As people and societies were forced to compete fiercely for economic output, religion's set of ethical norms would come in handy to help societies cohere. God would be called upon to provide a supernatural narrative, a balm that reconciled humanity to its un-improvable lot; or maybe to help in war and conquest as access to resources became a zero-sum game.

To many in this dystopian future, faith would be worth the price, whatever sacrifices religion demanded in return.

# CHAPTER NINE

# The Price of the Future

**FOR MORE THAN** a century, economics has been known as the dismal science, peddling doom and despair, with little hope to offer. It owes this reputation to the work of the Scottish reverend Thomas Robert Malthus, who two hundred years ago delivered a crippling blow to his era's burgeoning optimism about the prospects for human progress. In *An Essay on the Principle of Population as It Affects the Future Improvement of Society*, published in 1798, the economist and demographer shook the self-confidence of the British Empire by arguing that the limited nature of the earth's endowments would condemn humankind to poverty. Civilization would be kept in check by an inevitable scarcity of food.

The process was straightforward: unable to control their reproductive urges, families would respond to any increase in their income by having more children. Feeding and clothing them would eat up their income gains, ensuring that they remained at the edge of subsistence forever. Human misery was the unavoidable outcome of a population that was growing geometrically—Malthus expected it to double every quarter century—yet was dependent on a food supply that grew much more slowly as new land was added to production and agricultural productivity increased at a snail's pace.

The price of food, of course, had to rise as demand expanded much faster than supply, until the "lower classes" couldn't afford it any longer. Either people killed each other off in some other way, or enough would die of hunger to bring the head count back into line with what the earth could feed.

"The vices of mankind are avid and able ministers of depopulation. They are the precursors of the great army of destruction, and often finish the dreadful work themselves," Malthus wrote. "But should they fail in this war of extermination, sickly seasons, epidemics, pestilence and plague, advance in terrific array and sweep off their thousands and ten thousands. Should success be still incomplete, gigantic inevitable famine stalks in the rear, and with one mighty blow, levels the population with the food of the world."

This kind of writing gave Malthus a gloomy reputation. The Victorian historian Thomas Carlyle characterized the controversy about population dynamics sparked by Malthus's work as "dreary, stolid, dismal, without hope for this world or next." But Malthus's prognostications were entirely reasonable. His brand of catastrophe had visited other corners of the world. The classical Mayan civilization collapsed around the ninth century of the Christian era, tearing itself apart in myriad wars over exhausted natural resources in the lowlands of what is now Guatemala, Honduras, Belize, and southeastern Mexico.

The Rapa Nui of Easter Island, famed carvers of huge monolithic heads called Moai, also collapsed after it exhausted its physical limits. A population that reached a peak of ten thousand in the early fifteenth century had withered to about two thousand when Captain James Cook visited the island in 1774. The surviving civilization had no idea how the monumental stone heads had come to be there.

The world in which Malthus lived seemed to have been stuck for years in a Malthusian quagmire. Over the prior two and a half centuries the world's average income per head had inched ahead at a pace of about 0.1 percent per year. Between 1500 and 1750 the world's population increased by only two thirds—to 720 million people. Humanity wasn't thriving.

Malthus's England was more prosperous than most of the world at the time. Still, an English baby born in 1750 could expect to die by his or her mid- to late thirties. England's population in 1750 remained roughly the same as in the year 1300, constrained by war, disease, and the food supply. It was virtually impossible to get ahead. Londoners in 1800 made about the same wages, in real terms, as their forefathers had four centuries before.

Nonetheless, Malthus got the future wrong. He made his predictions just as England and the rest of Europe were embarking upon a sustained period of unprecedented economic growth that would spread around the globe and drastically improve humanity's well-being over the following two centuries.

**THE REVOLUTION IN** productivity in Lancashire's cotton industry started as early as the 1730s, with a series of new inventions to spin yarn, such as John Kay's "flying shuttle," and continued through the 1770s with inventions such as Samuel Crompton's "spinning mule." The yarn revolution was followed by a weaving breakthrough. By the late 1700s Britain was starting to transform from a mostly rural nation into an industrial power, exporting textiles and metals. Then the spread of the steam engine in the nineteenth century led the Industrial Revolution to its apogee. Infant mortality declined sharply as living standards rose. But population growth was no match for the pace of material improvement. Between 1801 and 1901 the English population more than trebled, to around 30 million. Yet Londoners' real wages more than doubled over the period.

It is hard to overstate the importance of this economic transition. With the exception of newly settled colonies, never before had a country been able to achieve the double feat of a growing population and rising living standards. Yet England's prosperity spread in the nineteenth century as the ships made with British steel brought Europe closer to the abundant natural resources and the sparsely populated land of the New World. From 1820 to the year 2000 economic activity sustained by the planet multiplied by almost sixty: the world's population grew sixfold, to roughly 6 billion. Per capita income jumped by a factor of almost ten. Malthus's thesis about the world's grim future was buried under an avalanche of progress.

Overcoming the Malthusian nightmare more than two hundred years ago put spring in civilization's stride. The feat underscored the power of human ingenuity to overcome its environmental constraints. Yet despite our past success, the dismal reality predicted by Malthus over two hundred years ago seems once again to loom in the offing. Despite enormous advances in productivity, civilization appears to be reaching the physical limits of our natural environment, stretching the carrying capacity of the planet. This could portend a dire future. Just as China, India, and other developing countries seem poised for a surge of economic growth that would lift billions of people out of poverty, rising prices of oil, food, and other commodities suggest the earth's resources may not support all this prosperity. Nowhere is this more apparent than in our debate over what to do to forestall climate change—brought about by our voracious consumption of energy and our massive emissions of carbon.

The United States produces about twenty metric tons of $CO_2$ annually for each American. By contrast, China emits five tons per capita, India only one. As these nations industrialize they expect, reasonably, to consume more energy and emit more carbon. But if each of 1.33 billion Chinese and 1.17 billion Indians were to put the same amount of $CO_2$ into the atmosphere as Americans do, they would burden the environment with the equivalent of seven extra American economies, more than doubling the world's emissions of carbon into the air.

Our new Malthusian moment confronts us with a difficult question. How much can the global economy grow without generating unacceptable climate-driven damage in the future? It becomes more difficult to answer when one flips the question on its head: how much economic growth should we be willing to forgo to avoid producing this damage to the world's future ecosystems? Ultimately, the question boils down to this: what price are we willing to pay today to protect future generations?

## MISPRICING NATURE

The economist Jeffrey Sachs characterizes climate change as "an accident of chemistry." How could we have known that the carbon released into the atmosphere every time we step on the gas or fire up the furnace would linger there for years, capturing heat and slowly raising the planet's temperature to the point that it would threaten nature's precarious balance? But it is also a failure of the market system. Global warming, like the extinction of species, soil depletion, and all the other signs that the planet is having trouble sustaining the humanity that lives on it, underscores the global economy's inability to put a proper price on the endowments of nature.

In a market system prices are meant to allocate resources efficiently. When demand outpaces supply, prices can be expected to rise and smoothly readjust the balance—drawing more producers into the market and nudging some price-conscious consumers away. Yet this doesn't happen when it comes to nature's bounty. We often get that for "free," no matter how much we consume. As is the case with other free things, the lack of a price signal to modulate our consumption will lead us to consume too much, until we deplete the resource at hand.

This pricing aberration explains landfills overflowing with garbage, rivers laced with mercury, melting polar ice, and depleted cod stocks in the Atlantic. From the point of view of a fisherman, cod are free—his only costs are those of getting to wherever the fish are, finding them, and catching them. That means he will catch as many as he can. So will every other fisherman in the vicinity. Overfishing—pulling them out faster than they can reproduce—is the inevitable consequence.

We have done the same thing with most "free" resources of nature—from clean air to clean water. Water, mostly a public utility around the world, costs very little; its price doesn't rise to reflect its growing scarcity and encourage us to consume it prudently. The cost of dealing with nitrogen runoff into streams is usually not incorporated into the price of our crops. Lacking prices to ration their use, free clean water and free clean air have met the fate of free things everywhere: they have started to run out. We are scrambling to deal with the fallout. Nowhere does this dynamic present a more menacing threat to humanity's future than in the context of climate change.


**ENERGY IS PROBABLY** the most egregiously mispriced good. The cost of gas at the pump incorporates the cost to find the oil, pay rent to the rulers of whatever country sits atop it, pull it out of the ground, refine it into gasoline, and move it to your local gas station. But in most countries no part of the price accounts for the effect that carbon dioxide released by burning oil has on the atmosphere.

This is devilishly hard to measure, depending on many assumptions about the value of the damage caused by climate change to the natural environment. Yet a review of studies by the Environmental Protection Agency concluded that the "social cost" of $CO_2$ emissions—a measure of the burden that releasing one metric ton of $CO_2$ into the air will have on the environment over the next century—ranged between

$40 and $68 today and would rise to somewhere between $105 and $179 in 2040 as the air became more saturated with the stuff. Given that burning a gallon of gas produces some twenty pounds of $CO_2$, accounting for the environmental cost of driving would require a tax today of about sixty-two cents per gallon.

Americans spew about twenty tons of $CO_2$ per person per year. By the EPA's calculations, the United States is imposing an annual burden on the environment of up to $1,224 per American. And that may be low. Other estimates reviewed by the agency put the social cost today of one ton of $CO_2$ at $159. If we were presented with the bill, perhaps as a tax on energy use, we would in all likelihood use energy more sparingly.

Europeans do better, mostly thanks to hefty taxes that increase their price of energy. In 2009, German households paid almost €0.23 per kilowatt/hour of electricity, roughly three times the rate in the United States. They also pay about three times as much for their gas. And they are thriftier about their energy use. Germany consumes energy at a rate of somewhat above four tons of oil per person per year, roughly half the rate in the United States. German emissions of $CO_2$—about ten metric tons per capita—also amount to about half of what Americans disgorge.

Americans too could be made to emit less carbon. But to do that, they would have to be made to pay for their emissions. The United States is a nation of drivers. In 2000, nine out of ten Americans drove to work, up from two thirds in 1960. There are 820 motor vehicles tooling along the nation's roads and highways for every 1,000 Americans, compared with 623 for every 1,000 people in Germany, 557 in Canada, and 76 in Indonesia. The transport sector in the United States consumes almost twice the amount of gasoline per person as in Australia, nearly four times as much as in Britain, and thirty times as much as in China.

But though we love our cars, we can be persuaded to drive more efficient ones. A study of auto sales from 1999 to 2008 concluded that a one-dollar increase in gas prices boosted the market share of compact cars like the Toyota Corolla by 24 percent and reduced the share of pickups like the Ford F-150 by about 11 percent. That won't transform the United States into Britain. There, gasoline costs up to three times as much and the bestselling car in 2009 was the tiny Ford Fiesta, which emits only 158 grams of $CO_2$ per mile driven, compared with about 660 grams per mile emitted by Americans' beloved Ford F-150 pickup truck. But tripling the price of gas might persuade Americans to lead somewhat more energetically frugal lives.

**PRECISELY BECAUSE ENERGY** is not sufficiently taxed, humanity consumes it with abandon, spewing around 39 billion tons of $CO_2$ from energy use, 60 percent more than in 1980. Other dynamics, like deforestation, add another 20 billion tons. Because of this, the concentration of $CO_2$ in the atmosphere has risen by more than half since the dawn of the Industrial Revolution. And global temperatures have risen by about half a degree Celsius since then.

We have a lot more warming coming. According to the Intergovernmental Panel on Climate Change, a group of scientists studying warming around the world, on present trends greenhouse gas emissions will grow between 25 and 90 percent from 2000 to 2030. Along this path, the planet would warm at least 1.8 degrees Celsius and perhaps up to 6.4°C over the course of the current century.

For comparison, we are only 5°C warmer than we were during the last Ice Age.

It doesn't require a lot of warming to cause environmental havoc. Even if temperatures rose less than 2°C, warming would disrupt patterns of rainfall, causing both floods and drought in India, China, and South America. Parts of the Amazon rain forest could become a grassy savannah. Fifteen to 40 percent of the world's species of plants and animals would risk extinction.

If temperatures were allowed to increase further, damages could become catastrophic. As Greenland's ice pack melted, rising sea levels could cover the Netherlands, the alluvial planes of Bangladesh, and about one third of Florida and Louisiana. Regardless of how one personally values nature's ecosystems, this would be a problem. By 2050, the world is expected to have 2.5 billion more people. On present trends, they would have to feed themselves with 10 percent less fresh water.

Until recently, the call to arms against warming was couched in terms of lost species and melting polar ice. But a few years ago, a team led by Sir Nicholas Stern, former chief economist of the World Bank, changed the terms of the debate with a report for the British Treasury that detailed the cost of climate change in strict economic terms.

If we continue spewing carbon into the air at our present pace, Stern concluded, the damage inflicted on the planet later this century and the next would be frightening, "on a scale similar to those associated with the great wars and the economic depression of the first half of the 20th century."

*The Stern Review on the Economics of Climate Change,* published in 2006, estimated that the future cost of our folly would amount to at least 5 percent of the world's total economic production and perhaps up to 20 percent "now and forever." A fifth of the world's gross domestic product is about $12 trillion. Losing that would be equivalent to, say, losing four fifths of the American economy. Or losing the entire economies of China, Japan, and India.

## THE ETHICS OF TOMORROW

Shouldn't we be more worried?

I found the first reference to the concept of climate change in the *New York Times* in September of 1955, running above a story about an electronic brain that could search a dictionary for the right word. In October of 1958, George H. T. Kimble, chairman of the geography department of Indiana University, wrote an article in the *Times Magazine* titled "Why the Weird Weather," in which he mentioned $CO_2$, and sunspots, as potential culprits of strange weather patterns that included May snow in Portugal, a heat wave in Czechoslovakia, and Florida's wettest March on record. By February 14 of 1979 the *Times* science editor, Walter Sullivan, was writing that "there is a real possibility that some people now in their infancy will live to a time when the ice at the North Pole will have melted."

Thirty years later, shipping lines, mining companies, and oil firms are waiting with baited breath as the forbidding masses of ice over the North Pole thaw—opening up oil and mineral deposits as well as new shipping lanes over the top of the world. Yet despite the crescendo of warning, the world's people and its leaders have proved incapable of agreeing on a decisive course of action to drastically reduce emissions of carbon. In December 2009, world leaders left a supposedly crucial summit on global climate in Copenhagen much as they arrived, with no firm agreement to cut emissions of carbon dioxide. The Obama administration was unable to persuade the United States Senate to pass a cap and trade plan to limit carbon emissions in 2010.

Hammered by economic troubles, Americans appeared to lose interest in the perils of the weather. In early 2010, only 32 percent of Americans said global warming amounted to a serious threat, 16 percent thought the damages would not materialize in their life-time, and 19 percent thought it would never happen.

The notion that we must curb our carbon emissions has many natural foes. ExxonMobil alone spewed 306 million tons of green-house gases in 2007. The American Electric Power Company emit-ted more than 150 million. A forty-dollar levy on each ton of $CO_2$ would amount to almost half of the power company's revenue and six times its profits.

But opposition is broader than that. Republicans mostly oppose legislation to cut carbon emissions because of their ties to the energy industry. But their skepticism about climate change also has a geographic rationale. Republicans on the House Energy and Commerce Committee in the 110th Congress represented districts with carbon emissions per capita that were 21 percent higher, on average, than those in districts represented by committee Democrats. Fifty-nine percent of Oklahoma's carbon emissions from electricity generation come from coal-fired plants. So it should perhaps be unsurprising that Senator James Inhofe, a Republican from Oklahoma, called global warming the "greatest hoax ever perpetrated on the American people."

The poor are not enthusiastic about the prospect of an energy tax either. Americans in the top tenth of the income distribution emit 2.5 times as much carbon as people at the bottom. But families among the bottom tenth of the income pile spend more than a quarter of what they earn on energy—compared with only 3.6 percent for those at the top.

**OPPOSITION TO EFFORTS** to avert climate change is arrayed along similar lines around the world. Poor countries in the tropics stand to suffer the most from warming. In Brazil, agribusiness accounts for one quarter of the economy. Agriculture accounts for 21 percent of India's GDP, about seventeen times its share of the United States economy. By 2080, global warming is expected to reduce agricultural productivity across the developing world by 15 percent to 26 percent. By contrast, farmers working the vineyards of Germany's Mosel valley might welcome climate change: a 1°C increase in temperature could increase their annual revenue by 30 percent, boosting the ripeness of their grapes. A 3°C rise would more than double the value of their land.

The heat also disrupts industrial activity and even political stability in poorer countries. Studying the relationship between temperature fluctuations and economic performance since 1950, researchers found that a 1°C increase in temperature reduced economic growth in poor countries by 1.1 percentage points but had no discernible effect on richer nations. But though developing nations stand most to gain from slowing the earth's warming, they are the most resistant to accepting any new costs to effect change. They aspire to the same energy-intensive development strategies that the developed world used to get rich and have settled on an environmental strategy that consists of reminding the industrial world that climate change to date is its fault, so it has a moral obligation to fix it.

Rich countries face the flip side of this quandary. By the end of the century, more than 85 percent of the world's population will live in the developing world. When presented with the bill to avert climate change, voters in rich countries see a plan to save people who will be born far in the future and halfway around the world. Developed nations can't even bring themselves to push for aid for people alive in poor countries today. Despite commitments to raise their foreign aid budgets to at least 0.7 percent of their GDP, only Luxembourg, the Netherlands, Norway, Sweden, and Denmark have met the target. The United States and Japan, the two largest economies in the world, provide 0.2 percent and 0.18 percent of their GDP in development aid. Germany contributes 0.35 percent. What chance is there that they will agree to provide much more to help poor foreigners who haven't been born yet and won't be born for a while?

As the United States Congress debated endlessly over legislation to cap carbon emissions in the summer of 2009, Representative Joe Barton, the ranking Republican on the House Energy Committee, argued that "I'm concerned that we're giving China a ticket to become the world's greatest free rider, enjoying all of the benefits that developed countries enjoy without having to share any burden, and challenging American economic dominance in a way that hasn't been done by anybody since before World War II."


**FOR ALL THE** various opposing interests, I believe the main reason for our cavalier approach to climate change is our inability to relate to pain in the future. Reducing carbon emissions requires making hard choices today. The projected costs of climate change, by contrast, are mostly meant to happen in a distant tomorrow. The absence of an imminent threat has allowed people to act as if warming were someone else's problem.

Yet it is not entirely unreasonable that people would resist the proposition that combating climate change must be our paramount priority. It is difficult to estimate the environmental, social, and economic damages of warming. And slashing carbon emissions could be expensive, slowing economic growth and sucking money from things like providing education and investing in factories. How do we know this is the best way to address the problem? Helping poor countries industrialize and reduce their dependence on farming might provide their citizens a better future than trying to preempt future weather convulsions that could devastate their crops.

The calculation demanded of our generation is not about the value of greenery compared with having more stuff. It pits our needs for goods, services, and a working environment against the value we place on the needs of other people one hundred years from now.

In the 1970s, the environmental economist Talbot Page used a literary trick to alert us to the ethical conundrum brought about by our overuse of the environment. He suggested we put ourselves in the shoes of a young man growing up in a world about to come to an end due to the immoderate appetites of previous generations. "You might well call out to the ghosts of the first generation, demanding by what right it made its decision," he counseled. "It would hardly be satisfying to hear the answer, 'We took a vote of all those present and decided to follow our own time preferences.'"

Our own time preferences are not very nice on the future. In an influential study in the 1990s, people around the United States were asked about how they valued people in the future compared with those currently alive. Almost four out of ten said they would prefer to invest in a program that saved a hundred lives from pollution in the present to an alternative plan that would save four thousand lives twenty-five years down the road. Almost half thought saving one person in the present was worth more than saving seventy in a hundred years. Other studies have concluded our preference for the present isn't quite as stark. In a more recent survey, only 28 percent of respondents said a death a hundred years from now wasn't as bad as a death next year. Still, it is clear that people feel greater kinship with their contemporaries than with people of the future, who can come across as abstractions rather than people.

We act by these beliefs every day, ignoring the needs of our descendants. The old, who vote in large numbers, regularly get a better deal from the political system than the young, who do not vote. Government spending skews heavily in favor of the old. Social spending on the elderly amounted to $19,700 per person in 2000, according to one study; children got $6,380. And those who don't expect to be alive very far into the future care less about what warming will do to it.

Only a quarter of Americans over the age of sixty-five believe global warming is a very serious problem, according to a poll by the Pew Research Center. Among those aged eighteen to twenty-nine, almost half thought it was very serious. A poll in Europe also found that only one-third of those over sixty-five were very worried, compared with 40 percent of those aged twenty-five to forty-four, the prime childbearing age. Just over a fifth of the young were willing to pay a gas tax in order to curb carbon emissions, while only a tenth of the elderly were willing to do so.

**THIS IS NOT** merely a conflict pitting altruism against self-regard. Even if we were designing our choices to best serve others, we would still be left in an ethical quandary. Partha Dasgupta, a Bangladeshi-born professor of economics at Cambridge University, crafted his own moral story to illustrate the democratic dilemma posed by climate change. Suppose, he suggested, that some voter were genuinely concerned about the long-term implications of climate change due to rising carbon emissions. She isn't selfish—she knows that carbon emissions have massive social costs. She understands she can't rely on her private interest to take a position on the matter. She must take into account the effect of her choices on others. But how to take future others into account?

For those deeply invested in the environmental movement, the answer to this dilemma is obvious. They couch arguments to save the environment in terms that appeal to the baby-seal lovers they assume live within us all. The environment, they suggest, is as inherently valuable as humanity. Nature is not to be conserved out of some estimate of its instrumental value to humankind. We should care for its intrinsic value, because it is the only nature there is. If we kill the last bear there will be bears no more. Earth First! puts it thus: "No Compromise in Defense of Mother Earth." But it's difficult to think this way when the debate is over allocating resources among competing virtuous endeavors.

Maybe we should abide by a rule that says we should leave the earth exactly as we got it so the next bunch can enjoy its bounty, as did we. No generation, of course, has behaved in such a way. Starting with the first sapiens who roamed the plains of Africa, humans have continuously altered their physical environment. By this rule, if we were given the choice of spending $1 billion to save the environment or to develop a vaccine that would benefit all future generations, we would have to choose the former.

If instead we tweak the mandate and demand that we bequeath at least as much "social capital" as we got—mixing in environmental assets with other good things like hospitals, roads, and educated people—we're back at square one. How should we measure the value of the road against the damages caused by the exhaust from the cars and trucks traveling on it? Some things, like the extinction of the dodo, are going to be very difficult to value.

We might be moved to protect the future out of altruism. But if that is the case, should the urge to help unborn people two hundred years from now take precedence over the philanthropic inclinations we feel to help the unfortunate of the present generation? There are lots of priorities to choose from, including 33 million people living with HIV. In sub-Saharan Africa 9 mothers die for every 1,000 live births and 157 out of every 1,000 kids die before reaching the age of five. In Southern Asia, 46 percent of children under five are underweight and nearly a third of the working population earns less than one dollar a day.

John Rawls, perhaps the most influential American moral and political philosopher since World War II, argued that societies should strive to maximize the well-being of the least fortunate among them. No society that I know of has ever met this goal. But most democratic governments today redistribute income in some way, through taxes and spending programs, from the rich to the poor.

The recommendations to combat climate change in the *Stern Review* stand uncomfortably alongside this principle of social justice. If income per person were to grow by 1 percent a year over the next two centuries, less than half the pace of growth of the last century, people in the year 2200 would be 6.3 times as rich as they are today. Why should the poorer people of the present scrimp and save in order to protect the environment for their richer descendants, who could afford more environmental investments than we can?

## THE PRICE OF THE FUTURE

Even if we were to decide that we should invest present resources to save future people from the perils of a warmer planet, another crucial question remains: how much?

The bill could be fairly high. The *Stern Review*, published in 2006, put the price tag on the worldwide effort to combat climate change at about 1 percent of the entire globe's economic output. That amounts to about $600 billion a year.

With this investment, Stern suggested, we could stabilize the concentration of greenhouse gases in the atmosphere at somewhere in the upper end of the range of 450 and 550 parts per million, compared with 430 ppm today, conserving energy and switching into more expensive nonfossil fuels. He said this should keep global temperatures from rising more than 2.5°C. It wouldn't prevent all environmental damages, of course. Stern estimated that allowing 550 ppm of greenhouse gases in the atmosphere would cause losses amounting to about 1.1 percent of the world's economic product. That's the equivalent of losing Indonesia or Turkey.

And there is a fair chance that the bill to avoid catastrophic warming is even higher. Vulnerable countries like the Maldives, a small archipelago of low-lying islands that rise only a few feet above sea level, are suggesting even a lower cap on carbon concentrations in the atmosphere. A couple of years after his initial report, Stern suggested that concentrations of greenhouse gases should best be kept below 500 ppm, an endeavor that would cost 2 percent of the world's gross domestic product.

That is a lot to spend. Stern's conclusion that the investment is worthwhile is based on a proposition that is either obvious or radically controversial about the value of human life. Stern assumes that the welfare of a person hundreds of years from now is worth the same as the welfare of a person alive today. Not everybody agrees.

Stern allows two modest adjustments to this equality. He acknowledges that the value of money to people is inversely proportional to how much they have. An extra dollar is worth less to an investment banker in New York than to a subsistence farmer in Michoacán. What's more, there is a minuscule chance that a meteorite will strike a devastating blow to the earth at some point in the future and kill everyone on it. In this case the welfare of humans beyond that point in time would fall to zero. We would have no justification to spend anything to enhance their welfare because by then humanity would be extinct. Those tweaks aside, the bedrock concept of the equal value of human welfare across time leads Stern to a straightforward rule of thumb: devoting a given share of the current generation's income to forestall global warming is justified if it produces a benefit amounting to at least the same share of that future generation's income no matter how many hundreds of years down the line.

This approach sounds reasonable when taken at face value. But it has a problem: it places too little value on the people of the present by making the future extremely expensive. That's because there isn't just one future generation to save at the present generation's expense, but many. Say we were justified in protecting future people from the damages of warming as long as the benefits, as a share of their future incomes, were greater than our investment was, as a share of our incomes now. Adding up the bill for the rescue over a large number of future generations would justify humongous spending today.

This kind of counting allows the *Stern Review* to estimate that the future costs of climate change are equivalent to a fifth of the world's income "now and forever." He reaches this price tag by adding very small costs in the near future with larger and larger costs in faraway centuries.

**IF WE WERE** to apply the most common economic techniques to value the future, we would not accept this conclusion. Outside the debate over climate change, money today is worth more than the same amount of money tomorrow. That's not just because of inflation: a businessman will make an investment only if it generates a higher return than putting the money in the bank to earn interest.

The return on corporate investments in the United States, before taxes, has averaged 6.6 percent per year over the past four decades. Government agencies are directed to use a "discount rate" of 7 percent to compare the expected future benefit of some programs with their up-front cost. This choice assumes that, excluding the effects of inflation, a dollar today—if applied productively—will be worth $1.07 next year, $1.145 the year after that, and $752,932 two centuries down the road. It means that to spare damages of $752,932 in two hundred years we should spend no more than $1 today.

One can transport this rationale to environmental issues. A forest in which 100 trees will produce 7 new ones next year has a 7 percent discount rate. Saving 100 trees from loggers this year has the same value as saving 107 trees next year.

Thinking in these terms, Stern's approach amounts to using an extremely low discount rate. The idea that averting a dollar's worth of damage in the future is worth spending a dollar today would amount to choosing a discount rate of zero. Stern chooses a slightly higher one, just a smidgen above the rate at which people's income is growing.

William Nordhaus of Yale University, one of the most prominent American economists working on climate-change models, disagrees pretty radically with Stern. Like Stern, he argues we must reduce emissions of greenhouse gases to try to get a grip on climate change. But he puts a much higher bar on how much we should be willing to invest in the endeavor. He points out that more than half the damages forecast by the *Stern Review* are expected to occur after the year 2800. Why, he asks, should we sacrifice a substantial share of our current welfare to avert costs that are so far off in the future?

Nordhaus argues that in estimating future damages we should use a rate that reflects the productivity of long-term investments. He argues it would be dumb to use present-day money to undertake an investment to tackle warming if it produced a lower return. That's because we could achieve a higher profit investing it in something else. We could use the returns of our investment to tackle warming in the future and we would still have money left over. "The discount rate is high to reflect the fact that investments in reducing future climate damages to corn and trees and other areas should compete with investments in better seed, improved rotation, and many other high-yield investments," Nordhaus writes in his book *A Question of Balance,* about options to combat climate change.

Future generations will take advantage too of the fecundity of these investments. Millions of poor farmers on Bangladesh's vast alluvial plains would surely welcome investments to stop the sea level from rising and swallowing their farms. But the Bangladeshis of the future, like those of the present, might be better served if the money were allocated instead to develop their economy so they could get a better job outside agriculture farther up the hill.

Using Nordhaus's discount rate, which he estimates at 4 percent per year, leads to a radically different view from Stern's about the merits of expensive interventions to save the future earth. Say we are deciding how much to spend to avoid a climate shock that would generate damages amounting to 13.8 percent of the world's gross domestic product in the year 2200—which happens to be the estimate for that year in the *Stern Review*'s bad scenario. If economic growth over the next 190 years replicates the seventy-five-fold jump of the past 190 years, the damages would amount to about $640 trillion in today's money. Using a discount rate of just above 1 percent, as Stern suggests, we would be justified to spend up to nearly $80 trillion to save the day 190 years down the road. But at a 4 percent discount rate, as Nordhaus uses, it would make sense to invest in this effort only if we could do it for about $385 billion. If we couldn't do it for that amount, we would be better off deploying the money on some other, more productive objective.

## TORN BETWEEN TWO PRICES

If she is listening to economists, Dasgupta's hypothetical voter is probably dizzy by now. President Harry Truman famously called for a one-armed economist to get around the profession's penchant for analysis of the "on the one hand, on the other hand" variety. Nordhaus and Stern fit the bill—each offering up one clear choice. But they do have two hands between them. Stern's analysis calls for a big immediate investment to combat climate change. He suggests that we start by setting a price of about seventy-five dollars per ton on emissions of carbon dioxide—sixty-eight cents per gallon of gas. He expects people and companies would dash to conserve energy, develop energy-efficient technologies, and switch into alternative, nonfossil fuels. As these technologies got cheaper, the levy on emissions could fall to about twenty-five dollars per ton of $CO_2$ by the year 2050.

Using a similar set of climatic facts, Nordhaus advises us to address the problem more gradually. He proposes that the levy on $CO_2$ today should start around $10 per ton and rise as the impact of carbon concentrations in the atmosphere increase, to about $200 at the end of this century. To the average American, who consumes 20 tons of $CO_2$ annually, the bill would start at around $200 per year.

Nordhaus would tolerate more climate change than Stern. He would allow $17 trillion in climate-related damages to happen simply because he estimates we would need to spend more than that to eliminate them. By 2100, temperatures would be about 2.6 degrees Celsius hotter than in preindustrial times. But though we would suffer more damage, we would get value for money from our investments: avoid $5 trillion in damages at a cost of $2 trillion. In Nordhaus's analysis, which does not contemplate the fast technological progress assumed by Stern, the cost of Stern's strategy to cap warming at 1.5 degrees could balloon to nearly $30 trillion in present value, and prevent only $12.5 trillion worth of damages to the earth. And we'd still be left with $9 trillion worth of climate-related damage.

The European Climate Exchange, a market for companies to buy and sell permits to emit $CO_2$, which was launched in 2005 as part of Europe's efforts to reduce carbon emissions, suggests that investors believe the world's policy makers are closer to adopting Nordhaus's views than Stern's. In the summer of 2010, the future contract for December priced one ton of $CO_2$ at about €15 a ton—about $18.75.

What should our voter instruct her elected representatives to do? Dasgupta doesn't quite know. And he is well versed in the economics of climate change. Perhaps, he suggests, cost-benefit considerations should be eschewed in favor of what is known as the precautionary principle, which would support large-scale spending to curb carbon emissions on the grounds that there is a chance, even if highly uncertain, of an Armageddon-like climatic catastrophe if we don't.

He argues it might be more politically feasible than we think to mobilize resources to save future generations. If voters in rich countries saw ourselves as directly responsible for future generations' plight, we might overcome our hostility toward foreign aid, which stems from the belief that the developing world's poverty is, to some extent, the developing world's fault.

Our voter could seek the high ethical ground by tweaking the parameters—maybe trimming Nordhaus's 4 percent by a point or two. After all, even though it's probably right to discount the value of money, environmental goods are likely to become more valuable as they become scarcer. So the monetary discount rate should be adjusted to take into account the rising value of environmental "goods." Saving that forest with 107 trees next year will be worth more than saving the 100-tree forest today because though we will have more money next year there will be fewer forests to go around. So each surviving tree will be more valuable to us.

Maybe our hypothetical voter should just follow her belly. Ultimately, Dasgupta argues, "it is a 'gut feeling' about the awful things that could occur if the global mean temperature were to rise another 5 degrees that should make us very scared." And there's no parameter to tell us precisely how to price this fear.

## SALVATION ON THE CHEAP

Or maybe she could cross her fingers and hope we will devise some clever technology to stop us from colliding head-on with the limits of the planet. Some scientists have been toying with the idea that geo-engineering might save the day from climate change: putting mirrors in orbit to reflect part of the sun's energy away from the earth, or pumping sulfur dioxide into the stratosphere. This would replicate the effects of the 1991 eruption of Mount Pinatubo in the Philippines—which sent up so much stuff into the air it blocked the sun and reduced surface temperatures by half a degree Celsius over the next two years.

Unfortunately, some studies suggest this strategy could trigger catastrophic drought in parts of the world. Still, it has the advantage that if it works, it would work fast. Moreover, it is cheap: a few billion at the most. This approach would fit what we have done, at least since Malthus's day. Every time we have faced physical constraints, we have deployed technology to squeeze more out of the finite resources of the planet.

Only forty years ago, as concern over population growth and environmental degradation was shaping into an environmental movement, the economist Julian Simon decided to challenge the prevailing concern about the state of the earth and dared the Stanford ecologist Paul R. Ehrlich, a noted prophet of doom, to a bet.

Ehrlich had built his reputation dusting off Malthus's expectation of impending environmental collapse. "In the 1970s the world will undergo famines—hundreds of millions of people are going to starve to death," he wrote in *The Population Bomb* in 1968. In *The End of Affluence,* published in 1974, he forecast "a genuine age of scarcity" by 1985. Simon would have none of it. In 1980 he challenged Ehrlich to choose any natural resource he wanted—from coal to copper to corn. If these commodities were to become scarce as the world's population grew, their price would naturally rise. Simon bet that the price of whatever Ehrlich chose would, instead, decline over the next decade.

Ehrlich bet $1,000 on a basket of five metals—chromium, copper, nickel, tin, and tungsten. He scoffed that explaining to an economist the inevitability of rising commodity prices was like "attempting to explain odd-day-even-day gas distribution to a cranberry." But Simon won. The world's population grew by 800 million people over the decade. But phone companies abandoned copper wire for fiber optics. Tin cans were displaced by aluminum. And the price of every one of the metals in Ehrlich's chosen basket fell, after accounting for inflation. Tin and tungsten plummeted 71 percent.

Ehrlich sent Simon his winnings: a check for $576.07—which amounted to the extent of the fall in the basket's price. Ever since, the wager has provided a victorious narrative for the school of thought that we can ride global warming out without enormous sacrifices. Opponents of efforts to reduce emissions of carbon into the atmosphere wield Simon's wager as a weapon. After his death in 1998, the Competitive Enterprise Institute in Washington, which spends much of its time and resources in denying climate change, created the Julian L. Simon Memorial Award to bestow upon fellow skeptics.

IT SEEMS RISKY to trust our ingenuity at this stage. Around the world, the planet is showing signs of stress to sustain 7 billion humans living on it.

It was barely over two years ago, in the spring and summer of 2008, just before banks across the rich world started buckling under the weight of bad mortgages, that the price of corn, wheat, and soybeans shot to unprecedented heights on the board of the Chicago Mercantile Exchange. There were food riots in Egypt and Bangladesh. In Haiti's sprawling slum of Cité Soleil, mud cookies—a mixture of dirt, salt, and vegetable shortening—became the food of choice as the price of rice soared out of most Haitians' reach. Prices of iron and steel jumped too. On July 3, Brent crude oil from the North Sea peaked at $143.95 a barrel—94 percent higher than its price just twelve months before.

We were momentarily saved from this catastrophe by a global recession of which we had not seen the like since the 1930s. But as soon as the world started growing again, we started hitting some of the same constraints. Oil prices, which dropped to a trough of

$33.73 a barrel after Christmas in 2008, were back above $80 in April of 2010. In August, on fears of a global shortage, the Food and Agriculture Organization's food price index surged to its highest level since September 2008. Martin Wolf, the usually serene economic columnist for the *Financial Times*, wrote that limits to economic growth could topple civilization. A world that over the past two hundred years had grown itself out of many of its problems could easily slip back to a zero-sum reality in which one group's gain would result in another's loss, in which the only chance to get ahead would be to steal, repress, and plunder. Democracy and peace work in a world of increasing opportunities where people can invest and trade their way to prosperity. If there are limits to growth, Wolf warned, "The political underpinning of our world falls apart."

And if there is any doubt that resources in the future will be more expensive than they were in the past, one need go no further than Ehrlich's basket. Between 1990 and 2008 the basket roughly doubled in price, after inflation. The price of tungsten zoomed up 150 percent. The price of chromium jumped 138 percent. Simon got lucky in his choice of decade. But it would seem foolhardy for us to trust that our luck will hold forever.

# When Prices Fail

**THERE'S A WEB SITE** called Zillow that will spit out a price estimate for pretty much any house in the country. Its algorithm, based on the sales history, the prices of homes sold nearby, and other public data, has a fair track record. In New York and Los Angeles, its estimates have a median error of about 12 percent.

I used to visit Zillow to keep an eye on the Los Angeles condo that my wife and I lived in before moving to New York in 2004. It's a pretty town house a ten-minute walk from the beach, with a windswept roof deck full of cacti and a view of the ocean. But it's not the house I pined over. I was nostalgic about the financial gamble, possibly the best deal I will ever make. We bought the place for $369,000 and sold it for $575,000 less than three years later. That is a $206,000 return, on a down payment of only $70,000. Like looking at the worn snapshot of a loved one, keeping an eye on the price of my old home brought me closer to that odd burst of luck. Perversely, it taunted me with the hint that I could have made more.

Financial ruminations of this sort can produce whiplash, however. I felt a pang of envy as the place zoomed past $800,000 a year after we sold it. Then it dipped, reassuringly, seesawed, shot back up past $900,000, dropped precipitously, bounced, and ended 2009 around $700,000. The roller-coaster ride has taught me one thing: it's hard to tell how much a home is worth. The rise and fall of my former L.A. condo offers a bigger lesson: prices can fail. They can get it wrong in a very big way, in fact—steering our decisions in unprofitable directions.

These decisions can be very costly. Skyrocketing house prices persuaded many to spend all their money on homes they would never be able to sell at a profit. Billions of dollars coursed through the Los Angeles real estate market every day. The fortunes of millions of people depended on the price of their homes. But evidently nobody had a clue about what houses in Los Angeles were really worth. So it was across the country, as house prices went for a feverish ride and took our prosperity with them.

The financial disaster unleashed by the collapse of housing led to the sharpest economic contraction in the United States since the 1930s—pushing unemployment above 10 percent for the first time in more than a quarter century. Ricocheting around the world, it knocked $3.3 trillion off the world economy in 2009. Who knew the price of houses could pack such destructive power?

**PRICES DO A** pretty decent job organizing the world, much of the time. Both shaping human behavior and shaped by it, prices distill people's knowledge, beliefs, and preferences about the choices that lie before them. A quarter century ago, an economist at UCLA published a study titled "Orange Juice and Weather," which showed that the prices of orange-juice concentrate futures did a better job predicting the weather in Florida than the National Weather Service. Concentrate prices incorporated what investors knew about the prospects for the orange crop. If they had reliable data that the weather would be favorable, they would bet on low prices. If instead it seemed a cold snap was around the corner, they would bet prices of concentrate would rise. Distilled from a large set of investors' decisions, the prices amalgamated the world's collective knowledge about Florida's weather.

Prices provide the most important signals in an economy, guiding people's decisions on where to invest their resources to get the best return they can. People who shop around to get the best possible price for their plasma TV are doing us all a favor. They get a better machine, have more money left over to buy other things, and improve the odds of success of the company that makes good products for less, boosting the economy's efficiency. Successful technology companies that profit from the work of highly qualified workers will offer higher wages—a higher price—to attract better-qualified applicants. Workers will keep raising their qualifications as long as the return—measured in better wages—is worth the investment in time, money, and effort.

This virtuous cycle, however, depends on relative prices being right. They must do a good job assessing the relative costs and benefits of different types of TVs. When prices go wrong, these decisions are distorted, often to devastating effect. This, unfortunately, happens depressingly often. Between 2000 and 2006, housing sucked in an unprecedented share of U.S. resources, as Americans rushed to buy a home in the belief that home prices would rise forever. The rush of money boosted house prices by some 70 percent on average. Builders rushed to build more. Then the bubble popped. Home prices fell almost a third from their peak in the spring of 2006 to their trough in early 2009.

The enormous bubble that lifted home prices skyward before slamming them down again didn't do much for homeownership. The share of Americans who owned their home increased by 1.5 percentage points between 2000 and 2004, to a peak of 69.4 percent. By the end of 2009 it had fallen back to 67.3 percent, where it was in the spring of 2000 before the party started. The fall, however, was devastating. For a few scary months, the world economy tottered perilously near disaster. The most hallowed institutions of American capitalism were humbled. The share prices of Citigroup and Bank of America fell more than 90 percent from their peaks. General Motors, whose chief executive had claimed more than half a century earlier that "what was good for the country was good for General Motors and vice versa," collapsed into the government's arms—unable to borrow money or sell cars.

And this wasn't an exclusively American drama. Between 2000 and 2007 house prices rose by some 90 percent in Britain and Spain. By the end of 2009, British home prices had fallen about 16 percent from their peak and Spanish homes about 13 percent.

## WHEN PRICES GO OFF THE RAILS

The housing bubble might be the most painful case of financial excess in recent memory, but it surely isn't the only one. Through the ages, virtually every potentially profitable new frontier opened up to investment has led to a speculative bubble, as investors have scrambled to tap into its promise only to stampede in retreat a few years later. A decade before the housing crisis we experienced the dot-com bubble. The NASDAQ index, heavy with technology stocks, quadrupled between 1996 and March of 2000. Drunk on information technology's promise, people poured retirement savings into companies like Pets.com, which achieved fame, though never profit, on the strength of a cute ad with a sock puppet. In 2000, AOL could use its pricey stock to take over media goliath Time Warner, which had more than five times its revenue. By October of 2002 the NASDAQ was back where it had been in 1996. In 2010, Time Warner quietly spun off AOL for a tiny fraction of its price a decade before.

The dot-com crash was preceded by the Asian financial crisis, with subsidiary bubblettes from Russia to Brazil, when a surge of money into promising "emerging markets" abruptly went into reverse. Similar dynamics caused investors to pummel the Mexican peso during the tequila crisis a few years before. Japan's Nikkei 225 stock index tripled in real terms between January 1985 and December 1989, only to fall 60 percent over the next two and a half years.

The very concept of a financial bubble is three hundred years old, added to the vernacular of finance in 1720 when French, Dutch, and British investors succumbed to euphoria over the potential of new trade routes across the Atlantic—pushing up stock prices before they ended in a precipitous crash. The British South Seas Company was established to buy the debt of the crown. To make money, it was given a royal charter to exploit trade routes between Africa, Europe, and Spain's colonies in America. Spain and Britain being at war, the routes were of dubious value. But that didn't stop investors from jumping on the vaunted opportunity. The share price of the South Seas Company soared. So did the shares of the maritime insurers covering its trips. Pretty soon, every investment looked like a great deal. Newspaper ads were offering a chance to invest in "a company for carrying out an undertaking of great advantage, but nobody to know what it is."

In a move ostensibly implemented to curb the rampant speculation but aimed in fact at protecting the royally chartered trading companies and maritime insurers from competition, in June of 1720 the British Parliament passed a law barring companies that didn't have a license from the Crown from raising money on the stock market. It also barred chartered companies from changing the purpose of their charter. The law was officially called "An Act to Restrain the Extravagant and Unwarrantable Practice of Raising Money by Voluntary Subscription For Carrying on Projects Dangerous to the Trade and Subjects of the United Kingdom." But it came to be known as the Bubble Act. And many analysts have suggested that this single act precipitated the bubble's rupturing. By September it had crashed, and in December, Jonathan Swift penned "The South-Sea Project," which started:

> *Ye wise philosophers, explain*
> *What magic makes our money rise,*
> *When dropt into the Southern main;*
> *Or do these jugglers cheat our eyes?*

And ended:

> *The nation then too late will find,*
> *Computing all their cost and trouble,*
> *Directors' promises but wind,*
> *South Sea, at best, a mighty bubble.*

**A REGULARITY THAT** stands out in these spurts of overenthusiastic invention is the exuberance of the institutions providing finance. This can be prompted by newly discovered investment opportunities—like the Internet or the transatlantic slave trade. But it can also be fueled by changes in the rules governing financial institutions. During the housing boom, financial inventions like floating rate and reverse amortization mortgages were instrumental in bringing less solvent buyers into the American housing market, creating a whole new class of financial product—the subprime loan. In the years of the bubble's rise, the monthly payments needed to buy a $225,000 house with a standard thirty-year, fixed-rate mortgage and a 20 percent down payment were about $1,079 a month. With an interest-only adjustable-rate mortgage, payments would fall to $663. With a negative amortization mortgage, initial monthly payments could fall all the way to $150.

Mortgage banks wanted to lend but weren't much interested in their borrowers' ability to pay. They were slicing up the mortgages and gluing them back together into structured products called "Residential Mortgage-Backed Securities"—RMBS in the jargon—that they sold to other financial institutions, who often had no idea of what they contained. By 2007 the mortgage-backed securities market was worth $6.9 trillion, from $3 trillion in 2000. This euphoria had little to do with hard-nosed analysis of the "real" value of homes.

Some eighty years ago the great British economist John Maynard Keynes provided a subtle explanation of how investors can take prices badly astray. In his book *The General Theory of Employment, Interest and Money,* Keynes compared picking stocks to a reverse beauty contest in which investors didn't have to choose the most beautiful face but the face that was most popular among other investors. "It is not a case of choosing those [faces] which, to the best of one's judgment, are really the prettiest, nor even those which average opinion genuinely thinks the prettiest," Keynes wrote. "We have reached the third degree where we devote our intelligences to anticipating what average opinion expects the average opinion to be." It wouldn't be smart, Keynes observed, to simply buy shares of the company the investor believed to be a good investment. Regardless of the company's merits, its stock wouldn't rise if other investors didn't share his belief.

In the late 1990s, every investor was a sheep looking for the herd—paying top dollar for dubious Internet stocks in the belief that the next investor along would pay a higher price, regardless of the underlying companies' profitability. It made little sense for an investor to bet against the flock. When there were enough fools who believed eToys would become the largest toy store in the United States and should be worth eighty dollars per share, it made perfect sense for the most hardheaded dot-com skeptic to buy the shares for fifty dollars even though he or she believed the company was around the corner from bankruptcy.

So it was during the housing bubble. I doubt that at any point in the cycle of euphoria there was a banker who didn't suspect home prices would eventually stop rising. Still, the dynamics driving investment into the sector depended on prices going up forever. To be able to keep paying the mortgage bill, the financially shaky subprime homeowners needed house prices to keep rising. That way they could either sell and plow the profit into a new property, or refinance at a higher price and pull "equity" from their home to make ends meet. Yet even those who knew that the music would eventually stop couldn't drop out of this game of financial musical chairs.

In the summer of 2007, as mortgage default rates were rising and the "subprime" mortgage market was starting to falter, the chief executive of Citigroup, Charles Prince, argued that "as long as the music is playing, you got to get up and dance. We're still dancing." Months later, Prince was ejected from his post. But he wasn't wrong. He was referring to a long-acknowledged feature of finance: even if an investor were to correctly call a bubble, it could be expensive to bet against it. If other investors were still carried away by their enthusiasm, the bubble could stay inflated longer than the contrarian investor could remain solvent.

## SHOULD WE POP THEM?

Bubbles leave no end of hardship in their wake: banking crises, recessions, and unemployment spikes, as well as more subtle consequences. One study found that the geographic mobility of people whose houses are underwater—worth less than the value of their mortgages—is about half that of homeowners in better financial condition. University students who graduate during a recession earn

less throughout much of their careers. A study of Canadian graduates in the 1980s and 1990s found that those entering the labor market during a recession suffered lower earnings for up to ten years.

Some social scientists have predicted the current crisis could favor
extreme right-wing politics in Europe and the United States in coming years, as lower growth leads to hostility toward governments and
taxes—spawning movements like the populist Tea Party in the United
States. A study of the impact of economic shocks on politics between
1970 and 2002 concluded that a one-percentage-point decline in economic growth leads to a one-percentage-point increase in the share
of the vote going to right-wing and nationalist parties.

Still, it's hard to know what to do about bubbles, even when we
know they are going to pop up time and again. The cycle of investment surge and bust can bankrupt many investors but can also do
good along the way. Investment booms built upon technological
breakthroughs like electricity, railways, or the Internet ultimately
revolutionized the world economy—fueling surges of productivity
that could—at least temporarily—justify the exuberance.

The long-standing American approach, shared by the chairman
of the Federal Reserve, Ben Bernanke, as well as his predecessor,
Alan Greenspan, has been that bubbles should be dealt with only
after the fact. The Fed should be ready to pick up the pieces after
they burst—flooding the economy with cheap money to encourage
lending and help debtors avoid bankruptcy as the value of their
assets deflates. But the government should do nothing to the bubbles themselves. Their point is that we can't tell when a bubble is a
bubble.

This, to critics, sounds as crazy as a bout of euphoric investment
in single-family homes. Why not lean against a bubble by gradually
raising interest rates and cutting the flow of money into the new
investment before things get out of hand? Allowing it to grow will
ensure that the fallout from its implosion will be that much more
painful. Yet while this seems clear-cut after the collapse of the

housing bubble has sent us careening to the edge of another Great Depression, it's not quite as easy to figure out beforehand what to prick and when to prick it.

Economists still debate whether Greenspan was wrong to have kept interest rates low to boost employment as the United States emerged from recession from 2001 to 2003. Raising interest rates would have taken the air out of the incipient housing bubble, but it would have also slowed the economy, lengthening the recession and boosting unemployment. Had housing growth stalled, lots of construction-sector jobs—which provided a livelihood for many workers—wouldn't have existed. "Whenever in the future the US finds itself in a situation like 2003, should it try to keep the economy near full employment even at some risk of a developing bubble?" wondered the economic historian J. Bradford Delong. "I am genuinely unsure as to which side I come down on in this debate."

Beyond the immediate impact on aggregate employment, what would happen with innovation if every time investors swooped upon a new technology the emergent bubbles were preemptively pricked? Big jumps in asset prices can lead to misallocated investments that squander productive resources. Bubbles generate enormous economic volatility as they inflate and burst. The damage is always most acute among the most vulnerable, who lose their jobs, lose their houses, and lose control over their lives. But speculation can also increase investment in risky ventures, which often yields benefits to society. The Internet is no bad thing to have.

In 1922 James Edward Meeker, the economist of the New York Stock Exchange, wrote: "Of all the peoples in history the American people can least afford to condemn speculation in those broad sweeping strokes so beloved of the professional reformer. The discovery of America was made possible by a loan based on the collateral of Queen Isabella's crown jewels, and at interest, beside which even the call rates of 1919–1920 look coy and bashful. Financing an unknown foreigner to sail the unknown deep in three cockleshell boats in the hope of discovering a mythical Zipangu cannot, by the wildest exercise of language be called a 'conservative investment.'" What's more, whatever we do to prevent financial turmoil, we must acknowledge an important limitation: we are unlikely to stamp out bubbles and crashes entirely.

Financial crises spawned by investment surges, credit booms, and asset bubbles appear to be a standard feature of the landscape of capitalism. Economists Carmen Reinhart and Kenneth Rogoff found that of the world's sixty-six major economies—including developed nations and the largest developing countries—only Portugal, Austria, the Netherlands, and Belgium had avoided a banking crisis between 1945 and 2007. By the end of 2008 no country was unscathed.

Every time investors become enthusiastic about some new investment proposition, they assure us that this time will be different. During the dot-com bubble the surge of productivity enabled by information technology allowed us to believe that the historical moment was unique. During the housing boom, we were sure that high-tech financial engineering would protect us from financial risks, spreading them among investors who knew how to handle them. Each time the Pollyannas were wrong.

## WHAT RATIONALITY?

Interestingly, there are economists—prominent ones—who believe bubbles don't exist. Indeed, during the past four decades the prevailing view among many if not most economists was that prices could never be wrong. The insight that prices set in a free exchange between willing buyers and sellers can allocate resources to where they would be most profitably used somehow transformed into a blind belief in the infallibility of markets. According to this model of reality, processes that took prices way above their reasonable, true value, luring people into big mistakes, could not possibly exist.

The seeds of this ideology were laid in nineteenth-century Vienna before settling in the middle of the twentieth at the University of Chicago, perhaps the most influential school of economics of the last thirty years. It held that the free market was the only legitimate way to organize society because it started with individuals' free will. Markets would organize the world impeccably by assigning relative values to goods, services, and individual courses of action. Humans being rational—meaning that they had a consistent set of preferences and beliefs about how their choices would improve their well-being—their decisions had to be the right ones. Government intervention, imposing the will of the state upon the people it ruled, was in this view necessarily inefficient and wrong.

To be sure, the so-called rational actor model has been enormously powerful in understanding people's choices. Its simple core idea, that we set out to maximize our well-being, provides a convincing immediate explanation of people's behavior. And it meshes with our understanding of the evolutionary processes shaping the development of species: if each decision we make leads to a set of probable outcomes with different odds of genetic survival, natural selection would shape preferences in such a way as to maximize biological fitness. But our faith in this theory went much too far. In the 1970s, the rational actor model was extended into the theory of "rational expectations." This adapted the belief in humanity's rationality to the fact that we cannot predict the future and thus must make decisions based only on what we expect the consequences of our actions will be, fitting the probable outcomes of our choices to our set of preferences. For instance, it posits that we plan our lives by coolly estimating our likely future income paths, adjusting our savings accordingly in order to smooth our consumption through our entire lifetimes—consuming less during our peak earning years in order to be able to consume more in retirement.

This was a perfect perch for a theory of perfect prices to latch on to. It posited that the price at which rational people would trade an asset, like orange juice futures, would reflect the available information affecting the asset, such as the weather and its impact on the orange crop. If a set of unusual expectations led a group of investors to push prices away from this rational path, the other investors in the market would make money by betting against them and bring prices back to reason. Economists called this the hypothesis of "efficient markets." These views reached their zenith in the 1980s, after Ronald Reagan and Margaret Thatcher rose to power in the United States and Britain amid the economic stagnation and high inflation produced by the oil crisis of the 1970s. They were on a mission to reduce the role of government in the economy. And the Chicago economists served them with a body of theory.

TO THE EFFICIENT-MARKETS crowd, the financial zigzags that often look like crazy booms and busts are the natural outcomes of the actions of rational investors who face an uncertain future and have to constantly update their expectations in response to new information about the potential profitability of investments. In this land the dot-com bubble was only a bubble in hindsight. In 1999 it might have made sense to put all one's money into the online grocer Webvan. It did go bankrupt two years later. But in 1999 one could believe it might evolve into the next Microsoft. As the economy reeled following the collapse of the housing bubble, the leading lights of Chicago stuck to their guns. "Economists are arrogant people. And because they can't explain something, it becomes irrational," said Eugene Fama, one of the leading economists of this school. "The word 'bubble' drives me nuts."

Yet in the wake of the disaster sparked by the frenzied lurch of housing prices, the assumption of rational investors relentlessly driving prices to their true value looks either wrong or irrelevant.

A Cambridge don and Bloomsbury habitué, a British representative to the peace talks in Versailles, where he argued that imposing tough reparation payments on Germany after World War I would impoverish Germans and lead them to extremism, Keynes was also a savvy investor who made a lot of money in the market. His experience in finance informed his perception that most of the time investors don't know what they are doing. Investment decisions, he thought, are the result of "animal spirits—of a spontaneous urge to action rather than inaction, and not as the outcome of a weighted average of quantitative benefits multiplied by quantitative probabilities."

Robert Shiller, an economist at Yale, has proposed a model based on Keynes's insight. In it, rationality takes a hike: a plausible new economic opportunity—say the Internet or new trade routes across the Atlantic—leads early investors to make a lot of money. This generates enthusiasm. The prices of the hot new asset—dot-com stocks, shares in shipping companies, whatever—are bid up as investors rush to partake of the profits. This leads to euphoria. Eventually the investments overrun the underlying logic. Investors see the price of stocks go up and assume they will continue to do so. They construct a narrative about how the new economic opportunity changes the conventional rules of the game, justifying stratospheric valuations. They borrow to double up on their investments.

Unfortunately, pessimism inevitably sets in when it turns out that the world was not really transformed by the new investment opportunity but operates in the same way it used to. Then the bubble bursts. Prices fall, begetting more pessimism and further price declines. Investors are forced to liquidate their depreciating portfolios to cover their debts, so asset prices fall further. It ends badly. As I watched estimates for my old Los Angeles condo soar above $900,000, two and a half times what I paid for it, I couldn't help thinking that home buyers and the banks that financed them were insane. But they could all justify their strategies by pointing to what other investors were doing. And their justification made some sense at the time. It doesn't make any sense now.

## ECONOMICS FOR A NEW WORLD

The financial disaster spawned in the American housing market is changing economics. Forced to reassess, many economists have suddenly acknowledged that we've known for a long time that the proposition of unerring reason has limitations. We know that sometimes people's preferences do not increase their welfare. Preferences can change unpredictably in response to events. And our belief about what set of choices will lead to our preferred outcomes is also a moving target. Add to that our limited ability to process information and compute the probable outcomes of our decisions, and the notion that we should always allow people's individual preferences to guide prices across society starts looking reckless. Change is even coming to the Booth School of Business at the University of Chicago, the cathedral of efficient markets. The school recently took out an ad in the *Financial Times* trumpeting that despite its reputed belief in boundless rationality, it actually has psychologists on staff too, studying what happens when rationality fails.

Belief in unbounded rationality is not economics' only flaw. The self-serving *Homo economicus*—willing to relentlessly pursue her individual preferences—is too narrow a being. The model fails to explain behaviors that are a fundamental part of who we are. Wedded to the notion that individuals will only do something if they get something in return, economics cannot properly explain why people help strangers whom they will never see again. It believes that people who reject free money must be crazy. But there are many instances of people rejecting payment for doing things they believe to be intrinsically good for society. In one experiment, Swedish women who were offered fifty kroner for their blood donations cut their donation rates in half. It was as if the payment crowded out an intrinsic nonmonetary incentive to give.

*Homo economicus* must be stripped of unbridled selfishness and modeled to fit a world where the relative distribution of prosperity is often more important than individual satisfaction. It must incorporate how the social norms built over evolutionary time to enhance societies' ability to survive feed into people's preferences even though they may not contribute to their immediate well-being. A comprehensive model of humankind must understand that people pursue not what they want but what they think they want, and how these objectives can diverge. It must include people who will pay an exorbitant price for a license plate precisely because its price is exorbitant, as if sticker shock were a desirable attribute. It must incorporate people's persistent lack of self-control, even when they know that indulging their appetites—whether smoking, overeating, or forgetting to save for a rainy day—will carry a high price in the end.

Including all these dimensions of humanity is likely to turn economics into a messier, less mathematically elegant discipline than the one we've been used to for the past half century, which thought that one simple process—a relentless drive to maximize our objective well-being—could explain every human behavior. It will have to tag on other considerations, and understand how they interact with self-gratification. It is likely to be more tentative. But, in exchange, the new economics will provide a more comprehensive understanding of the world. Also important, it will be able to grapple with the many ways in which the decisions we make based on the prices arrayed before us can take us in directions that, individually or as a society, we would rather avoid.

**BEYOND THE CHANGE** of the discipline of economics, the more interesting question is how the global meltdown will change capitalism itself. In 2008, as the financial disaster spread outward from New York to London, Zurich, and around the world, many announced the end of the era of so-called Anglo-Saxon capitalism of small government and unfettered markets. "Self-regulation is finished, *laissez-faire* is finished, the idea of an all powerful market which is always right is finished," said France's president, Nicolas Sarkozy. Peer Steinbrück, Germany's finance minister at the time, argued that "the US will lose its status as the superpower of the world financial system." Some policy makers have touted a Chinese model of capitalism, in which the state exerts direct control over huge swaths of economic activity, including credit allocation and the price of the nation's currency, to fuel export-led development. As the global economic balance shifts—the OECD club of industrial nations estimates that nonmembers will make up 57 percent of the world economy by 2030, up from 49 percent today—perhaps the liberal model of democracy and market capitalism that powered prosperity in the West will lose influence.

I am somewhat skeptical that China could provide a model for countries that are not accustomed to totalitarian rule. But it seems inevitable that the rules of the economic order will change as we incorporate the lessons of the crash. Crashes like the one we just experienced affect people's attitudes deeply. Opinion surveys in the United States over the past few decades suggest that Americans who experienced a deep recession between the ages of eighteen and twenty-five were more likely to grow up to believe that success is achieved through luck rather than effort and were more likely to support redistributing income from the lucky rich to the unlucky poor. Paradoxically, the shock also diminished their trust in public institutions, like the presidency and Congress, so even as they demanded more of government, they doubted government's ability to deliver necessary services.

History has many examples of crises causing deep changes in economic and political governance. At the beginning of the twentieth century, France was a highly evolved capitalist economy. The market capitalization of companies listed on the Parisian bourse reached 78 percent of French GDP, more than the value of the firms on the New York Stock Exchange as a share of the American economy. But the Great Depression and the German occupation delivered a shock to the faith of the French in the Third Republic. And their faith in laissez-faire capitalism suffered a permanent blow too.

The history of capitalism is punctuated by changes of direction in response to crises. In the 1930s, even as most major economies were mired in what would come to be known as the Great Depression, economic orthodoxy had it that government had no role to play in economic management. After the stock-market crisis of 1929 Secretary of the Treasury Andrew Mellon argued that government should stay out. According to the memoirs of President Herbert Hoover, Mellon's formula was "liquidate labor, liquidate stocks, liquidate farmers, liquidate real estate . . . It will purge the rottenness out of the system." Keynes, who proposed vigorous government spending to replace collapsing private demand, had a hard time being heard. There is a document in the archive of the British Treasury that shows the reaction of the permanent secretary of the Treasury to Keynes's proposal for government spending to boost Britain's economy, scribbled in three words: "Extravagance, Inflation, Bankruptcy." By the end of the decade, however, Keynes's work had become the basis for a new economic orthodoxy that persisted until the 1970s, based on the view that governments had a substantial role to play in economic management. And Keynes was the hero who saved the world.

**THE STAGFLATION OF** the 1970s and early 1980s provided a similar shock to the world's economic organization, but in the opposite direction. Sparked by a combination of skyrocketing oil prices and bad economic management by overconfident governments willing to print money at will to meet their spending requirements, a combination of high inflation and high unemployment that the world had never seen before fatally undermined people's trust in the state. This laid the stage for a three-decade-long period of government withdrawal. Starting with the election of Margaret Thatcher in Britain in 1979 and of Ronald Reagan in the United States a year later, governments around the world cut taxes, privatized state enterprises, and deregulated economies. Even in France, where President François Mitterrand nationalized the banking system, increased government employment, and raised public-sector pay, soon after being elected in 1981, the new orthodoxy ultimately prevailed. In 1983, President Mitterrand did a complete U-turn, froze the budget, and put in place a policy regime he called "La Rigueur": The Austerity.

The financial crisis of 2008–9 has all the markings of such a momentous watershed moment. But what will the new era on the other side of it look like? The crisis squarely undermined the belief that markets are always better than policy makers at allocating resources, setting prices freely by force of supply and demand. Could it point us toward a more aggressive social democracy, with a more active role for government in allocating resources and steering the economy? Could unfettered market capitalism have sung its last hurrah?

The Obama administration seems to be trying to steer such a course. It is apparent in the Federal Communications Commission's efforts to establish oversight over access to the Internet and in the increasingly activist stance of the trustbusters at the Federal Trade Commission and the Department of Justice. It is evident in the president's ultimately successful battle to extend health insurance to all Americans. So, too, governments around the world have been working on new rules to further regulate and constrain the activities of banks—forcing them to amass bigger precautionary cushions of money, limiting the kinds of businesses they can engage in, and targeting them for special taxes to pay for the potential costs of any future financial disaster.

But it would be naive to believe that industrial nations will inevitably move back to a Big Government era, clipping bankers' horns, clamping down on monopolies, and generally taking a decisive role in shaping the economic order. Bank shares jumped the day after the U.S. Congress passed a new law to regulate the financial industry. They surged again after global regulators agreed on new, higher capital cushions. Both jumps suggest the new rules will do little to curtail banks' risk taking.

What's more, President Obama's efforts to reform health insurance and stimulate the economy with government spending provoked a furious populist backlash. Forty-eight percent of Americans tell Gallup their taxes are too high. As I write this passage, the loudest protesters on the streets are not railing against bankers. They are members of the Tea Party, who accuse President Obama of being a "socialist" out to undermine the nation's values. In Europe, faith in government is not doing much better. Following the battering of the bonds of weaker countries like Greece and Spain in the spring of 2010, European Union governments virtually across the board declared it was time to start slashing their budget deficits. This, despite the fact that employment was still contracting, unemployment remained around 10 percent, and there was no plausible alternative source of demand to take the place of the spending that governments planned to withdraw from their economies. In other words, they risked a deeper economic downturn just for the sake of pulling the government out of the economy.

These are early days. Little more than two years have passed since the demise of Lehman Brothers. Finding a new equilibrium between government action and private markets was always going to take longer than that. And citizens' mistrust of their governments seems about as high as their mistrust of bankers. But if we learn only one thing from the economic disaster of the last two years, it should be this: we should never again accept unchallenged the notion that the prices set by unfettered markets must inevitably be right. Sometimes they are. Sometimes they are not.

Consider the testimony before Congress of Alan Greenspan, the former chairman of the Federal Reserve, on October 23, 2008. Greenspan was known as "the Maestro" for his seemingly deft management of monetary policy, evidenced by a long tenure during which the United States experienced low inflation, long economic expansions, and short and shallow recessions. He was also one of the main architects of economic policy as the housing bubble inflated toward its climax. A follower of the libertarian, antigovernment thinker Ayn Rand, he was considered the high priest of unfettered markets, prone to righteous expressions of faith in their ability to properly price financial assets and allocate resources efficiently.

But when he was dragged before the House of Representatives' government oversight committee on October 23, Mr. Greenspan shocked the world by admitting he had been wrong. Henry Waxman, the Democrat from California who chaired the committee, goaded him, "You found that your view of the world, your ideology, was not right, it was not working." And to most people's surprise, Greenspan answered, "Absolutely, precisely." Indeed, even Greenspan learned just how badly prices can fail and send our decisions and our lives astray.

# Acknowledgments

**I HAVE BEEN** writing for a living for two decades. Never before did writing seem to be such a quest. As with any great adventure, the success of this book relied on a large cast of characters.

I couldn't have started without the help—sometimes inadvertent, involuntary, even posthumous—of economists, psychologists, and even the occasional biologist, demographer, and sociologist.

Some of these scholars were particularly generous. In no particular order, I would like to thank Monica Dasgupta and Vijayendra Rao of the World Bank, Robert Frank from Cornell, Claudia Goldin and David Laibson from Harvard, and Justin Wolfers from the University of Pennsylvania's Wharton School, who patiently talked me through some of their work and helped me grasp sometimes difficult concepts.

But my gratitude extends to the hundreds of scientists who have offered their lives' work to understanding some of the bigger questions about humanity: how do we choose between our options? Why do we behave the way we do? I built this project upon their insights and discoveries.

I am grateful to the team at Portfolio. Adrian Zackheim saw promise in this project before I knew where it would lead. He and Courtney Young provided sharp and concise advice along the way and a deft editing touch at the end. Will Weisser and Maureen Cole provided marketing and publicity expertise. And I thank Lance Fitzgerald for pushing this book around the world, so it can be read in many places I have never been. Jason Arthur and Drummond Moir at RH/Heinemann in London were wonderfully supportive.

I will be always grateful to Cressida Leyshon, Steve Fishman, Adam Cohen, Nick Kristof, and Charlie Duhigg, who read portions of the book—providing much needed advice and helping steer me back to coherence when my writing lost its purpose and my ideas went astray. And I thank Tim Sullivan, whose patient ear and sound counsel helped me craft a jumble of thoughts into a coherent idea. Beyond the rather substantial help of my friends, I relied on the able work of some sharp research assistants: Avi Salzman, Miriam Gottfried, April Rabkin, and Alejandra Pérez Grobet. If there are any errors in this book, it is nobody's fault but my own. There would be more if not for the eagle eye of three great fact checkers—Joshua Friedman, Susan Kirby, and Jane Cavolina.

I would also like to thank all my colleagues at the *New York Times,* in the newsroom and on the editorial board. It is a privilege to work with them every day. I owe special gratitude to my boss, Andy Rosenthal, whose forbearance allowed this book to happen.

Some superspecial thanks are in order: First of all to my mother, who has always been there, through thick and thin, ready to provide the sort of unconditional love and encouragement that only mothers can. This book happened only because of the persistence of my old friend and agent, Zoë Pagnamenta, who not only believed I had a book in me but helped me figure out what it was about. She has been a doggedly enthusiastic advocate for this book and an indispensable guide, always ready to provide needed directions to navigate the seas of publishing. I also thank Simon Trewin of United Agents in London.

Most of all, I owe an enormous debt of gratitude to my family, who had to bear with me as I reorganized my life and theirs around my exciting new adventure. Gisele, my wonderful wife, not only agreed to be a sounding board, providing thoughtful advice and reassurance through the uncertain early stages of the book, she gamely shouldered new burdens so I could focus on writing, filling as best she could the hole left in our family by my absence. Mateo, our son, might remember this stage of his life as the time when his father wasn't allowed to have any fun. He doesn't know yet how much fun I had. He should know too the crucial role he played in this project. His raw love and indiscriminate joy gave me an endless supply of light and heat. And he is a great partner to kick the ball around with in the yard. I couldn't have done this without him.

# Notes

**General note:** Unless otherwise noted, prices in U.S. dollars are converted to 2009 dollars using the Consumer Price Index.

**1–4 Prices Are Everywhere:** The data on how people value garbage is drawn from: Annegrete Bruvoll and Karine Nyborg, "On the Value of Households' Recycling Efforts," Statistics Norway Research Department Discussion Paper, March 2002 (http://papers.ssrn.com/sol3/papers.cfm?abstract_id=310320, accessed 08/01/2010); Roland K. Roberts, Peggy V. Douglas, and William M. Park, "Estimating External Costs of Municipal Landfill Siting Through Contingent Valuation Analysis: A Case Study," *Southern Journal of Agricultural Economics,* Vol. 23, Issue 2, December 1991; Derek Eaton and Thea Hilhorst, "Opportunities for Managing Solid Waste Flows in the Peri-Urban Interface of Bamako and Ouagadougou," *Environment and Urbanization,* Vol. 15, No. 1, April 2003; and Papiya Sarkar, "Solid Waste Management in Delhi—A Social Vulnerability Study," in Martin J. Bunch, V. Madha Suresh, and T. Vasantha Kumaran, eds., *Proceedings of the Third International Conference on Environment and Health,* Chennai, India, December 15–17, 2003 (Chennai, India: Department of Geography, University of Madras and Faculty of Environmental Studies, York University), pp. 451–464. Evidence of the different Swiss and Chinese attitudes toward the environment is drawn from the 2005–2008 wave of the World Values Survey (http://www.worldvaluessurvey.org/, accessed 08/01/2010). The relation between sulfur-dioxide emissions and income is found in Gene Grossman and Alan Krueger, "Economic Growth and the Environment," *Quarterly Journal of Economics,* Vol. 110, No. 2, 1995 (converted to 2009 dollars using GDP deflator). $SO_2$ emissions in the United States are drawn from the Environmental Protection Agency (http://www.epa.gov/air/sulfurdioxide/, accessed 08/01/2010). The tale of the Larry Summers memo is drawn from Noam Scheiber, "Free Larry Summers: Why the White House Needs to Unleash Him," *New Republic,* April 1, 2009; "Let Them Eat Pollution," *Economist,* February 8, 1992; and James A. Swaney, "What's Wrong with Dumping on Africa?," *Journal of Economic Issues,* Vol. 28, No. 2, June 1994, pp. 367–377.

**5–8 The Price of Crossing Borders:** Comparative gender gaps are drawn from: Bijayalaxmi Nanda, "The Ladli Scheme in India: Leading to a Lehenga or a Law Degree?" Presentation, Department of Political Science, Miranda House, Delhi University (http://www.undp-povertycentre.org/pressroom/files/ipc126 .pdf, accessed 08/13/2010). The analysis of illegal immigration into the United States draws from: Raúl Hinojosa-Ojeda, "Raising the Floor for American Workers: The Economic Benefits of Comprehensive Immigration Reform," Center for American Progress, January 2010 (http://www.immigrationpolicy. org/special-reports/raising-floor-american-workers, accessed 08/01/2010); the Mexican Migration Project database (http://mmp.opr.princeton.edu/results/ 001costs-en.aspx, accessed on 06/30/2010); Maria Jimenez, "Humanitarian Crisis: Migrant Deaths at the U.S.-Mexico Border," American Civil Liberties Union, Washington, 2009 (http://www.aclu.org/immigrants-rights/humanitarian-crisis-migrant-deaths-us-mexico-border, accessed 08/08/2010); Patricia Cortes, "The Effect of Low-Skilled Immigration on U.S. Prices: Evidence from CPI Data," *Journal of Political Economy*, Vol. 116, No. 3, June 2008; and Department of Homeland Security, Office of Immigration Statistics, "Estimates of the Unauthorized Immigrant Population Residing in the United States: January 2009" (http://www.dhs.gov/xlibrary/assets/statistics/publications/ois_ill_pe_2009 .pdf, accessed 07/27/2010).

**8–10 Prices Rule:** The data on cigarette prices comes from the Campaign for Tobacco Free Kids (http://tobaccofreekids.org/reports/prices/, accessed 8/13/2010); and the Centers for Disease Control and Prevention (http:// www.cdc.gov/tobacco/data_statistics/tables/economics/trends/index.htm, accessed 8/13/2010). Illegal drug prices and consumption drawn from Arthur Fries, Robert W. Anthony, Andrew Cseko, Jr., Carl C. Gaither, and Eric Schulman, "The Price and Purity of Illicit Drugs: 1981–2007," Institute for Defense Analysis for the Office of National Drug Control Policy (http://www.whitehousedrugpolicy.gov/publications/price_purity/price_purity07.pdf, accessed 08/08/2010). The analysis relating gas prices and housing draws from Edward L. Glaeser and Matthew E. Kahn, "Sprawl and Urban Growth," NBER Working Paper, May 2003; and Census Bureau, *American Housing Survey of the United States*, 2007 and 1997 editions (found at http://www.census.gov/hhes/www/ housing/ahs/nationaldata.html, accessed 08/13/2010). The comparison of urban patterns in Moscow with those of other cities draws from Alain Bertaud and Renaud Bertrand, "Cities Without Land Markets, Location and Land Use in the Socialist City," the World Bank, Policy Research Working Paper 477, June 1995, in *Journal of Urban Economics*, Vol. 41, No. 1, January 1997, pp. 137–151.

**11–12 When Prices Misfire:** The anecdote about incentives and births in Australia comes from Joshua Gans and Andrew Leigh, "Born on the First of July: An (Un)natural Experiment in Birth Timing," *Journal of Public Economics*, Vol. 93, 2009. Data on the window tax come from the Wolverhampton Archives (http://www.wolverhamptonarchives.dial.pipex.com/windowtax.htm, accessed 08/13/2010). The analysis of the effects of the 55-mph speed limit draws from Paul Grimes, "Practical Traveler: The 55-m.p.h. Speed Limit," *New York Times*,

December 26, 1982; and M. C. Jensen and W. H. Meckling, "The Nature of Man," *Journal of Applied Corporate Finance*, Vol. 7, No. 2, Summer 1994, pp. 4–19. The data on wages and gas prices was drawn from the Bureau of Labor Statistics and the Energy Information Administration. Data on gas mileage was drawn from the Environmental Protection Agency's *1974 Gas Mileage Guide for Car Buyers.*

**15–22 The Price of Things:** The experiment on placebo effects is found in Dan Ariely, Baba Shiv, Ziv Carmon, and Rebecca Waber, "Commercial Features of Placebo and Therapeutic Efficacy," *Journal of the American Medical Association*, Letters, Vol. 299, No. 9, 2008, pp. 1016–1017. The relation between lap-dancer tips and menstrual cycles is drawn from Geoffrey Miller, Joshua Tybur, and Brent Jordan, "Ovulatory Cycle Effects on Tip Earnings by Lap Dancers: Economic Evidence for Human Estrus?," *Evolution and Human Behavior*, Vol. 28, 2007, pp. 375–381. The impact of *Sesame Street* characters on children's preferences is found in The Sesame Workshop, "If Elmo Eats Broccoli, Will Kids Eat It Too?," Press Release, September 20, 2005. Evidence on people's willingness to travel across town to save twenty dollars comes from "Conversation Between Economists Glenn Lowry and Sendhil Mullainathan," Bloggingheads TV, March 22, 2010 (http://bloggingheads.tv/diavlogs/26877, accessed 08/13/2010). Wine preferences are drawn from Eileen Brooks, "Products and Prejudice: Measuring Country-of-Origin Bias in U.S. Wine Imports," University of California Santa Cruz Center for International Economics Working Paper, 2003; Hilke Plassmann, John O'Doherty, Baba Shiv, and Antonio Rangel, "Marketing Actions Can Modulate Neural Representations of Experienced Pleasantness," *Proceedings of the National Academy of Sciences*, Vol. 105, No. 3, January 2008, pp. 1050–1054; and Robin Goldstein, Johan Almenberg, Anna Dreber, John W. Emerson, Alexis Herschkowitsch, and Jacob Katz, "Do More Expensive Wines Taste Better? Evidence from a Large Sample of Blind Tastings," Stockholm School of Economics Working Paper, April 2008. The story about pricey license plates in Dubai comes from Margaret Corker, "Read My License Plate: It Cost Me a Fortune—Oil Rich Persian Gulf Drivers Take Vanity Tags to a Whole New Level," *Wall Street Journal*, July 1, 2008. The history of diamond marketing draws from Edward Epstein, "Have You Ever Tried to Sell a Diamond?," *Atlantic*, February 1982; IDEX Online Research, "Bridal Jewelry Business High-Growth & Less Seasonal," April 19, 2007; and *IDEX Magazine*, "The Key Facts About Diamond Engagement Rings," No. 240, April 29, 2010 (http://www.idexonline.com/portal_FullMazalUbracha.asp?id=33915, accessed 08/05/2010).

**22–24 A History of Prices:** The discussion of the concept of process from Aristotle to Marx draws from Eric Roll, *A History of Economic Thought* (London: Faber and Faber, 1992). Marx's statement about value relations is drawn from Karl Marx, *Capital: A Critique of Political Economy*, Vol. 1 (Chicago: Charles H. Kerr and Company, 1915), p. 83.

**25–30 Taming Prices:** The analysis on the value of sports-club subscriptions draws from: Stefano Della Vigna and Ulrike Malmendier, "Overestimating

Self-control: Evidence from the Health Club Industry," NBER Working Paper, September 2004. The data on the costs of printing are found in www.hp.com; www .riteaid.com; Jeff Bertolucci, "How Much Ink Is Left in That Dead Cartridge?" *PC World*, November 2, 2008 (http://www.pcworld.com/article/152953/ how_much_ink_is_left_in_that_dead_cartridge/html, accessed 08/13/2010); and Stephen Shankland, "HP Sues Firms That Refill Ink Cartridges," CNET, March 28, 2005 (http://news.cnet.com/HP%20sues%20firms%20that%20 refill%20ink%20cartridges/2100-1041_3-5643687.html?tag=techdirt, accessed 08/13/2010). Families' reaction to high gas prices drawn from Dora Gicheva, Justine Hastings, and Sofia Villas-Boas, "Revisiting the Income Effect: Gasoline Prices and Grocery Purchases," NBER Working Paper, November 2007. The analysis of companies' reaction to changes in food prices draws from Anne Kadet, "Who Shrunk the Cereal?," *Smart Money*, November 6, 2008; Stuart Elliot, "Food Brands Compete to Stretch a Dollar," *New York Times*, May 10, 2009; and *Adweek*, "French's Puts 'Fun,' 'Value' on Menu," May 11, 2009. Data on phone prices drawn from Federal Communications Commission, *The Industry Analysis Division's Reference Book of Rates, Price Indices and Expenditures for Telephone Service*, July 1998 (http://www.fcc.gov/Bureaus/Common_ Carrier/Reports/FCC-State_Link/IAD/ref98.pdf, accessed 08/13/2010); www .att.com; and http://www.productsandservices.bt.com/consumerProducts/ displayTopic.do?topicId=25500. Sandra Kurtzig's tale is drawn from http:// venturehacks.com/articles/pricing, accessed 08/13/2010. Airlines' reaction to Southwest Airways is found in Austan Goolsbee and Chad Svyerson, "How Do Incumbents Respond to the Threat of Entry? Evidence from the Major Airlines," *Quarterly Journal of Economics*, Vol. 123, No. 4, November 2008, pp. 1611–1633. Discussion of the effect of Walmart on competitors and prices draws from Jerry Hausman and Ephraim Leibtag, "Consumer Benefits from Increased Competition in Shopping Outlets: Measuring the Effect of Wal-Mart," NBER Working Paper, December 2005; Vishal P. Singh, Karsten T. Hansen, and Robert C. Blattberg, "Market Entry and Consumer Behavior: An Investigation of a Wal-Mart Supercenter," *Marketing Science*, September 1, 2006; Emek Basker, "Selling a Cheaper Mousetrap: Wal-Mart's Effect on Retail Prices," *Journal of Urban Economics*, Vol. 58, No. 2, September 2005, pp. 203–229; Emek Basker, "The Causes and Consequences of Wal-Mart's Growth," *Journal of Economic Perspectives*, Vol. 21, No. 3, Summer 2007, pp. 177–198; and Jerry Hausman and Ephraim Leibtag, "CPI Bias from Supercenters: Does the BLS Know That Wal-Mart Exists?," NBER Working Paper, August 2004.

**30–32 Keeping Competition at Bay:** The discussion of automakers' employee discount plans comes from Meghan R. Busse, Duncan Simester, and Florian Zetelmeyer, "The Best Price You'll Ever Get: The 2005 Employee Discount Pricing Promotions in the U.S. Automobile Industry," NBER Working Paper, May 2007. The data on price dispersion at Israeli stores comes from Saul Lach, "Existence and Persistence of Price Dispersion: An Empirical Analysis," NBER Working Paper, January 2002. Price obfuscation online drawn from Glenn Ellison and Sara Fisher Ellison, "Search, Obfuscation, and Price Elasticities on the Internet," NBER Working Paper, June 2004.

**33–37 Searching for Fools:** The quote on fools by Daniel Kahneman is found in Lee Young Han and Ulrike Malmendier, "The Bidder's Curse," NBER Working Paper, December 2007. The attitude of private-equity firms toward auctions comes from "Auction Process Roundtable," *Mergers and Acquisitions*, December 2006, pp. 31–32. Prices paid by Denver shoppers are found in Mark Aguiar and Erik Hurst, "Lifecycle Prices and Production," Federal Reserve Bank of Boston Discussion Paper, July 2005. The price of appetizers in romantic restaurants is discussed in I. P. L. Png and Wang Hao, "Buyer Uncertainty and Two-Part Pricing of Felicitous vis-à-vis Distress Goods: Theory with Evidence from New York Restaurants," Working Paper, April 2008. Airline ticket pricing is discussed in Severin Borenstein and Nancy L. Rose, "How Airline Markets Work . . . Or Do They? Regulatory Reform in the Airline Industry," NBER Working Paper, September 2007; and Steven Puller, Anirban Sengupta, and Steven Wiggins, "Testing Theories of Scarcity Pricing in the Airline Industry," NBER Working Paper, December 2009. Evidence of price discrimination in the concert industry is in Pascal Courty and Mario Pagliero, "The Impact of Price Discrimination on Revenue: Evidence from the Concert Industry," CEPR Discussion Paper, January 2009; and Pascal Courty and Mario Pagliero, "Price Discrimination in the Concert Industry," CEPR Discussion Paper, January 2009. Price discrimination by Coke from Constance Hays, "Variable-Price Coke Machine Being Tested," *New York Times*, October 28, 1999. Price discrimination by Amazon from Joseph Turow, Lauren Feldman, and Kimberly Meltzer, "Open to Exploitation: American Shoppers Online and Offline," University of Pennsylvania Annenberg Public Policy Center, June 2005 (http://www.annenbergpublicpolicycenter.org/Downloads/Information_And_Society/Turow_APPC_Report_WEB_FINAL.pdf, accessed 08/01/2010). Data on airlines' falling fares and financial problems is found in Air Transport Association, Annual Passenger Yield (http://www.airlines.org/Economics/DataAnalysis/Pages/AnnualPassengerYieldUSAirlines.aspx, accessed 08/13/2010); and Bureau of Transportation Statistics (http://www.TranStats.bts.gov/Data_Elements.aspx?Data=6, accessed 08/13/2010).

**38–39 Protect Us from What We Buy:** The dubious value of presents is found in Joel Waldfogel, "Does Consumer Irrationality Trump Consumer Sovereignty?," *Review of Economics and Statistics*, Vol. 87, No. 4, 2005, pp. 691–696. Price fans will pay for basketball tickets from Ziv Carmon and Dan Ariely, "Focusing on the Forgone: How Value Can Appear So Different to Buyers and Sellers," *Journal of Consumer Research*, Vol. 27, December 2000, pp. 360–370; and Drazen Prelec and Duncan Simester, "Always Leave Home Without It: A Further Investigation of the Credit Card Effect on Willingness to Pay," *Marketing Letters*, Vol. 12, 2001, pp. 5–12. The story about the invention of ninety-nine-cent stores is in Tim Arango, "Bet Your Bottom Dollar on 99 Cents," *New York Times*, February 8, 2009. Kahneman's opinion on paternalistic interventions is found in Daniel Kahneman, "New Challenges to the Rationality Assumption," *Journal of Institutional and Theoretical Economics*, Vol. 150, No. 1, 1994, pp. 18–36.

**40–41 The Price of Life:** The Jewish teachings are mentioned in Peter Singer, "Why We Must Ration Health Care," *New York Times Magazine*, July 19, 2009. The various prices placed on life come from Chris Dockins, Kelly Maguire, Nathalie Simon, and Melonie Sullivan, "Value of Statistical Life Analysis and Environmental Policy," White Paper for Presentation to Science Advisory Board—Environmental Economics Advisory Committee, U.S. Environmental Protection Agency, National Center for Environmental Economics, April 21, 2004; United Kingdom Department for Environmental, Food and Rural Affairs, "An Economic Analysis to Inform the Air Quality Strategy," Updated Third Report of the Interdepartmental Group on Costs and Benefits, July 2007; Ramanan Laxminarayan, Eili Klein, Christopher Dye, Katherine Floyd, Sarah Darley, and Olusoji Adeyi, "Economic Benefit of Tuberculosis Control," World Bank Policy Research Working Paper, 2007.

**41–44 Paying for the Dead:** Kenneth Feinberg's experience at the helm of the September 11th Victim Compensation Fund comes from Kenneth Feinberg, "What Is Life Worth?," *Public Affairs*, 2005; Frances Romero, "Kenneth Feinberg: Compensation Czar," *Time*, June 10, 2009; Kenneth Feinberg, Camille Biros, Jordana Harris Feldman, Deborah E. Greenspan, and Jacqueline Zins, "Final Report of the Special Master for the September 11th Victim Compensation Fund of 2001," Vol. 1, p. 98 (http://www.columbia.edu/cu/lweb/indiv/usgd/wtc.html#exec, accessed 08/08/2010); and Benjamin Weiser, "Value of Suing Over 9/11 Deaths Is Still Unsettled," *New York Times*, March 13, 2009.

**44–47 Valuing Citizens' Safety:** The cost-benefit analysis of flame-resistant mattresses is found in Consumer Product Safety Commission, "Final Rule: Standard for the Flammability (Open Flame) of Mattress Sets," *Federal Register*, Vol. 71, No. 50, March 15, 2006, Rules and Regulations. The analysis of costs and benefits of seat belts in school buses is in William L. Hall, "Seat Belts on School Buses: A Review of Issues and Research," paper for the North Carolina School Bus Safety Conference, February 29, 1996. Approaches to cost-benefit analysis by the Environmental Protection Agency and the Food and Drug Administration are discussed in Fred Kuchler and Elise Golan, "Assigning Values to Life. Comparing Methods for Valuing Health Risks," USDA Agricultural Economic Report No. 784, November 1999. Costs and benefits of Homeland Security spending are discussed in Mark G. Stewart and John Mueller, "Assessing the Costs and Benefits of United States Homeland Security Spending," University of Newcastle Center for Infrastructure Performance and Reliability Research Report, 2009; and Mark G. Stewart and John Mueller, "A Risk and Cost-Benefit Assessment of Australian Aviation Security," *Security Challenges*, Vol. 4, No. 3, Spring 2008, pp. 45–61. The high cost of some government regulations in the United States is discussed in John F. Morrall III, "Saving Lives: A Review of the Record," AEI-Brookings Joint Center for Regulatory Studies Working Paper, 2003; Government Accountability Office, "Superfund: Funding and Reported Costs of Enforcement and Administration Activities," July 18, 2008; and W. Kip Viscusi and James Hamilton, "Cleaning Up Superfund," *Public Interest*, Summer 1996. The costs and benefits of WHO's strategy to combat tuberculosis are laid out in Ramanan Laxminarayan, Eili Klein, Christopher Dye, Katherine Floyd, Sarah Darley, and Olusoji Adeyi, "Economic Benefit of Tuberculosis Control,"

World Bank Policy Research Working Paper, 2007. The data on deaths from tuberculosis come from the United Nations Millennium Development Indicators' data set.

**48–51 Price Your Own Life:** The value of life and the risk of dying in a car crash are discussed in "New Crash Tests Demonstrate the Influence of Vehicle Size and Weight on Safety in Crashes; Results Are Relevant to Fuel Economy Policies," Insurance Institute for Highway Safety News Release, April 14, 2009; and Orley Ashenfelter and Michael Greenstone, "Using Mandated Speed Limits to Measure the Value of a Statistical Life," NBER Working Paper, August 2002. Thomas Schelling's proposal on valuing life is in Thomas Schelling, "The Life You Save May Be Your Own," in S. B. Chase, ed., *Problems in Public Expenditure and Analysis* (Washington, D.C.: Brookings Institution, 1968), pp. 127–162. Bike helmets, cancer risks, and the value of life are discussed in W. Kip Viscusi and Joseph Aldy, "The Value of a Statistical Life: A Critical Review of Market Estimates Throughout the World," *Journal of Risk and Uncertainty*, Vol. 27, No. 1, 2003, pp. 5–76. The United States Department of Agriculture's evaluation of the cost of salmonella is in http://www.ers.usda.gov/data/foodborneillness/, accessed 08/13/2010). The value of health warnings on cigarette packs in Australia is in "Cost-Benefit Analysis of Proposed New Health Warnings on Tobacco Products," Report Prepared for the Commonwealth Department of Health and Ageing, December 2003 (http://www.treasury.gov.au/contentitem .asp?ContentID=794&NavID, accessed on 08/08/2010).

**51–54 Do We Know How Much We Are Worth?:** The value of an old life versus a young life is debated in Cass Sunstein, "Lives, Life-Years and Willingness to Pay," University of Chicago John M. Olin Law and Economics Program Working Paper, June 2003; Joseph Aldy and W. Kip Viscusi, "Age Differences in the Value of Statistical Life Revealed Preference Evidence," Resources for the Future Discussion Paper, April 2007; and John Graham, "Benefit-Cost Methods and Lifesaving Rules," Memorandum from the White House's Office of Information and Regulatory Affairs to the President's Management Council, May 2003. The comparison of the value of a life saved from terrorism with a life saved from a hurricane is in W. Kip Viscusi, "Valuing Risks of Death from Terrorism and Natural Disasters," Vanderbilt University Law School, Law and Economics Working Paper, March 13, 2009. The assessment of the value of life for the rich and the poor, the white and the black is in Thomas Schelling, op. cit.; W. Kip Viscusi, "Racial Differences in Labor Market Values of a Statistical Life," Harvard Law School Center for Law, Economics, and Business Discussion Paper (April 2003); James Hammitt and María Eugenia Ibarrarán, "The Economic Value of Reducing Fatal and Non-Fatal Occupational Risks in Mexico City Using Actuarial- and Perceived-Risk Estimates," *Health Economics*, Vol. 15, No. 12, 2006, pp. 1329–1335; James Hammitt and Ying Zhou, "The Economic Value of Air-Pollution-Related Health Risks in China: A Contingent Valuation Study," *Environmental and Resource Economics*, Vol. 33, No. 3, 2006, pp. 399–423; Cass Sunstein, "Are Poor People Worth Less Than Rich People? Disaggregating the Value of Statistical Lives," University of Chicago, Olin Law and Economics

Program Research Paper, February 2004. Data on deaths on the *Titanic* is in http://www.ithaca.edu/staff/jhenderson/titanic.html.

**54–58 The Price of Health:** Data on cervical cancer in Mexico is found in Cristina Gutiérrez-Delgado, Camilo Báez-Mendoza, Eduardo González-Pier, Alejandra Prieto de la Rosa, and Renee Witlen, "Relación costo-efectividad de las intervenciones preventivas contra el cáncer cervical en mujeres mexicanas," *Salud Pública Méx*, Vol. 50, No. 2, 2008, pp. 107–118; Olga Georgina Martinez M., "Introducing New Health Commodities into National Programs: Mexico's Experience with the HPV Vaccine," Presentation at the Microbicide Access Forum, Mexico City, August 3, 2008; Liliana Alcántara and Thelma Gomez, "Papiloma, Vacuna de la Discordia," *El Universal*, March 5, 2009. New Zealand's policy on vaccines against pneumococcal disease is in Richard Milne, "Economic Evaluation of New Vaccines," presentation at the New Zealand Immunization Advisory Centre Conference, Te Papa, September 15, 2007. World Health Organization guidelines on the affordability of medical treatment are from http://www.who.int/choice/costs/en/. The discussion about rationing treatment for renal cancer in Britain draws from NICE Technology Appraisal Guidance 169, "Sunitinib for the First-Line Treatment of Advanced and/or Metastatic Renal Cell Carcinoma," March 2009; Kate Devlin, "Kidney Cancer Patients Should Get Sutent on the NHS, says NICE," *Daily Telegraph*, February 4, 2009; Joseph J. Doyle Jr., "Health Insurance, Treatments and Outcomes: Using Auto Accidents as Health Shocks," *Review of Economics and Statistics*, Vol. 87, No. 2, May 2005, pp. 256–270; Gardiner Harris, "British Balance Benefit vs. Cost of Latest Drugs," *New York Times*, December 3, 2008. Health-care spending and health-care outcomes in the United States are discussed in Douglas Elmendorf, "Options for Controlling the Cost and Increasing the Efficiency of Health Care," Congressional Budget Office Testimony Before the Subcommittee on Health, Committee on Energy and Commerce, U.S. House of Representatives, March 2009; Organisation for Economic Cooperation and Development, "Society at a Glance—OECD Social Indicators 2009" (www.oecd.org/els/social/indicators/SAG, accessed on 08/08/2010); Ryan D. Edwards and Shripad Tuljapurkar, "Inequality in Life Spans and a New Perspective on Mortality Convergence Across Industrialized Countries," *Population and Development Review*, Vol. 34, No. 4, December 2006; *OECD Factbook 2009*; Congressional Budget Office, "Research on the Comparative Effectiveness of Medical Treatments: Issues and Options for an Expanded Federal Role," December 2007.

**59–64 The Price of Happiness:** The impact of *Los Ricos También Lloran* is discussed in Sam Quiñones, "A Real-Life Soap Opera for Mexican TV Star: Network Dumps Queen of 'Telenovelas,' Latin America's Best-Known Actress," *San Francisco Examiner*, September 27, 1999; Sam Quiñones, *True Tales from Another Mexico* (Albuquerque: University of New Mexico Press, 2001); and Helen Womack, "Mexican Soap Washes Away Russian Woes," *Independent*, September 8, 1992. Schopenhauer statement can be found in Arthur Schopenhauer, "Psychological Observations," in *The Essays of Arthur Schopenhauer* (General Books

LLC, 2010), p. 78. Bobby Kennedy's speech can be found in the John F. Kennedy Presidential Library (at http://www.jfklibrary.org/Historical+Resources/ Archives/Reference+Desk/Speeches/RFK/RFKSpeech68Mar18UKansas.htm, accessed 08/16/2010). The "Report by the Commission on the Measurement of Economic Performance and Social Progress," by Joseph Stiglitz, Amartya Sen, and Jean-Paul Fitoussi for the French government can be found at www .stiglitz-sen-fitoussi.fr. The account of Bhutan's gross national happiness draws from Seth Mydans, "Recalculating Happiness in a Himalayan Kingdom," *New York Times*, May 7, 2009; the Center for Bhutan Studies (grossnationalhappiness. com/gnhIndex/intruductionGNH.aspx, accessed 08/12/2010); Swaminathan S. Anklesaria Aiyar, "Bhutan's Happiness Is Large Dam, Fast GDP," *Times of India*, November 1, 2009; and Ben Saul, "Cultural Nationalism, Self-Determination and Human Rights in Bhutan," *International Journal of Refugee Law*, Vol. 12, No. 3, July 2000, pp. 321–353. Data on Bhutan and India's GDP per person is drawn from International Monetary Fund statistics (www.imf.org/external/datamapper/ index.php). Statistics on the impact of income on happiness come from Andrew Oswald and Nattavudh Powdthavee, "Does Happiness Adapt? A Longitudinal Study of Disability with Implications for Economists and Judges," IZA Discussion Paper, July 2006; Paul Frijters, David W. Johnston, and Michael A. Shields, "Happiness Dynamics with Quarterly Life Event Data," IZA Discussion Paper, July 2008; Gallup Organization, "About One in Six Americans Report History of Depression," October 22, 2009 (www.gallup.com/poll/123821/One-Six-Americans-Report-History-Depression.aspx, accessed 08/16/2010); Ronald Inglehart, Roberto Foa, Christopher Peterson, and Christian Welzel, "Development, Freedom and Rising Happiness, A Global Perspective (1981–2007)," *Perspectives on Psychological Science*, Vol. 3, No. 4, 2008, pp. 264–285; and Angus Deaton, "Income, Aging, Health and Wellbeing Around the World: Evidence from the Gallup World Poll," *Journal of Economic Perspectives*, Vol. 22, No. 2, Spring 2008.

**64–66 What Happiness Is:** Examples of the link between happiness and other measures of well-being are in: David Blanchflower and Andrew Oswald, "Hypertension and Happiness Across Nations," *Journal of Health Economics*, Elsevier, Vol. 27, No. 2, March 2008, pp. 218–233; Daniel Kahneman and Alan B. Krueger, "Developments in the Measurement of Subjective Well-Being," *Journal of Economic Perspectives*, Vol. 20, No. 1, Winter 2006, pp. 3–24. Examples of the difficulty of defining happiness are found in Daniel Gilbert, *Stumbling on Happiness* (New York: Vintage Books, 2005); Norbert Schwarz and Fritz Strack, "Evaluating One's Life: A Judgment Model of Subjective Well-Being," in Fritz Strack, Michael Argyle, and Norbert Schwarz, eds., *Subjective Well-Being, An Interdisciplinary Perspective* (New York: Pergamon Press, 1991), p. 36. Sigmund Freud quote is from Sigmund Freud, *Civilization and Its Discontents* (New York: W. W. Norton, 2005), p. 52. The inconsistent choices of overweight Americans are found in Jeffrey M. Jones, "In U.S., More Would Like to Lose Weight Than Are Trying To," Gallup, November 20, 2009 (www.gallup.com/poll/124448/ in-u.s.-more-lose-weight-than-trying-to.aspx, accessed on 08/08/2010). Abraham Lincoln's tale is in Ben Bernanke, "The Economics of Happiness," Speech at the University of South Carolina Commencement Ceremony, May 8, 2010 (found at www.federalreserve.gov/newsevents/speech/bernanke20100508a .pdf, accessed 08/16/2010).

**67–70 Happiness Is a Concrete Floor:** The link between sex and happiness is described in David Blanchflower and Andrew Oswald, "Money, Sex and Happiness: An Empirical Study," *Scandinavian Journal of Economics,* Vol. 106, No. 3, 2004, pp. 393–415. The data on happy Republicans comes from Paul Taylor, "Republicans: Still Happy Campers," Pew Research Center, 2008; and Jaime Napier and John Jost, "Why Are Conservatives Happier Than Liberals?," *Psychological Science,* Vol. 19, No. 6, June 2008, pp. 565–572. The data on happiness in East Germany are found in Paul Frijters, John Haisken-DeNew, and Michael Shields, "Money Does Matter! Evidence from Increasing Real Incomes and Life Satisfaction in East Germany Following Reunification," *American Economic Review,* Vol. 94, No. 3, June 2004, pp. 730–740. The data on happiness in Russia come from Richard Easterlin, "Lost in Transition: Life Satisfaction on the Road to Capitalism," SOEP Papers, DIW Berlin, the German Socio-Economic Panel (SOEP), April 2008; and Elizabeth Brainerd, "Economic Reform and Mortality in the Former Soviet Union: A Study of the Suicide Epidemic in the 1990s," IZA Discussion Paper, January 2001. The story about the impact of a concrete floor on happiness in Mexico's Coahuila state is in Matias Cattaneo, Sebastian Galiani, Paul Gertler, Sebastián Martínez, and Rocio Titiunik, "Housing Health and Happiness," World Bank Policy Research Paper, April 2007. The data on happiness among the rich and the poor come from Rafael Di Tella and Robert MacCulloch, "Gross National Happiness as an Answer to the Easterlin Paradox?" *Journal of Development Economics,* Vol. 86, No. 2, April 2008, pp. 22–42. Robert Frank's statement is in Robert Frank, "Does Absolute Income Matter?" in P. L. Porta and L. Bruni, eds., *Economics and Happiness* (New York: Oxford University Press, 2005), p. 67. The data on income and happiness in Brooklyn and San Jose, California, is found in Census Bureau, American Community Survey 2006–2008 estimates (factfinder.census.gov/servlet/DatasetMainPageServlet?_ program=ACS&_submenuId=&_lang=en&_ts=, accessed on 08/08/2010) and the Gallup-Healthways Well-Being Index (at www.ahiphiwire.org/wellbeing/, accessed 08/16/2010).

**70–72 The Treadmill of Happiness:** How happiness adapts to positive and negative shocks is discussed in Andrew Oswald and Nattavudh Powdthavee, "Does Happiness Adapt? A Longitudinal Study of Disability with Implications for Economists and Judges," Warwick University Working Paper, July 2006; Andrew E. Clark, Ed Diener, Yannis Georgellis, and Richard E. Lucas, "Lags and Leads in Life Satisfaction: A Test of the Baseline Hypothesis," *Economic Journal,* Vol. 118, June 2008, pp. F222–F243. Richard Easterlin's finding on Americans' stagnant happiness is in Richard Easterlin, "Does Economic Growth Improve the Human Lot? Some Empirical Evidence," in Paul A. David and Melvin Reder, eds., *Nations and Households in Economic Growth: Essays in Honor of Moses Abramowitz* (New York: Academic Press, 1974), p. 89. The data on the impact on happiness of your neighbors' wealth are in Erzo Luttmer, "Neighbors as Negatives:

Relative Earnings and Well-Being," *Quarterly Journal of Economics*, Vol. 120, No. 3, August 2005, pp. 963–1002; and Mary Daly and Dan Wilson, "Keeping Up with the Joneses and Staying Ahead of the Smiths: Evidence from Suicide Data," Federal Reserve Bank of San Francisco Working Paper, April 2006. The thesis about how stagnant happiness may confer evolutionary advantages is in Luis Rayo and Gary Becker, "Evolutionary Efficiency and Happiness," *Journal of Political Economy*, Vol. 115, No. 2, 2007. Adam Smith's quote about happiness as deception is in Adam Smith, *The Theory of Moral Sentiments*, 11th edition (Edinburgh: printed for Cadell and Davies et al., 1812), p. 317. Easterlin's views about the pointlessness of growth are in Richard Easterlin, "Feeding the Illusion of Growth and Happiness: A Reply to Hagerty and Venhoven," *Social Indicators Research*, Vol. 74, No. 3, 2005, pp. 429–443.

**73–77 The American Trade-Off:** Data on Americans' stagnant happiness are found in Bruno Frey and Alois Stutzer, "What Can Economists Learn from Happiness Research?" *Journal of Economic Literature*, Vol. 40, No. 2, June 2002, pp. 402–435; and the Organisation for Economic Co-operation and Development, "Society at a Glance," 2009 edition, p. 121. Evidence on how happiness increases as income rises around the world is in Ronald Inglehart, Roberto Foa, Christopher Peterson, and Christian Welzel, "Development, Freedom, and Rising Happiness, A Global Perspective (1981–2007)," *Perspectives on Psychological Science*, Vol. 3, No. 4, 2008, pp. 264–285; Ronald Inglehart, Roberto Foa, and Christian Welzel, "Social Change, Freedom and Rising Happiness," *Journal of Personality and Social Psychology*, Internet Appendix (www.worldvalues survey.org/wvs/articles/folder_published/article_base_106/files/trends .doc, accessed 08/16/2010); Betsey Stevenson and Justin Wolfers, "Economic Growth and Subjective Well-Being: Reassessing the Easterlin Paradox," *Brookings Papers on Economic Activity*, Spring 2008; and Daniel Kahneman and Angus Deaton, "High Income Improves Evaluation of Life but Not Emotional Well-Being," *Proceedings of the National Academy of Sciences*, advance online publication, September 7, 2010 (www.pnas.org/cgi/doi/10.1073/pnas.1011492107, accessed 09/07/2010). Data on wealth and happiness in the United States and Europe is found in the International Monetary Fund's *World Economic Outlook* of October 2009 (www.imf.org/external/pubs/ft/weo/2009/02/weodata/ index.aspx, accessed 08/16/2010); "L'Opinion publique dans l'Union Européenne—Automne 2009," Eurobarométre, February 2010 (ec.europa.eu/ public_opinion/archives/eb/eb72/eb72_en.htm, accessed 08/16/2010); and General Social Survey (www.norc.org/GSS+Website/Browse+GSS+Variables/ Collections/, accessed 08/16/2010). Data on inequality and happiness in the United States come from Claudia Goldin and Lawrence Katz, "Long-Run Changes in the Wage Structure: Narrowing, Widening, Polarizing," *Brookings Papers on Economic Activity*, Spring 2007); Betsey Stevenson and Justin Wolfers, op. cit.; and OECD, op. cit. The study on Texan women is found in Daniel Kahneman and Alan Krueger, "Developments in the Measurement of Subjective Well-Being," *Journal of Economic Perspectives*, Vol. 20, No. 1, Winter 2006, pp. 3–24. The relation between leisure time and happiness in rich nations draws from "Measuring Leisure in OECD Countries," in Organisation for Economic

Co-operation and Development, *Society at a Glance—OECD Social Indicators 2009* (www.oecd.org/els/social/indicators/SAG, accessed 08/08/2010), pp. 19–41; Rafael Di Tella and Robert MacCulloch, "Gross National Happiness as an Answer to the Easterlin Paradox?," *Journal of Development Economics*, Vol. 86, No. 1), pp. 22–42, April 2008. Data on happiness over the life cycle are found in David Blanchflower and Andrew Oswald, "Is Well-being U-shaped over the Life-Cycle?," *Social Science and Medicine*, Vol. 66, 2008, pp. 1733–1749. Data on how we work too much, sleep too little, and spend too little time on meals are found in Mathias Basner, Kenneth M. Fomberstein, Farid M. Razavi, Siobhan Banks, Jeffrey H. William, Roger R. Rosa, and David F. Dinges, "American Time Use Survey: Sleep Time and Its Relationship to Waking Activities," *Sleep*, Vol. 30, No. 9, 2007; Stephen S. Roach, "Working Better or Just Harder?," *New York Times*, February 14, 2000; and Dan Hammermesh, "Time to Eat: Household Production Under Increasing Income Inequality," *American Journal of Agricultural Economics*, Vol. 89, No. 4, November 2007, pp. 852–863.

**77–78 La Joie de Vivre:** The impact of higher taxes and stronger unions on working hours in Europe is discussed in Edward Prescott, "Why Do Americans Work So Much More Than Europeans?," *Federal Reserve Bank of Minneapolis Quarterly Review*, Vol. 28, No. 1, July 2004, pp. 2–13; Alberto Alesina, Edward Glaeser, and Bruce Sacerdote, "Work and Leisure in the U.S. and Europe: Why So Different?" NBER Working Paper, April 2005; and Olivier Blanchard, "The Many Dimensions of Work, Leisure, and Employment: Thoughts at the End of the Conference," comments on papers presented at the Rodolfo DeBenedetti conference on "Are Europeans Lazy, or Are Americans Crazy?" Portovenere, Italy, June 2006. Data on the impact of time use on happiness is from Ronald Inglehart, Roberto Foa, and Christian Welzel, "Social Change, Freedom and Rising Happiness," *Journal of Personality and Social Psychology*, Internet Appendix (at www.worldvaluessurvey.org/wvs/articles/folder_published/article_base_106/files/trends.doc, accessed 08/16/2010); "Measuring Leisure in OECD Countries," in Organisation for Economic Co-operation and Development, op. cit.; and Alan Krueger, Daniel Kahneman, David Schkade, Norbert Schwarz, and Arthur Stone, "National Time Accounting: The Currency of Life," Princeton University Department of Economics Working Paper, March 2008.

**79–86 The Price of Women:** Data on the popularity of polygamy through history found in Walter Scheidel, "Monogamy and Polygamy in Greece, Rome, and World History," Princeton/Stanford Working Papers in Classics, June 2008; Theodore Bergstrom, "Economics in a Family Way," *Journal of Economic Literature*, Vol. 34, 1996, pp. 1903–1934; and Gary Becker, *A Treatise on the Family*, enlarged edition (Cambridge, Mass.: Harvard University Press, 1993), p. 81. God's insistence on King Solomon's marrying only Hebrew women comes from the Bible, 1 Kings 11:1–2. Support for the genetic basis of polygamy found in M. F. Hammer, F. L. Mendez, M. P. Cox, A. E. Woerner, and J. D. Wall, "Sex-Biased Evolutionary Forces Shape Genomic Patterns of Human Diversity," *PLoS Genetics*, Vol. 4, No. 9, 2008 (www.plosgenetics.org/article/info%3Adoi%2F10.1371%2Fjournal.pgen.1000202, accessed 08/08/2010).

The views of David Hume and Ayatollah Ruhollah Khomeini on polygamy are found in David Hume, *Essays Moral, Political and Literary*, Part I, Essay XIX, in *The Philosophical Works of David Hume*, Vol. 3, edited by Adam Black, William Tait, and Charles Tait, 1826; and Oriana Fallaci, "An Interview with Khomeini," *New York Times Magazine*, October 7, 1979. Mating strategies of bonobos and birds can be found in Matt Ridley, *The Red Queen* (London: Penguin Books, 1993), pp. 203–235. Insights on men and women's adulterous choices can be found in Lena Edlund, "Marriage: Past, Present, Future?" *CESifo Economic Studies*, Vol. 52, No. 4, 2006, pp. 621–639. Information on the purpose and prevalence of bride prices can be found in Steven Gaulin and James Boster, "Dowry as Female Competition," *American Anthropologist*, Vol. 92, 1992, pp. 994–1005; Monique Borgerhoff Mulder, "Women's Strategies in Polygamous Marriage," *Human Nature*, Vol. 3, No. 1, 1992, pp. 45–70; Monique Borgerhoff Mulder, "Kipsigis Bridewealth Payments," in Laura Betzig, Monique Borgerhoff Mulder, and Paul Turke, eds., *Human Reproductive Behavior* (Cambridge, England: Cambridge University Press, 1988), pp. 65–82; Monique Borgerhoff Mulder, "Bridewealth and Its Correlates: Quantifying Changes over Time," *Current Anthropology*, Vol. 36, No. 4, August/October 1995, pp. 573–603. Benefits of banning polygamy are laid out in Michele Tertilt, "Polygyny, Fertility, and Savings," *Journal of Political Economy*, Vol. 113, December 2005. Laura Betzig's sentiments on being John Kennedy's third wife are in Matt Ridley, op. cit., p. 178. The insight that women are valued more in polygamous societies comes from Theodore C. Bergstrom, "On the Economics of Polygamy," University of California at Santa Barbara Working Paper, 1994; and Steven Gaulin and James Boster, "Dowry as Female Competition," *American Anthropologist*, Vol. 92, 1992, pp. 994–1005. The discussion on why polygamy disappeared is drawn from Eric D. Gould, Omer Moav, and Avi Simhon, "The Mystery of Monogamy," *American Economic Review*, Vol. 98, No. 1, 2008; Walter Scheidel, op. cit.; and Erik Eckholm, "Boys Cast Out by Polygamists Find Help," *New York Times*, September 9, 2007.

**86–93 The Value of Women's Work:** Data on the price of divorce in ancient Sumer can be found in James Baker, *Women's Rights in Old Testament Times* (Salt Lake City: Signature Books, 1992). The code of Hammurabi can be found at www.wsu.edu/~dee/MESO/CODE.HTM. The discussion of adultery in the Trobriand Islands is in Bronislaw Malinowski and Havelock Ellis, *The Sexual Life of Savages in North Central Melanesia*, Kessinger Publishing, 1929, p. 143. Arthur Lewis's quote is in Arthur Lewis, *The Theory of Economic Growth* (London: Allen and Unwin, 1963), p. 422. The description of the pattern of how women join the workforce as countries develop is drawn from Claudia Goldin, "The U-Shaped Female Labor Force Function in Economic Development and Economic History," NBER Working Paper, April 1994; Francine Blau, Marianne Ferber, and Anne Winkler, *The Economics of Men, Women and Work*, 5th edition (Upper Saddle River, N.J.: Pearson Prentice Hall, 2006), p. 21; and Sudhin K. Mukhopadhyay, "Adapting Household Behavior to Agricultural Technology in West Bengal, India: Wage Labor, Fertility, and Child Schooling Determinants," *Economic Development and Cultural Change*, Vol. 43, No. 1, October 1994, pp. 91–115. The narrative of women's march into the workplace in the United States is drawn from Betsey Stevenson, "Divorce Law and Women's Labor Supply," NBER Working Paper, September 2008; Claudia Goldin, "The Quiet Revolution That Transformed Women's Employment, Education and Family," Ely Lecture, American Economic Association Annual Meeting, January 2006; Paul Douglas and Erika Schoenberg, "Studies in the Supply Curve of Labor: The Relation in 1929 Between Average Earnings in American Cities and the Proportions Seeking Employment," *Journal of Political Economy*, Vol. 45, No. 1, February 1937, pp. 45–79; Jacob Mincer, "Labor Force Participation of Married Women: A Study of Labor Supply," in H. Gregg Lewis, ed., *Aspects of Labor Economics* (Princeton: Princeton University Press, 1962), pp. 63–97. The description of Sandra Day O'Connor's job search is in Kamil Dada, "Supreme Court Justice Pushes Public Service," *Stanford Daily*, April 22, 2008. The impact of changes in the labor force on women's bodies is drawn from Nigel Barber, "The Slender Ideal and Eating Disorders: An Interdisciplinary 'Telescope' Model," *International Journal of Eating Disorders*, Vol. 23, 1998, pp. 295–307; Brett Silverstein, Lauren Perdue, Barbara Peterson, Linda Vogel, and Deborah A. Fantini, "Possible Causes of the Thin Standard of Bodily Attractiveness for Women," *International Journal of Eating Disorders*, Vol. 5, No. 5, 1986, pp. 907–916; Judith L. Anderson, Charles B. Crawford, and Tracy Lindberg, "Was the Duchess of Windsor Right? A Cross-Cultural Review of the Socioecology of Ideals of Female Body Shape," *Ethology and Sociobiology*, Vol. 13, 1992, pp. 197–227. The drastic changes in the expectations and achievements of American women over the last century are outlined in Claudia Goldin, Lawrence Katz, and Ilyana Kuziemko, "The Homecoming of American College Women: The Reversal of the College Gender GAP," Working Paper, September 2005; Francine Blau and Lawrence Kahn, "Changes in the Labor Supply Behavior of Married Women 1980–2000," NBER Working Paper, March 2005. Data on women's educational attainment are drawn from T. D. Snyder and S. A. Dillow, *Digest of Education Statistics 2009* (Washington, D.C.: National Center for Education Statistics, April 2010) (nces.ed.gov/Programs/digest/, accessed 08/08/2010). Data on men's and women's income are from the Census Bureau (www.census.gov/hhes/www/income/data/historical/people/index.html, table p. 5, accessed 08/17/2010). Analysis of the gender gap in labor participation is found in Bureau of Labor Statistics, "Labor Force Statistics from the Current Population Survey" (www.bls.gov/cps, accessed 08/08/2010). The discussion of the gender wage gap draws from Bureau of Labor Statistics, "Women's to Men's Earnings Ratio by Age, 2009" (www.bls.gov/opub/ted/2010/ted_20100708_data .htm, accessed 08/08/2010). The discussion about the gender gap among MBA graduates comes from Marianne Bertrand, Claudia Goldin, and Lawrence F. Katz, "Dynamics of the Gender Gap for Young Professionals in the Financial and Corporate Sectors," *American Economic Journal: Applied Economics*, Vol. 2, No. 3, July 2010, pp. 228–255.

**93–97 Renegotiating the Marriage Bargain:** The description of changes in women's attitudes toward career and household work draws from Valerie Ramey, "Time Spent in Home Production in the 20th Century: New Estimates from Old Data," *Journal of Economic History*, Vol. 69, No. 1, March 2009, pp. 1–47;

Samuel Preston and Caroline Sten Hartnett, "The Future of American Fertility," NBER Working Paper, November 2008. Data about changes in fertility patterns come from the Centers for Disease Control and Prevention, *National Vital Statistics Report*, Vol. 57, No. 12, March 18, 2009; Samuel H. Preston and Caroline Sten Hartnett, op. cit.; American Time Use Survey, 2009 (www.bls.gov/ tus/tables/a1_2009.pdf, accessed 07/18/2010); and U.S. Census Bureau, "The Fertility of American Women: 2006," Washington, August 2008 (Supplemental tables 1 and 2). Statistics on fiancée and spouse visas are drawn from Department of Homeland Security, Office of Immigration Statistics, "2008 Yearbook of Immigration Statistics," Washington, August 2009. The leftward tilt of American women's political preferences is described in Lena Edlund, Laila Haider, and Rohini Pande, "Unmarried Parenthood and Redistributive Politics," *Journal of the European Economic Association*, Vol. 3, No. 1, March 2005, pp. 95–119. The gender difference in votes for President Barack Obama in the 2008 elections is detailed in "Women's Vote Clinches Election Victory: 8 Million More Women Than Men Voted for Obama," Institute for Women's Policy Research Press Release, November 6, 2008 (at www.iwpr.org/pdf/08ElectionRelease .pdf, accessed 08/18/2010). Data on women's labor supply around the world comes from the Organisation for Economic Co-operation and Development's Factbook (www.oecd-ilibrary.org/content/book/factbook-2010-en, accessed 07/18/2010). Data on fertility in the industrial countries is drawn from the Population Reference Bureau (at www.prb.org/Datafinder/Topic/Bar.aspx?so rt=v&order=d&variable=117, accessed 07/18/2010).

**97–101 The New Mating Market:** The story about *The Quiverfull* was aired by National Public Radio on *Morning Edition* on March 25, 2009 (www.npr .org/templates/story/story.php?storyId=102005062&ft=1&f=1001, accessed 07/18/2010). Data on government pension replacement rates and their impact on fertility comes from Olivia S. Mitchell and John W. R. Phillips, "Social Security Replacement Rates for Alternative Earnings Benchmarks," University of Michigan Retirement Research Center Working Paper, May 2006; and Francesco C. Billari and Vincenzo Galasso, "What Explains Fertility? Evidence from Italian Pension Reforms," CEPR Discussion Paper, October 2008. Arguments about work's impact on fertility in Europe are drawn from Bruce Sacerdote and James Feyrer, "Will the Stork Return to Europe and Japan? Understanding Fertility Within Developed Nations," NBER Working Paper, June 2008; and Samuel Preston and Caroline Sten Hartnett, op. cit. Evidence of the financial benefits of marriage is found in Martin Browning, Pierre-André Chiappori, and Arthur Lewbel, "Estimating Consumption Economies of Scale, Adult Equivalence Scales, and Household Bargaining Power," Economics Series Working Paper, Oxford University Department of Economics, August 2006; Graziella Bertocchi and Marianna Brunetti, "Marriage and Other Risky Assets: A Portfolio Approach," CEPR Discussion Paper, February 2009; Libertad González and Berkay Özcan, "The Risk of Divorce and Household Saving Behavior," IZA Working Paper, September 2008. Data on the relative earnings of husbands and wives are found in Census Bureau, Current Population Survey, "Annual Social and Economic Supplements, Table F-22: Married-Couple Families with

Wives' Earnings Greater Than Husbands' Earnings: 1988 to 2008" (www.census
.gov/hhes/www/income/data/historical/families/index.html, accessed 07/18/
2010). Data on increased marriage rates among college graduates come from
Justin Wolfers and Betsey Stevenson, "Marriage and Divorce, Changes and
Their Driving Forces," *Journal of Economic Perspectives*, Vol. 21, No. 2, Spring
2007, pp. 27–52; and Adam Isen and Betsey Stevenson, "Women's Education
and Family Behavior: Trends in Marriage, Divorce and Fertility," NBER Working Paper, February 2010. Evidence of mothers' recent change in attitudes
toward work is found in Pew Research Center, "Fewer Mothers Prefer Full-time
Work," July 2007; and Sharon R. Cohany and Emy Sok, "Trends in Labor Force
Participation of Married Mothers of Infants," *Bureau of Labor Statistics Monthly
Labor Review*, February 2007 (www.bls.gov/opub/mlr/2007/02/art2abs.htm,
accessed 08/08/2010). The data on American fertility are from the Centers
for Disease Control and Prevention (www.cdc.gov/nchs/births.htm, accessed
07/18/2010). Data on growing numbers of forty-year-old mothers come from
Claudia Goldin, personal communication.

**101–104 The Cheapest Women:** Indian men's preference for women from the
same caste is discussed in Abhijit Banerjee, Esther Duflo, Maitreesh Ghatak,
and Jeanne Lafortune, "Marry for What? Caste and Mate Selection in Modern
India," NBER Working Paper, May 2009. The analysis of dowry payments in
India and Bangladesh draws from Francis Bloch and Vijayendra Rao, "Terror
as a Bargaining Instrument: A Case-Study of Dowry Violence in Rural India,"
*American Economic Review*, Vol. 92, No. 4, September 2002, pp. 1029–1043; Siwan
Anderson, "The Economics of Dowry and Brideprice," *Journal of Economic Per-
spectives*, Vol. 21, No. 4, Fall 2007, pp. 151–174; Vijayendra Rao, "The Rising
Price of Husbands: A Hedonic Analysis of Dowry Increases in Rural India,"
*Journal of Political Economy*, Vol. 101, No. 4, 1993, pp. 666–671; Vijayendra Rao,
"The Economics of Dowries in India," in Kaushik Basu, ed., *Oxford Companion
to Economics in India* (New Delhi: Oxford University Press, 2007); and Luciana
Suran and Sajeda Amin, "Does Dowry Make Life Better for Brides? A Test of
the Bequest Theory of Dowry in Rural Bangladesh," Policy Research Division
Working Paper, Population Council, New York, 2004.

**104–106 Killing Girls:** The decline in the abortion of female fetuses in South
Korea and the impact of ultrasound technology on such abortions in India are
discussed in Woojin Chung and Monica Das Gupta, "The Decline of Son Preference in South Korea: The Roles of Development and Public Policy," *Population and Development Review*, Vol. 33, No. 4, December 2007, pp. 757–783. Data
on gender imbalances in South Korea and China are drawn from Monica Das
Gupta, Jiang Zhenghua, Li Bohua, Xie Zhenming, Woojin Chung, and Bae
Hwa-Ok, "Why Is Son Preference So Persistent in East and South Asia? A Cross-
Country Study of China, India and the Republic of Korea," *Journal of Development Studies*, Vol. 40, No. 2, December 2003, pp. 153–187; and "China Faces
Growing Sex Imbalance," BBC News, 01/11/2010 (at news.bbc.co.uk/2/hi/
asia-pacific/8451289.stm, accessed 07/18/2010). Data on gender imbalances
among Indian, Chinese, and Korean families in the United States are found in

Douglas Almond and Lena Edlund, "Son-biased Sex Ratios in the 2000 United States Census," *Proceedings of the National Academy of Sciences*, Vol. 105, No. 15, April 15, 2008, pp. 5681–5682.

**106–109 Missing Brides:** The discussion of the consequences of China's gender imbalance draws from Avraham Ebenstein and Ethan Jennings, "The Consequences of the Missing Girls of China," *World Bank Economic Review*, Vol. 23, No. 3, November 2009, pp. 399–425; "China Faces Growing Sex Imbalance," BBC News, 01/11/2010 (at news.bbc.co.uk/2/hi/asia-pacific/8451289.stm, accessed 07/18/2010); Shang-Jin Wei and Xiaobo Zhang, "The Competitive Saving Motive: Evidence from Rising Sex Ratios and Savings Rates in China," NBER Working Paper, June 2009. The analysis of the positive influence of women on development in China and Taiwan draws from "Women and Men in China, Facts and Figures, 2004," Department of Population, Social Science, and Technology, National Bureau of Statistics, China, April 2004; Zhang Ye, "Hope for China's Migrant Women Workers," *China Business Review*, April 2002; Nancy Qian, "Missing Women and the Price of Tea in China: The Effect of Sex-Specific Earnings on Sex Imbalance," CEPR Discussion Paper, December 2006; and Andrew M. Frances, "Sex Ratios and the Red Dragon: Using the Chinese Communist Revolution to Explore the Effect of the Sex Ratio on Women and Children in Taiwan," Emory University Working Paper, November 2008.

**110–114 The Price of Work:** Data on labor coercion are found in International Labor Organization, "The Cost of Coercion," Report of the Director General, International Labour Conference, 2009. Data on the labor share of national income is drawn from Bureau of Economic Analysis, National Income and Product Accounts, Table 1.12: National Income by Type of Income. The analysis of the evolution of slavery through history draws from Jonathan Conning, "On the Causes of Slavery or Serfdom and the Roads to Agrarian Capitalism: Domar's Hypothesis Revisited," Hunter College Department of Economics Working Paper, City University of New York, November 2004; Nils-Petter Lagerlöf, "Slavery and Other Property Rights," *Review of Economic Studies*, Vol. 76, No. 1, January 2009, pp. 319–342; Evsey Domar, "The Causes of Slavery or Serfdom: A Hypothesis," *Economic History Review*, Vol. 30, No. 1, March 1970, pp. 18–32; Kevin O'Rourke and Ronald Findlay, *Power and Plenty: Trade, War and the World Economy in the Second Millennium* (Princeton: Princeton University Press, 2007), p. 130; and Daron Acemoglu and Alexander Wolitzky, "The Economics of Labor Coercion," NBER Working Paper, December 2009. Data on the impact of slavery on productivity and economic growth is drawn from Nathan Nunn, "Slavery, Inequality, and Economic Development in the Americas: An Examination of the Engerman-Sokoloff Hypothesis," MPRA Paper, University Library of Munich, Germany, October 2007; Peter Mancall, Joshua Rosenbloom, and Thomas Weiss, "South Carolina Slave Prices, 1722–1809," NBER Historical Paper, March 2000; Peter Mancall, Joshua Rosenbloom, and Thomas Weiss, "Agricultural Labor Productivity in the Lower South, 1720–1800," *Explorations in Economic History*, Vol. 39, No. 4, October 2002, pp. 390–424. The impact of illegal immigration on capital investments in American agriculture is discussed in Eduardo Porter, "In Florida Groves, Cheap Labor Means Machines," *New York Times*, March 22, 2004. Data on wages in Vietnam comes from Vu Trong Khanh and Leigh Murray, "Inflation Fears After Vietnam Boosts Wages," *Wall Street Journal*, March 26, 2010.

**114–118 What's Fair Pay?:** Data on the cost of goods measured in terms of the average worker's wage comes from United States Bureau of Labor Statistics, "100 Years of U.S. Consumer Spending: Data for the Nation, New York City, and Boston," May 2006; J. Bradford Delong, "Cornucopia: Increasing Wealth in the Twentieth Century," NBER Working Paper, March 2000. The value of speaking English in India is found in Mehtabul Azam, Aimee Chin, and Nishith Prakash, "The Returns to English-Language Skills in India," IZA Discussion Paper, 2010. The discussion of the higher wages of the tall and the beautiful draws from Anne Case and Christina Paxson, "Stature and Status: Height, Ability, and Labor Market Outcomes," *Journal of Political Economy*, Vol. 116, No. 3, 2008, pp. 499–532; Daniel Hammermesh and Jeff Biddle, "Beauty and the Labor Market," *American Economic Review*, Vol. 84, 1994, pp. 1174–1194; and Peter Lundborg, Paul Nystedt, and Dan-Olof Rooth, "The Height Premium in Earnings: The Role of Physical Capacity and Cognitive and Non-Cognitive Skills," IZA Working Paper, June 2009. The stories about George Eastman and Henry Ford's labor policies are drawn from Sanford M. Jacobi, *Modern Manors: Welfare Capitalism Since the New Deal* (Princeton: Princeton University Press, 1997); "Eastman Charted Path for Industry," *New York Times*, March 15, 1932; Daniel Raff and Lawrence Summers, "Did Henry Ford Pay Efficiency Wages?" *Journal of Labor Economics*, Vol. 5, October 1987, pp. S57–86. The analysis of the number of American jobs that could be sent offshore is found in Alan Blinder and Alan Krueger, "Alternative Measures of Offshorability: A Survey Approach," NBER Working Paper, August 2009. Chinese economic data comes from the International Monetary Fund (www.imf.org/external/pubs/ft/weo/2010/01/weodata/index.aspx, accessed 08/09/2010) and the United Nations Millennium Indicators (at mdgs.un.org/unsd/mdg/Default.aspx, accessed 08/09/2010). Data on unionization in the United States comes from the Bureau of Labor Statistics (www.bls.gov/news.release/union2.nr0.htm, accessed 07/18/2010); and Barry Hirsch and David Macpherson, *Union Membership and Earnings Data Book* (Arlington, Va.: The Bureau of National Affairs, Inc., 2010).

**118–121 Paying Superman:** Data on pay in Major League Baseball are drawn from the *USA Today* baseball salary database (content.usatoday.com/sports/baseball/salaries/default.aspx, accessed 07/18/2010). Data on corporate pay is drawn from Thomas Piketty and Emmanuel Saez, "Income Inequality in the United States, 1913–1998," *Quarterly Journal of Economics*, Vol. 118, 2003, pp. 1–39, updated tables and figures (at clsa.berkeley.edu/~saez/TabFig2010.xls, accessed 07/18/2010); Carola Frydman and Raven Saks, "Executive Compensation: A New View from a Long-Term Perspective, 1936–2005," NBER Working Paper, June 2008, Table 3; and Xavier Gabaix and Augustin Landier, "Why Has CEO Pay Increased so Much?," NYU Working Paper, 2006. Sherwin Rosen's analysis is in Sherwin Rosen, "The Economics of Superstars," *American Economic*

*Review,* Vol. 71, No. 5, December 1981, pp. 845–858. The analysis of the fast growth of earnings at the top in pop music, Hollywood, and soccer draws from Alan Krueger, "The Economics of Real Superstars: The Market for Rock Concerts in the Material World," *Journal of Labor Economics,* Vol. 23, January 2005, pp. 1–30; the IMDB database (at www.imdb.com/name/nm0000129/bio and http://www.imdb.com/title/tt0120755/, accessed 07/18/2010); Edward Jay Epstein, "Tom Cruise Inc.: The Numbers Behind His Celebrity," *Slate,* June 27, 2005; Claudia Eller, "Tom Cruise Sees Box Office Share Scaled Back," *Los Angeles Times,* February 17, 2010; Matthew Saltmarsh, "European Soccer Revenue Climbs, but So Do Salaries," *New York Times,* June 8, 2010; Garry Jenkins, *The Beautiful Team* (New York: Simon & Schuster, 2006); Futebolfinance.com; Christina Settimi, "Soccer's Highest Earners," Forbes.com, April 21, 2010; and Fédération Internationale de Football Association (www.fifa.com/aboutfifa/marketing/factsfigures/tvdata.html). Data on the earnings of the richest families comes from Piketty and Saez, op. cit.

**121–125 Farmers and Financiers:** Data on bankers' bonuses come from the office of the Comptroller of New York State (www.osc.state.ny.us/press/releases/feb10/bonus_chart_2009.pdf, accessed 07/18/2010.) Data on banks' profits drawn from the Bureau of Economic Analysis (www.bea.gov). Faylene Whitacker's comments about immigrant laborers are in Eduardo Porter, "Who Will Work the Farms?" *New York Times,* March 23, 2006. Data on international migration is drawn from the Migration Policy Institute (www.migrationinformation.org/datahub/charts/6.1.shtml, accessed 07/18/2010). Data on growing inequality in China are in Anthony B. Atkinson, Thomas Piketty, and Emmanuel Saez, "Top Incomes in the Long Run of History," NBER working paper, October 2009. Analysis on the impact of inequality on economic growth draws from Dan Andrews, Christopher Jencks, and Andrew Leigh, "Do Rising Top Incomes Lift All Boats?," Harvard University John F. Kennedy School of Management Working Paper, 2009. Data on economic growth per person in the United States is from the International Monetary Fund (http://www.imf.org/external/pubs/ft/weo/2010/01/weodata/weorept.aspx?pr.x=37&pr.y=1 2&sy=1980&ey=2015&scsm=1&ssd=1&sort=country&ds=.&br=1&c=111&s=NG DPRPC%2CNGDPPC&grp=0&a=, accessed 08/09/2010). International comparisons of inequality are found in Organisation for Economic Co-operation and Development, *Growing Unequal? Income Distribution and Poverty in OECD Countries* (OECD Publishing, October 2008), pp. 77–92. Data on the impact of income inequality on health and segregation are drawn from Richard Wilkinson and Kate Pickett, *The Spirit Level: Why More Equal Societies Almost Always Do Better* (New York: Bloomsbury Press, 2010); and Joseph Gyourko, Christopher Mayer, and Todd Sinai, "Superstar Cities," NBER Working Paper, July 2006.

**125–127 The Vanishing Middle:** The discussion of the impact of education on income growth draws from Claudia Goldin and Lawrence Katz, *The Race Between Education and Technology* (Cambridge, Mass.: Belknap Press of Harvard University Press, 2008); David Autor and David Dorn, "Inequality and Specialization: The Growth of Low-Skill Service Jobs in the United States," NBER working paper, November 2008; Congressional Budget Office, "Changes in the Distribution of Workers' Annual Earnings Between 1979 and 2007," October 2009; Francine Blau, Marianne Ferber, and Anne Winkler, *The Economics of Women, Men and Work*, 5th edition (Upper Saddle River, N.J.: Pearson Prentice Hall, 2006); Bureau of Labor Statistics (www.bls.gov/news.release/wkyeng.t05.htm, accessed 08/08/2010); Census Bureau, "Income, Poverty, and Health Insurance Coverage in the United States," 2008 (www.census.gov/prod/2009pubs/p60-236.pdf, accessed 08/09/2010); Bureau of Labor Statistics, "100 Years of U.S. Consumer Spending: Data for the Nation, New York City, and Boston," May 2006 (www.bls.gov/opub/uscs/home.htm, accessed 08/09/2010); and Bureau of Labor Statistics (www.bls.gov/bls/wages.htm, accessed 08/08/2010).

**127–129 A Banker's Paradise:** The narrative about financial deregulation and the rise of bankers' pay draws from Thomas Philippon and Ariell Reshef, "Wages and Human Capital in the U.S. Financial Industry: 1909–2006," NBER working paper, January 2009. The data on banks' share of corporate profits comes from the Bureau of Economic Analysis, NIPA Tabes No. 6.16A-D (www.bea.gov/national/nipaweb/Index.asp, accessed 08/09/2010). The data on university graduates taking jobs in finance comes from Claudia Goldin and Lawrence F. Katz, "Transitions: Career and Family Lifecycles of the Educational Elite," *American Economic Association Papers and Proceedings*, May 2008, pp. 363–366; and Princeton University, Office of Career Services, Class of 2008 Career Survey Report.

**130–133 The Price of Free:** The discussion about the success of Radiohead's *In Rainbows* draws from *Billboard* (www.billboard.com/#/); and Daniel Kreps, "Radiohead Publishers Reveal 'In Rainbows' Numbers," *Rolling Stone*, October 15, 2008. Analysis about the value of viewers' attention to broadcast television is drawn from Eduardo Porter, "Television Is Not Free and Does Not Want to Be," *New York Times*, March 8, 2010; and Ernest Miller, "Top Ten New Copyright Crimes," *Lawmeme*, May 2, 2002 (lawmeme.research.yale.edu/modules.php?name=News&file=article&sid=198, accessed 07/18/2010).

**133–137 The Allure of the Free:** The origin of the "no free lunch" saying is taken from William Safire, "On Language: Words Out in the Cold," *New York Times*, February 14, 1993. The psychological impact of receiving something for free comes from David Adam Friedman, "Free Offers: A New Look," *New Mexico Law Review*, Vol. 38, Winter 2008, pp. 49–94; Kristina Shampanier, Nina Mazar, and Dan Ariely, "Zero as a Special Price: The True Value of Free Products," *Marketing Science*, Vol. 26, No. 6, November/December 2007, pp. 742–757. Adrian Johns makes his point on the importance of information to the economy of the twenty-first century in *Piracy: The Intellectual Property Wars from Gutenberg to Gates* (Chicago: University of Chicago Press, 2009). Comments on gift-giving rituals among marginal cultures draws from Marcel Mauss, *The Gift: The Form and Reason for Exchange in Archaic Societies* (New York: W. W. Norton, 1990), p. 30. Data on spam volumes and costs drawn from Messagelabs (www

.messagelabs.com/resources/press/45666, accessed 7/18/2010); Chris Kanich,
Christian Kreibich, Kirill Levchenko, Brandon Enright, Geoffrey Voelker, Vern
Paxson, and Stefan Savage, "Spamalytics: An Empirical Analysis of Spam Mar-
keting Conversion," *Communications of the Association for Computing Machinery*,
Vol. 52, No. 9, September 2009, pp. 99–107; Marco Caliendo, Michel Clement,
Dominik Papies, and Sabine Scheel-Kopeinig, "The Cost Impact of Spam Filters:
Measuring the Effect of Information System Technologies in Organizations," IZA
Working Paper, October 2008. German wages are from Eurostat (epp.eurostat
.ec.europa.eu/portal/page/portal/eurostat/home/, accessed 7/18/2010). The
Korean reaction to spam is in Robert Kraut, Shyam Sunder, Rahul Telang, and
James Morris, "Pricing Electronic Mail to Solve the Problem of Spam," Yale ICF
Working Paper, July 2005.

**137–141 Napstering the World:** The falling prices of computers are found
in Bureau of Economic Analysis, NIPA table 1.5.4, Price Indices for GDP,
expanded detail (www.bea.gov/national/nipaweb/TableView.asp?SelectedTable=
34&ViewSeries=NO&Java=no&Request3Place=N&3Place=N&FromView=YES&
Freq=Year&FirstYear=1980&LastYear=2009&3Place=N&Update=Update&Java
Box=no#Mid, accessed on 08/16/2010). The explosion of free music downloads is detailed in Amanda Lenhart and Susannah Fox, "Downloading Free
Music," Pew Internet and American Life Project, September 28, 2000. Stewart
Brand's quote is in Jack Fuller, *What Is Happening to News: The Information Explosion and the Crisis in Journalism* (Chicago: University of Chicago Press, 2010),
p. 104. Chris Anderson's thoughts can be found in *Free: The Future of a Radical
Price* (New York: Hyperion, 2009). Data on the declining sales of music record-
ings come from the Recording Industry Association of America (awww.riaa.
org) and the International Federation of the Phonographic Industry (www.ifpi
.org). The stories about the music industry's losing battle against free music
are drawn from Eric Pfanner, "Court Says File-Sharing Site Violated Copyright,"
*New York Times*, April 18, 2009; John Schwartz, "Tilting at Internet Barrier, a
Stalwart Is Upended," *New York Times*, August 11, 2009; Joseph Plambeck, "Idea
Man of LimeWire at a Crossroads," *New York Times*, May 23, 2010; "The State
of Online Music: Ten Years After Napster," Pew Internet and American Life
Project, June 15, 2009; Hilmar Schmundt, "Darth Vader and the Vikings: The
Rise of Sweden's Pirate Party," *Der Spiegel* Online, June 19, 2009; IFPI Digital
Music report 2009 (www.ifpi.org/content/section_resources/dmr2009.html,
accessed 07/18/2010); Tim Arango, "Despite iTunes Accord, Music Labels Still
Fret," *New York Times*, February 1, 2009. Data on how free downloads are mak-
ing inroads in Hollywood are drawn from "The Cost of Movie Piracy," Motion
Picture Association of America, 2005; IFPI Digital Music Report 2009; and
Brian Stelter and Brad Stone, "Digital Pirates Winning Battle with Studios," *New
York Times*, February 4, 2009. The discussion of the top sources of news about
Michael Jackson's death is found in "Protect, Point, Pay: An Associated Press
Plan for Reclaiming News Content Online," Associated Press internal memo-
randum, unpublished, July 2009. Data on newspapers' declining advertising
revenue come from the Newspaper Association of America (at www.naa.org).
Google's financial data come from the company.

**141–144 Profiting from Ideas:** The story of Brunelleschi's patent on *Il Badalone* is in Paul Robert Walker, *The Feud That Sparked the Renaissance: How Brunelleschi and Ghiberti Changed the Art World* (New York: William Morrow, 2002), pp. 117–118. Data on the pharmaceutical industry's investments are in Joseph DiMasi, Ronald Hansen, and Henry Grabowski, "The Price of Innovation: New Estimates of Drug Development Costs," *Journal of Health Economics*, Vol. 22, 2003, pp. 151–185. Details of Brazil's compulsory licensing of antiretroviral drugs are found in "Timeline on Brazil's Compulsory Licensing," Program on Information Justice and Intellectual Property, American University, Washington College of Law, April 2008 (www.ggp.up.ac.za/human_rights_access_to_medicines/syllabus/2009/day2/2PIJIPBrazilTimeline.pdf, accessed 08/08/2010). Changes in Indian patent law are described in Donald McNeil Jr., "India Alters Law on Drug Patents," *New York Times*, March 24, 2005. The impact of patent expiry on the prices and market share of branded drugs is discussed in Laura Magazzini, Fabio Pammolli, and Massimo Riccaboni, "Dynamic Competition in Pharmaceuticals: Patent Expiry, Generic Penetration, and Industry Structure," *European Journal of Health Economics*, Vol. 5, June 2004, pp. 175–182; Frank R. Lichtenberg and Gautier Duflos, "Time Release: The Effect of Patent Expiration on U.S. Drug Prices, Marketing, and Utilization by the Public," Manhattan Institute Center for Policy Research, Medical Progress Report No. 11, October 2009 (www.manhattan-institute.org/pdf/mpr_11.pdf, accessed 08/08/2010). The impact of patents on the creation and diffusion of innovations is discussed in William Baumol, "Intellectual Property: How the Right to Keep It to Yourself Promotes Dissemination," *Review of Economic Research on Copyright Issues*, Vol. 2, No. 2, pp. 17–23; Steve Lohr, "Now, an Invention Inventors Will Like," *New York Times*, September 21, 2009.

**144–148 The Case for Bookaneering:** Paul McCartney's quote is found in David Bennahum, *The Beatles: After the Break-up: In Their Own Words* (London: Omnibus Press, 1991), p. 19. The tale about the origins of copyright in Britain and its controversial application in the United States is drawn from Hal Varian, "Copying and Copyright," *Journal of Economic Perspectives*, Vol. 19, No. 2, Spring 2005, pp. 121–138; Robert Spoo, "Ezra Pound's Copyright Statute: Perpetual Rights and the Problem of Heirs," *UCLA Law Review*, Vol. 56, 2009; Charles C. Mann, "The Heavenly Jukebox," *Atlantic Monthly*, September 2000; Ezra Pound, "Copyright and Tariff," *New Age*, Vol. 23, October 13, 1918, p. 363. Paulo Coelho's fondness for sharing his books online is discussed in Torrent Freak, "Best-Selling Author Turns Piracy into Profit," May 12, 2008 (torrentfreak.com/best-selling-author-turns-piracy-into-profit-080512/, accessed 07/18/2010). Analysis of the impact of file sharing on the market for music draws from Rafael Rob and Joel Waldfogel, "Piracy on the High C's: Music Downloading, Sales Displacement, and Social Welfare in a Sample of College Students," *Journal of Law and Economics*, Vol. 49, No. 1, April 2006, pp. 29–62; Alejandro Zentner, "Measuring the Effect of File Sharing on Music Purchases," *Journal of Law and Economics*, Vol. 49, No. 1, April 2006; Martin Peitz and Patrick Waelbroeck, "The Effect of Internet Piracy on Music Sales: Cross-Section Evidence," *Review of Economic Research on Copyright Issues*, 2004, Vol. 1, No. 2, 2004, pp. 71–79; Sudip Bhattacharjee,

Ram Gopal, Kaveepan Lertwachara, James Marsden, and Rahul Telang, "The Effect of Digital Sharing Technologies on Music Markets," *Management Science*, Vol. 53, No. 9, September 2007, pp. 1359–1374. The analysis of the impact of music downloads on bands that haven't yet made the A-list is drawn from Alan Krueger, "The Economics of Real Superstars: The Market for Rock Concerts in the Material World," *Journal of Labor Economics*, Vol. 23, January 2005, pp. 1–30; Marie Connolly and Alan Krueger, "Rockonomics: The Economics of Popular Music," NBER Working Paper, April 2005; "The State of Online Music: Ten Years After Napster," Pew Internet and American Life Project, June 15, 2009, pp. 13–14; Greg Sandoval, "Trent Reznor: Why Won't People Pay $5?," CNET News, January 10, 2008 (at news.cnet.com/8301-10784_3-9847788-7. html, accessed 07/18/2010).

**149–152 Stealing Sneakers:** Stan Liebowitz's analysis of the economics of copyright is found on his Web site at the University of Texas at Dallas (at www .utdallas.edu/~liebowit/, accessed 07/18/2010); Stan Liebowitz, "Testing File-Sharing's Impact by Examining Record Sales in Cities," University of Texas at Dallas School of Management, Department of Finance and Managerial Economics Working Paper, April 2006; Stan Liebowitz, "Economists' Topsy-Turvy View of Piracy," *Review of Economic Research on Copyright Issues*, Vol. 2, No. 1, 2005, pp. 5–17. Artists' reactions to Google's request for free art is found in Andrew Adam Newman, "Use Their Work Free? Some Artists Say No to Google," *New York Times*, June 15, 2009. The story about free lawyers is in Elie Mystal, "It's Come to This: Unpaid Internships for Lawyers with One–Three Years Experience," *Above the Law*, September 30, 2009 (abovethelaw.com/2009/09/its-come-to-this-unpaid-internships-for-lawyers-with-one-three-years-experience/, accessed 07/18/2010). Hal Varian's suggestion on how newspapers can make money is in Hal R. Varian, "Versioning Information Goods," University of California Berkeley Working Paper, March 13, 1997. The online pricing strategy of the *Newport Daily News* in Rhode Island is described in Joseph Tartakoff, "Taking the Plunge: How Newspaper Sites That Charge Are Faring," Paid Content. org, September 2, 2009 (paidcontent.org/article/419-taking-the-plunge-how-newspaper-sites-that-charge-are-faring/, accessed on 08/16/2010).

**152–154 Where Information Goes to Die:** Data on music sales in France is in IFPI, "Digital Music Report," 2009. Experts' trust in the inevitable demise of copyright is drawn from "The Future of the Internet III," Pew Internet and American Life Project, December 14, 2008. Tales about the battle against the piracy of sheet music in the nineteenth century are found in Adrian Johns, *Piracy: The Intellectual Property Wars from Gutenberg to Gates* (Chicago: University of Chicago Press, 2009), p. 329.

**155–162 The Price of Culture:** The data on the spread of democracy is drawn from Freedom House, "Democracy's Century: A Survey of Global Political Change in the 20th Century," 1999 (http://www.freedomhouse.org/ template.cfm?page=70&release=75, accessed 08/09/2010). The data on vote buying in Thailand and São Tomé and Príncipe comes from Frederic Charles

Schaffer, "Vote Buying in East Asia," Transparency International Corruption Report, 2004; Pedro Vicente, "Is Vote Buying Effective? Evidence from a Field Experiment in West Africa," Oxford University Working Paper, 2007; and Pedro Vicente, "Does Oil Corrupt? Evidence from a Natural Experiment in West Africa," Oxford University Working Paper, 2006. Tales about vote buying in Britain and the United States in the nineteenth century come from E. Anthony Smith, "Bribery and Disfranchisement: Wallingford Elections, 1820–1832," *English Historical Review*, Vol. 75, No. 297, October 1960, pp. 618–630; Gary Cox and J. Morgan Kousser, "Turnout and Rural Corruption: New York as a Test Case," *American Journal of Political Science*, Vol. 25, No. 4, 1981; and David Kirkpatrick, "Does Corporate Money Lead to Political Corruption?," *New York Times*, January 23, 2010. The data on campaign spending in the 2008 presidential election in the United States comes from the Center for Responsive Politics (www.opensecrets.org/pres08/index.php, accessed 07/18/2010); and Federal Election Commission, 2008 Official Presidential General Election Results (www.fec.gov/pubrec/fe2008/2008presgeresults.pdf, accessed 07/18/2010). The discussion of the limited returns to contemporary campaign spending is in Steven Levitt, "Using Repeat Challengers to Estimate the Effects of Campaign Spending on Electoral Outcomes in the U.S. House," *Journal of Political Economy*, Vol. 102, 1994, pp. 777–798. The comparison between corruption and lobbying draws from Bard Harstad and Jakob Svensson, "Bribes, Lobbying and Development," CEPR Discussion Paper, 2006; the Center for Responsive Politics ( www.opensecrets.org/lobby/index.php, accessed 07/18/2010); the Center for Responsive Politics, "Banking on Connections," June 3, 2010; Erich Lichtblau and Edward Wyatt, "Financial Overhaul Bill Poses Big Test for Lobbyists," *New York Times*, May 22, 2010; Henrik Kleven, Martin Knudsen, Claus Kreiner, Søren Pedersen, and Emmanuel Saez, "Unwilling or Unable to Cheat? Evidence from a Randomized Tax Audit Experiment in Denmark," NBER Working Paper, February 2010; Nauro Campos and Francesco Giovannoni, "Lobbying, Corruption and Other Banes," CEPR Discussion Paper, 2008; "Daimler Agrees to Pay $185m After Admitting Bribery," BBC News, April 1, 2010 (news.bbc.co.uk/go/pr/fr/-/2/hi/business/8600241.stm, accessed 07/18/2010); and Politische Datensbank ( www.parteispenden.unklarheiten. de/?seite=datenbank_show_k&db_id=25&kat=3&sortierung=start, accessed 07/15/2010); and Vanessa Fuhrman and Thomas Catan, "Daimler to Settle with U.S. on Bribes," *Wall Street Journal*, March 24, 2010. Tim Groseclose and Jeff Milyo discuss how members of Congress value their seats in "Buying the Bums Out: What's the Dollar Value of a Seat in Congress?" Stanford University Graduate School of Business Research Paper, 1999.

**162–165 What Culture Does:** The working habits among daughters of immigrants to the United States are found in Raquel Fernandez, "Women, Work, and Culture," NBER Working Paper, February 2007. The impact of fines in Israeli day-care centers is discussed in Uri Gneezy and Aldo Rustichini, "A Fine Is a Price," *Journal of Legal Studies*, Vol. 29, No. 1, January 2000, pp. 1–17. The statistic about Japan's high prices comes from Robert Lipsey and Birgitta

Swedenborg, "Explaining Product Price Differences Across Countries," NBER Working Paper, July 2007.

**165–168 Where Culture Comes From:** Discussion of the economic implications of trust draws from Jeff Butler, Paola Giuliano, and Luigi Guiso, "The Right Amount of Trust," CEPR Discussion Paper, September 2009; and the World Values Survey, 2005–2008 wave (www.wvsevsdb.com/wvs/WVSAnalizeSample.jsp, accessed 07/18/2010). Different views on the deformed lips of Mursi girls are from Mursi Online, Oxford University Department of International Development (www.mursi.org/); and Luigi Guiso, Paola Sapienza, and Luigi Zingales, "Does Culture Affect Economic Outcomes?," *Journal of Economic Perspectives*, Vol. 20, Spring 2006, pp. 23–48. The results of experiments using the Ultimatum Game around the world are described in Joseph Heinrich et al., "'Economic Man' in Cross-Cultural Perspective: Behavioral Experiments in 15 Small-Scale Societies," *Behavioral and Brain Sciences*, Vol. 28, 2005, pp. 795–855. The use of myth to manage caribou populations among the Chisasibi is described in Fikret Berkes, *Sacred Ecology*, 2nd edition (New York: Routledge, 2008), pp. 128–129. Data about cultural proximity between societies that share similar environments is found in Mathias Thoenig, Nicolas Maystre, Jacques Olivier, and Thierry Verdier, "Product-Based Cultural Change: Is the Village Global?," CEPR Discussion Paper, August 2009. The impact of the choice of economic system on the worldview of East and West Germans is drawn from Alberto Alesina and Nicola Fuchs-Schündeln, "Good-bye Lenin (or Not?): The Effect of Communism on People's Preferences," NBER Working Paper, October 2005.

**168–173 Who Can Afford Animal Rights?:** Data on attitudes toward premarital sex are drawn from Jesús Fernández-Villaverde, Jeremy Greenwood, and Nezih Guner, "From Shame to Game in One Hundred Years: An Economic Model of the Rise in Premarital Sex and Its Destigmatization," NBER Working Paper, January 2010; and Kaye Wellings, "Poverty or Promiscuity: Sexual Behaviour in Global Context," London School of Hygiene and Tropical Medicine, paper presented at the Training Course in Sexual and Reproductive Health Research, Geneva, Switzerland, February 23, 2009. The reasons for England's crummy cuisine are discussed in Paul Krugman, "Supply, Demand and English Food," *Fortune*, July 1988. International comparisons of the share of income devoted to food, the price elasticity of food demand, and preferences for treating farm animals humanely are drawn from the Economic Research Service of the United States Department of Agriculture (www.ers.usda.gov/Data/InternationalFood-Demand/Index.asp?view=PEF#IFD, accessed 07/18/2010); David Dickinson and DeeVon Bailey, "Experimental Evidence on Willingness to Pay for Red Meat Traceability in the United States, Canada, the U.K. and Japan," *Journal of Agricultural and Applied Economics*, Vol. 37, No. 3. December 2005, pp. 537–548; and World Values Survey, average of first four waves: 1981–2000 (www.wvsevsdb .com/wvs/WVSAnalizeSample.jsp, accessed 07/18/2010). The analysis of the relationship between the price of labor and the availability of services is in Robert Lipsey and Birgitta Swedenborg, "High-Price and Low-Price Countries: Causes and Consequences of Product Price Differences Across Countries," University of Pennsylvania Workshop Presentation, 2008; Robert Lipsey and Birgitta Swedenborg, "Explaining Product Price Differences Across Countries," NBER Working Paper, July 2007; and Robert Lipsey and Birgitta Swedenborg, "Wage Dispersion and Country Price Levels," NBER Working Paper, 1997. The commentary on the different views on fairness and luck in Europe and the United States draws from Roland Benabou and Jean Tirole, "Belief in a Just World and Redistributive Politics," NBER Working Paper, March 2005; and World Values Survey, 2005–2008 wave (http://www.wvsevsdb.com/wvs/WVSAnalizeStudy .jsp, accessed 08/09/2010). The discussion on racial diversity and support for redistributive policies draws from William Julius Wilson, *When Work Disappears: The World of the New Urban Poor* (New York: Vintage Books, 1997), p. 202. Data on tipping patterns in the United States come from Daniel Kahneman, Jack Knetsch, and Richard Thaler, "Fairness as a Constraint on Profit Seeking: Entitlements in the Market," *American Economic Review*, Vol. 76, September 1986, pp. 728–741; and Michael Lynn, "Tipping in Restaurants and Around the Globe: An Interdisciplinary Review," in Morris Altman, ed., *Handbook of Contemporary Behavioral Economics, Foundations and Developments* (Armonk, N.Y.: M .E. Sharpe Publishers, 2006), pp. 626–643.

**173–177 The Price of Repugnance:** Discussion on different attitudes about eating horse fillet are drawn from Alvin Roth, "Repugnance as a Constraint on Markets," *Journal of Economic Perspectives*, Vol. 21, No. 3, Summer 2007, pp. 37–58; maville.com, Caen et ça region (at www.caen.maville.com/actu/ actudet_-Cyril-ouvre-une-boucherie-chevaline-boulevard-Leroy-_loc-822159_ actu.htm, accessed 07/18/2010); and Tara Burghart, "Last US Horse Slaughterhouse to Close," *Huffington Post*, June 29, 2007 (www.huffingtonpost.com/ huff-wires/20070629/horse-slaughter/#, accessed 07/18/2010). The discussion about attitudes toward egg donations draws from the Ethics Committee of the American Society for Reproductive Medicine, "Financial Compensation of Oocyte Donors," *Fertility and Sterility*, Vol. 88, No. 2, August 2007, pp. 305–309; David Tuller, "Payment Offers to Egg Donors Prompt Scrutiny," *New York Times*, May 10, 2010; United Kingdom Human Fertilization and Embryology Authority, "Egg Donation and Egg Sharing" (at www.hfea.gov.uk/egg-donation-and-egg-sharing.html, accessed 07/18/2010); and Alvin Roth, op. cit. The discussion about opposition to dwarf tossing in France comes from Alvin Roth, op. cit. Brigitte Bardot's campaign against Koreans' taste for dog meat is discussed in William Saletan, "Wok the Dog," *Slate*, January 16, 2002. Data on kidney transplants are found in Scientific Registry of Transplant Recipients (at www.ustransplant .org/csr/current/nationalViewer.aspx?o=KI, accessed 07/18/2010). The discussion on how kidney sales would increase the supply of kidneys for transplant draws from Gary S. Becker and Julio Jorge Elías, "Introducing Incentives in the Market for Live and Cadaveric Organ Donations," *Journal of Economic Perspectives*, Vol. 21, Summer 2007, pp. 3–24; Anne Griffin, "Kidneys on Demand," *British Medical Journal*, Vol. 334, March 10, 2007, pp. 502–505; Ahad J. Ghods and Shekoufeh Savaj, "Iranian Model of Paid and Regulated Living-Unrelated

Kidney Donation," *Clinical Journal of the American Society of Nephrology*, Vol. 1, 2006, pp. 616–625; and Hassan Ibrahim, Robert Foley, LiPing Tan, Tyson Rogers, Robert Bailey, Hongfei Guo, Cynthia Gross, and Arthur Matas, "Long-Term Consequences of Kidney Donation," *New England Journal of Medicine*, Vol. 360, No. 5, January 2009, pp. 459–469.

**177–178 Darwin's Price System:** The experiments about monkeys' sense of fairness are described in Sarah Brosnan and Frans de Waal, "Monkeys Reject Unequal Pay," *Nature*, Vol. 425, September 18, 2003, pp. 297–299.

**179–181 The Price of Faith:** Pascal's wager is described in Blaise Pascal, *Pensées*, translated by W. F. Trotter, 1910, Section IV: On the Means of Belief, paragraph 233 (at oregonstate.edu/instruct/phl302/texts/pascal/pensees-contents.html, accessed 07/18/2010).

**182–185 The Benefits of Belief:** The discussion of mutual assistance patterns in religious groups draws from Eli Berman, "Sect, Subsidy and Sacrifice: An Economist's View of Ultra-Orthodox Jews," *Quarterly Journal of Economics*, Vol. 65, No. 3, 2003, pp. 905–953; David Landau, *Piety and Power: The World of Jewish Fundamentalism* (New York: Hill and Wang, 1992), p. 263; Buster Smith and Rodney Stark, "Religious Attendance Relates to Generosity Worldwide," Gallup Report, September 4, 2009 (www.gallup.com/poll/122807/religious-attendance-relates-generosity-worldwide.aspx, accessed 07/18/2010); Daniel Chen, "Club Goods and Group Identity: Evidence from Islamic Resurgence During the Indonesian Financial Crisis," *Journal of Political Economy*, Vol. 118, No. 2, 2010, pp. 300–354. The discussion about the impact of religious faith on trust, moral behavior, happiness, and mortality draws from Luigi Guiso, Paola Sapienza, and Luigi Zingales, "People's Opium? Religion and Economic Attitudes," *Journal of Monetary Economics*, Vol. 50, No. 1, pp. 225–282, 2003; Azim Shariff and Ayan Norenzayan, "God Is Watching You," *Psychological Science*, Vol. 18, No. 9, 2007, pp. 803–809; Steve Farkas, Jean Johnson, and Tony Foleno, "For Goodness Sake: Why So Many Want Religion to Play a Greater Role in American Life," *Public Agenda*, 2001; Robert Hummer, Richard Rogers, Charles Nam, and Christopher Ellison, "Religious Involvement and U.S. Adult Mortality," *Demography*, Vol. 36, No. 2, May 1999, pp. 273–285; Jonathan Gruber, "Religious Market Structure, Religious Participation, and Outcomes: Is Religion Good for You?" NBER Working Paper, May 2005; and Timothy Brown, "A Monetary Valuation of Individual Religious Behavior: The Case of Prayer," University of California Berkeley Working Paper, September 2009. The relation between religious attitudes and people's opportunities in the secular world is discussed in Jonathan Gruber and Daniel Hungerman, "The Church vs. the Mall: What Happens When Religion Faces Increased Secular Competition?" NBER Working Paper, July 2006; Jonathan Gruber, "Pay or Pray? The Impact of Charitable Subsidies on Religious Attendance," NBER Working Paper, March 2004; and Edward Glaeser and Bruce Sacerdote, "Education and Religion," NBER Working Paper, 2001.

**185–188 What Does It Cost?:** Maimonides' comment on circumcision is found in Moses Maimonides, *The Guide for the Perplexed*, translated from the original Arabic text by M. Friedlander, 2nd edition (Charleston, S.C.: Forgottenbooks. com, 2008), pp. 646–647. The description of the mystic religion of Pythagoras is in Bertrand Russell, *A History of Western Philosophy* (London: Routledge, 1991), p. 51. The survival rates of religious versus secular communes in the nineteenth century are found in Richard Sosis and Eric Bressler, "Cooperation and Commune Longevity: A Test of the Costly Signaling Theory of Religion," *Cross-Cultural Research*, Vol. 37, No. 2, May 2003, pp. 211–239.

**189–192 When Belief Is Cheap:** Efforts by the religious to segregate themselves from other groups are discussed in Laurence Iannaccone, "Introduction to the Economics of Religion," *Journal of Economic Literature*, Vol. 36, September 1998, pp. 1465–1496. The description of the emergence of ultra-Orthodox Judaism in Europe is drawn from Eli Berman, "Sect Subsidy and Sacrifice: An Economist's View of Ultra-Orthodox Jews," *Quarterly Journal of Economics*, Vol. 115, No. 3, August 2000, pp. 905–953. Membership in the Catholic Church is found in Carol Glatz, "Vatican: Priest Numbers Show Steady, Moderate Increase," *Catholic News Service*, March 2, 2009. *Time* magazine's famous God article is "Toward a Hidden God," *Time*, April 8, 1966. The discussion on the weakening of the Catholic Church since the 1960s is drawn from the Association of Religion Data Archives (www.thearda.com/Denoms/D_836.asp, accessed 07/18/2010); the Pew Global Attitudes Project, "The U.S. Stands Alone in Its Embrace of Religion," December 19, 2002; and the World Values Survey (www.wvsevsdb .com/wvs/WVSAnalizeSample.jsp, accessed 07/18/2010). Pope Benedict's reintroduction of plenary indulgences is described in Paul Vitello, "For Catholics, Heaven Moves a Step Closer," *New York Times*, February 10, 2009.

**192–195 What the Church Wants:** The medieval Catholic Church's tinkering with its rules, penalties, and prices is described in Robert Ekelund Jr., Robert Hébert, and Robert Tollison, "An Economic Analysis of the Protestant Reformation," *Journal of Political Economy*, Vol. 110, No. 3, 2002; and Robert Ekelund, Robert Tollison, Gary Anderson, Robert Hébert, and Audrey Davidson, *Sacred Trust: The Medieval Church as an Economic Firm* (New York: Oxford University Press, 1996), pp. 96–98.

**195–198 Sin vs. the Secular World:** The decline of the belief in God across the industrial world is documented in Ronald Inglehart and Pippa Norris, *Sacred and Secular: Religion and Politics Worldwide* (Cambridge, U.K.: Cambridge University Press, 2004). The divergence from this trend in the United States is discussed in Pew Research Center for the People and the Press, "U.S. Stands Alone in Its Embrace of Religion," Pew Global Attitudes Project, December 19, 2002; Roger Finke and Rodney Stark, "The Dynamics of Religious Economies," in Michele Dillon, ed., *Handbook of the Sociology of Religion* (Cambridge, U.K.: Cambridge University Press, 2004); and Association of Religion Data Archives (www .thearda.com/quickstats/qsdir.asp, accessed 08/19/2010).

**198–200 Will God Bounce Back?:** The relation between poverty and religion is discussed in Ronald Inglehart and Pippa Norris, op. cit.; and Eli Berman, op. cit. Data on fertility, poverty, and religious fervor in the United States is drawn from Census Bureau, Fertility of American Women 2006 (www.census.gov/prod/2008pubs/p20-558.pdf, accessed 08/19/2010); Census Bureau, State Median Family Income 2007 (www.census.gov/hhes/www/income/statemedfaminc.html, accessed 08/19/2010); and Frank Newport, "Religious Identity: States Differ Widely," Gallup Report, August 7, 2009 (www.gallup.com/poll/122075/religious-identity-states-differ-widely.aspx, accessed 07/19/2010).

**201–205 The Price of the Future:** The description of the Reverend Thomas Malthus is drawn from Robert Heilbroner, *The Worldly Philosophers*, revised 7th edition (New York: Touchstone, 1999), pp. 75–104. Malthus's quote is in Thomas Malthus, *An Essay on the Principle of Population: or, A View of Its Past and Present Effects on Human Happiness* (Cambridge, U.K.: Cambridge University Press, 1992), pp. 42–43. Carlyle's quote is in Thomas Carlyle, *Chartism* (New York: Wiley and Putnam, 1847), p. 383. The description of the collapse of ancient civilizations draws from Jared Diamond, "The Last Americans: Environmental Collapse and the End of Civilization," *Harper's*, June 2003; and James Brander and M. Scott Taylor, "The Simple Economics of Easter Island: A Ricardo-Malthus Model of Renewable Resource Use," *American Economic Review*, Vol. 88, No. 1, March 1998, pp. 119–138. The description of the world in the centuries up to Malthus's day and the economic transformation experienced since then draws from J. Bradford Delong, "Estimating World GDP, One Million B.C.–Present," May 1998, unpublished (at www.j-bradford-delong.net/TCEH/1998_Draft/World_GDP/Estimating_World_GDP.html, accessed 07/19/2010); David Cutler, Angus Deaton, and Adriana Lleras-Muney, "The Determinants of Mortality," NBER Working Paper, January 2006; Julie Jefferies, "The UK Population: Past, Present and Future," in *Focus on People and Migration*, UK Office for National Statistics, 2005 (at www.statistics.gov.uk/downloads/theme_compendia/fom2005/01_FOPM_Population.pdf, accessed 07/19/2010); Ronald Findlay and Kevin H. O'Rourke, *Power and Plenty: Trade, War and the World Economy in the Second Millennium* (Princeton: Princeton University Press, 2007), pp. 315–323; and Jeffrey Sachs, *The End of Poverty: Economic Possibilities of Our Time* (London: Penguin Books, 2006), pp. 27–37. The comparative data on carbon emissions in the United States, China, and India comes from the United States Energy Information Administration (www.eia.doe.gov/oiaf/ieo/pdf/ieorefcase.pdf, accessed 07/19/2010).

**205–209 Mispricing Nature:** Jeffrey Sachs's quote is in Jeffrey Sachs, *Common Wealth: Economics for a Crowded Planet* (New York: The Penguin Press, 2008), p. 67. The Environmental Protection Agency's evaluation of the social costs of $CO_2$ emissions is in the Environmental Protection Agency, "Technical Support Document on Benefits of Reducing GHG Emissions," June 12, 2008 (www.eenews.net/public/25/10084/features/documents/2009/03/11/document_gw_04.pdf, accessed 07/19/2010). Data on energy prices, energy consumption, and carbon emissions in Germany are drawn from Eurostat news release, "Household Electricity Prices in the EU27 Fell by 1.5% and Gas Prices by 16.0%," May 28, 2010 (epp.eurostat.ec.europa.eu/cache/ITY_PUBLIC/8-28052010-AP/ EN/8-28052010-ap-en.pdf, accessed 07/19/2010); United States Energy Information Administration (at www.eia.doe.gov/cneaf/electricity/epm/table5_3. html, accessed 07/19/2010); OECD Factbook (www.oecd-ilibrary.org/content/book/factbook-2010-en, accessed 07/18/2010); and International Energy Agency, "$CO_2$ Emissions from Fuel Combustion, Highlights," 2009, p. 89 (http://www.iea.org/co2highlights/, accessed 08/09/2010). American driving patterns and gas consumption compared with other countries is drawn from Edward Glaeser and Matthew Kahn, "Sprawl and Urban Growth," NBER Working Paper, May 2003; and World Bank, "World Development Indicators: Transport Sector Gasoline Fuel Consumption Per Capita" (data.worldbank .org/indicator/IS.ROD.SGAS.PC, accessed 07/19/2010) and "World Development Indicators: Motor Vehicles (per 1,000 people)" (data.worldbank.org/ indicator/IS.VEH.NVEH.P3, accessed 08/05/2010). The impact of gas prices on car sales is estimated in Meghan Busse, Christopher Knittel, and Florian Zettelmeyer, "Pain at the Pump: The Differential Effect of Gasoline Prices on New and Used Automobile Markets," NBER Working Paper, December 2009. Data on bestselling cars and their carbon emissions are from "New Car $CO_2$ Report," Society of Motor Manufacturers and Traders, London, March 2009 (http://www.smmt.co.uk/downloads/SMMT-Annual-CO2-report.pdf, accessed on 08/16/2010); Autodata (http://www.motorintelligence.com/m_frameset .html, accessed 01/15/2010); and www.fueleconomy.gov. Data on the path of $CO_2$ emissions and global warming is from the U.S. Energy Information Administration, "International Energy Outlook," May 2010; the Intergovernmental Panel on Climate Change, "Climate Change, 2007 Synthesis Report" (at www .ipcc.ch/pdf/assessment-report/ar4/syr/ar4_syr.pdf, accessed 07/19/2010); *The Stern Review: The Economics of Climate Change,* Executive Summary, London, October 2006 (webarchive.nationalarchives.gov.uk/+/www.hm-treasury.gov .uk/independent_reviews/stern_review_economics_climate_change/sternre view_index.cfm, accessed 07/19/2010). Estimates of population and the availability of water in 2050 are from a United Nations Press Conference on Key Issues Relating to Climate Change and Sustainable Development, November 6, 2009 (www.un.org/News/briefings/docs/2009/091106_Climate_Change.doc .htm, accessed 07/19/2010).

**209–216 The Ethics of Tomorrow:** Americans' declining concerns about climate change are discussed in Frank Newport, "Americans' Global Warming Concerns Continue to Drop," Gallup Report, March 11, 2010 (www.gallup .com/poll/126560/americans-global-warming-concerns-continue-drop.aspx, accessed 07/19/2010). Data on carbon emissions by selected companies and the impact of a carbon tax on their profits is found in Investor Responsibility Research Center, Institute for Corporate Responsibility, "Carbon Risks and Opportunities in the S&P 500," June 2009, and American Electric Company financial filings. The discussion of the rationale for Republicans' skepticism about the perils of climate change draws from Michael I. Cragg and Matthew

E. Kahn, "Carbon Geography: The Political Economy of Congressional Support for Legislation Intended to Mitigate Greenhouse Gas Production," NBER Working Paper, May 2009. Data on the impact of energy taxes on the poor are found in Dallas Burtraw, Rich Sweeney, and Margaret Walls, "The Incidence of U.S. Climate Policy: Where You Stand Depends on Where You Sit," Resources for the Future Discussion Paper, September 2008 (http://www.rff.org/rff/documents/rff-dp-08-28.pdf, accessed on 08/08/2010). The impact of climate change on agriculture is in William Cline, "Climate Change Economics 2008," Lecture presented at Colgate University, Center for Ethics and World Societies, Hamilton, New York, March 10, 2008; Orley Ashenfelter and Karl Storchmann, "Measuring the Economic Effect of Global Warming on Viticulture Using Auction, Retail and Wholesale Prices," American Association of Wine Economists Working Paper, May 2010; and Orley Ashenfelter and Karl Storchmann, "Using a Hedonic Model of Solar Radiation to Assess the Economic Effect of Climate Change: The Case of Mosel Valley Vineyards," NBER Working Paper, July 2006. The analysis of the impact of warming on industrial production in poor countries draws from Melissa Dell, Benjamin Jones, and Benjamin Olken, "Climate Change and Economic Growth: Evidence from the Last Half Century," NBER Working Paper, June 2008. Population projections for the end of the century come from "World Population in 2300," Report from the United Nations Department of Economic and Social Affairs, Population Division, 2003 (www.un.org/esa/population/publications/longrange2/Long_range_report.pdf, accessed 08/08/2010). The discussion of rich countries' likely reluctance to provide financial aid to help poor countries deal with the impact of climate change draws from the Organisation for Economic Co-operation and Development, "Development Co-operation Report 2010, Statistical Annex," (http://www.oecd.org/document/9/0,3343,en_2649_34447_1893129_1_1_1_1,00.html, accessed 07/18/2010); and Joe Barton, "How Congress's Drive to Stop Global Warming Is Fueling China's Drive to Out-Compete the U.S.," *The Hill*, July 7, 2009. The discussion about people's reluctance to sacrifice present resources to improve the lives of future people draws from Talbot Page, "Conservation and Economic Efficiency: An Approach to Materials Policy," (Baltimore: Johns Hopkins University Press, 1977), p. 169; Maureen Cropper, Sema Aydede, and Paul Portney, "Rates of Time Preference for Saving Lives," Economics of the Environment, *American Economic Association Papers and Proceedings*, Vol. 82, No. 2, May 1992, pp. 469–472; and Shane Frederick, "Measuring Intergenerational Time Preference: Are Future Lives Valued Less?," *Journal of Risk and Uncertainty*, Vol. 26, No. 1, 2003, pp. 39–53; Susmita Pati, Ron Keren, Evaline Alessandrini, and Donald Schwarz, "Generational Differences in U.S. Public Spending, 1980–2000," *Health Affairs*, Vol. 23, September/October 2004, pp. 131–141; Pew Research Center, "Fewer Americans See Solid Evidence of Global Warming," October 22, 2009; and W. Kip Viscusi and Joni Hersch, "The Generational Divide in Support for Climate Change Policies: European Evidence," Harvard Law School Working Paper, February 2005. Partha Dasgupta's democratic dilemma is discussed in Partha Dasgupta, "Discounting Climate Change," *Journal of Risk and Uncertainty*, Vol. 37, December 2008, pp. 141–169. Evidence that there are other priorities we could spend money on besides averting climate change is found in the United Nations Millennium Development Goals Report, 2008 (at www.un.org/millenniumgoals/pdf/The%20Millennium%20Development%20Goals%20Report%202008.pdf, accessed 07/18/2010).

**216–220 The Price of the Future:** Nicholas Stern's evaluation of the investments needed to avert catastrophic climate change is drawn from *The Stern Review: The Economics of Climate Change,* Chapter 13, "Towards a Goal for Climate Change Policy," p. 295 (webarchive.nationalarchives.gov.uk/+/www.hm-treasury.gov.uk/independent_reviews/stern_review_economics_climate_change/sternreview_index.cfm, accessed 07/19/2010); Lauren Morello, "Is 350 the New 450 When It Comes to Capping Carbon Emissions?," *New York Times* ClimateWire, September 28, 2009; and Juliette Jowit and Patrick Wintour, "Cost of Tackling Global Climate Change Has Doubled, Warns Stern," *Guardian,* June 26, 2008. Analysis of the discount rate is drawn from William Nordhaus, *A Question of Balance: Weighing the Options on Global Warming Policies* (New Haven: Yale University Press, 2008), pp. 9–11. Nordhaus's disagreement with Stern is discussed in William Nordhaus, "The Challenge of Global Warming: Economic Models and Environmental Policy," Yale University Working Paper, July 2007; and William Nordhaus, op. cit., p. 11. Estimates of economic growth over the past two hundred years come from Angus Maddison, "Historical Statistics for the World Economy: 1–2008 AD" (http://www.ggdc.net/maddison/Historical_Statistics/horizontal-file_02-2010.xls, accessed 08/11/2010).

**220–222 Torn Between Two Prices:** Stern's and Nordhaus's contrasting prescriptions are found in William Cline, "Climate Change Economics 2008," Lecture presented at Colgate University, Center for Ethics and World Societies, Hamilton, New York, March 10, 2008; and William Nordhaus, *A Question of Balance: Weighing the Options on Global Warming Policies* (New Haven: Yale University Press, 2008), especially pp. 1–29, 88–93, and 165–191. Data from the European Climate Exchange is at www.ecx.eu. Dasgupta's difficulty in reaching a conclusion on how much to spend to slow global warming is in Partha Dasgupta, op. cit.

**222–225 Salvation on the Cheap:** Comments about geo-engineering solutions to global warming are found in Catherine Brahic, "Hacking the Planet: The Only Climate Solution Left?," *New Scientist,* No. 2697, July 2009, pp. 8–10. The tale about the wager between Julian Simon and Paul Ehrlich is in John Tierney, "Betting on the Planet," *New York Times Magazine,* December 2, 1990. The price of Brent crude is drawn from the Energy Information Agency database (at tonto.eia.doe.gov/dnav/pet/hist/LeafHandler.ashx?n=Plastic&s=RBRTE&f=D, accessed 07/19/2010). Martin Wolf's despair is in evidence in Martin Wolf, "The Dangers of Living in a Zero-Sum World Economy," *Financial Times,* December 18, 2007. The price of the contents of Ehrlich's basket can be found in U.S. Geological Survey, "Historical Statistics for Mineral and Material Commodities in the United States" (minerals.usgs.gov/ds/2005/140/index.html, accessed 07/19/2010).

**226–229 When Prices Fail:** The estimate of the impact of the financial crisis on the world's economic output in 2009 is drawn from the International Monetary Fund, *World Economic Outlook*, April 2010 (http://www.imf.org/external/pubs/ft/weo/2010/01/weodata/weorept.aspx?pr.x=64&pr.y=7&sy=2008&ey=2015&scsm=1&ssd=1&sort=country&ds=.&br=1&c=001&s=NGDPD&grp=1&a=1, accessed 08/09/2010). The relationship between the price of orange juice and the weather is drawn from Richard Roll, "Orange Juice and Weather," *American Economic Review*, Vol. 75, No. 5, 1984. Data on the rise and fall of home prices is from the Standard & Poor's Case-Shiller Home Prices Index (www.standardandpoors.com/indices/sp-case-shiller-home-price-indices/en/us/?indexId=spusa-cashpidff—p-us, accessed 07/19/2010).

**229–233 When Prices Go Off the Rails:** Data on AOL's purchase of Time Warner draws from Saul Hansell, "America Online to Buy Time Warner for $165 Billion," *New York Times*, January 11, 2000. The discussion of the seventeenth century's financial bubbles and the United Kingdom's Bubble Act draws from Kevin Lansing, "Asset Price Bubbles," Federal Reserve Bank of San Francisco, Economic Letter, Number 2007-32, October 26, 2007; and Peter M. Garber, *Famous First Bubbles* (Cambridge, Mass.: MIT Press, 2000), pp. 50–64. "The South-Sea Project" is in *The Poems of Jonathan Swift, Vol. 1* (London: William Ernst Browning, 1910), pp. 198–207. The description of new high-tech mortgages and the boom of mortgage-backed securities is in Jane Dokko, Brian Doyle, Michael Kiley, Jinill Kim, Shane Sherlund, Jae Sim, and Skander Van den Heuvel, "Monetary Policy and the Housing Bubble," Federal Reserve Board, Finance and Economics Discussion Series, December 22, 2009. Keynes's description of the reverse beauty contest is in John Maynard Keynes, *The General Theory of Employment, Interest and Money* (New Delhi: Atlantic Publishers, 2006), p. 140. Charles Prince's view of dancing is reported in Michiyo Nakamoto and David Wighton, "Citigroup Chief Stays Bullish on Buy-outs," *Financial Times*, July 9, 2007.

**233–236 Should We Pop Them?:** Discussion of the potential social, economic, and political fallout from the financial crisis of 2008 draws from Fernando Ferreira, Joseph Gyourko, and Joseph Tracy, "Housing Busts and Household Mobility," NBER Working Paper, September 2008; Philip Oreopoulos, Till von Wachter, and Andrew Heisz, "The Short- and Long-Term Career Effects of Graduating in a Recession: Hysteresis and Heterogeneity in the Market for College Graduates," NBER Working Paper, April 2006; and Markus Brückner and Hans Grüner, "Economic Growth and the Rise of Political Extremism: Theory and Evidence," CEPR Discussion Paper, March 2010. The debate over whether bubbles should be popped draws from Brad Delong, "Sympathy for Greenspan," Project Syndicate, June 29, 2009 (at www.project-syndicate.org/commentary/delong91); Kevin J. Lansing, "Speculative Growth, Overreaction, and the Welfare Cost of Technology-Driven Bubbles," Federal Reserve Bank of San Francisco Working Paper, August 2009 (www.frbsf.org/publications/economics/papers/2008/wp08-08bk.pdf, accessed 08/08/2010); and James Edward Meeker,

*The Work of the Stock Exchange* (New York: The Ronald Press Company, 1922), p. 419. The tally of countries that have escaped banking crises is by Carmen Reinhart and Kenneth Rogoff, "Banking Crises: An Equal Opportunity Menace," NBER Working Paper, December 2008.

**236–239 What Rationality?:** Eugene Fama's quote is in Douglas Clement, "Interview with Eugene Fama," *The Region,* Federal Reserve Bank of Minnesota, December 2007. Keynes's quote is in John Maynard Keynes, *The General Theory of Employment, Interest and Money* (New York: Harcourt Brace and World, 1965), p. 161. Robert Shiller's theory is described in George Akerlof and Robert Shiller, *Animal Spirits: How Human Psychology Drives the Economy, and Why It Matters for Global Capitalism* (Princeton: Princeton University Press, 2010).

**240–246 Economics for a New World:** Limits to the assumption of human rationality and self-regard are discussed in Herbert Gintis, "Five Principles for the Unification of the Behavioral Sciences," Working Paper, May 13, 2008. The impact of payments on altruistic motivations is discussed in Carl Mellström and Magnus Johannesson, "Crowding Out in Blood Donation: Was Titmuss Right?," *Journal of the European Economic Association,* MIT Press, Vol. 6, No. 4, 2008, pp. 845–863; William Upton, "Altruism, Attribution and Intrinsic Motivation in the Recruitment of Blood Donors," doctoral dissertation, Cornell University, August 1973; and Dan Ariely, Anat Bracha, and Stephan Meier, "Doing Good or Doing Well? Image Motivation and Monetary Incentives in Behaving Prosocially," Federal Reserve Bank of Boston Working Paper, August 2007 (www.bos.frb.org/ economic/wp/wp2007/wp0709.pdf, accessed 08/08/2010). Data on the increasing economic clout of developing countries can be found in OECD Development Center, "Economy: Developing Countries Set to Account for Nearly 60% of World GDP by 2030, According to New Estimates," June 16, 2010 (at www .oecd.org/document/12/0,3343,en_2649_33959_45467980_1_1_1,00.html, accessed 07/19/2010). The potential impact of recession on the mind-set of Americans is discussed in Paola Giuliano and Antonio Spilimbergo, "Growing Up in a Recession: Beliefs and the Macroeconomy," NBER Working Paper, September 2009. The British Treasury's response to Keynes's suggestions during the Great Depression is in Anatole Kaletsky, *Capitalism 4.0* (New York: Public Affairs, 2010), p. 50. And Alan Greenspan's shock was recorded in Brian Knowlton and Michael Grynbaum, "Greenspan 'Shocked' That Free Markets Are Flawed," *New York Times,* October 23, 2008.

# Index

ABC, 132
Abell, O. J., 116
abortion (feticide), 5, 13, 63, 79, 84,
    104, 107, 168
Abu Dhabi, 20
Aché, 166–67
adaptation, 70–73, 167, 192
adultery, 82, 87
advertising, 21, 26–27, 60,
    101–2, 134, 137, 150, 157–58,
    230, 240
  news and, 140–41
  television, 132–33, 158
Africa, 47, 215, 216, 230
  polygamy in, 80, 83
  premarital sex in, 168–69
  slave trade in, 112, 166
Agent Orange, 42
agriculture, 1, 27, 122, 164, 219–20
  food prices and, 27–28, 183
  future of, 211, 213
  illegal immigrants and, 7, 113
  productivity in, 89, 111, 202, 211
  slavery and, 111, 112
Agriculture Department, U.S., 50,
    170
airlines, 29, 35–36, 37, 41, 44, 46
air pollution, 51, 53, 60, 67
airports, Hare Krishna in, 134
Aktion T-4, 57
alcohol, 19–20, 24, 39, 183, 184
altruism, 131, 214, 215
Amazon.com, 37, 134, 148
American Airlines, 35, 41, 44
American Association of Retired
    People, 52
American Indians, 79–80, 135, 167
American Society for Reproductive
    Medicine, 174

Amway, 133–34
Anabaptists, 86
Anderson, Chris, 137
anemia, 68, 69
animal welfare movements, 170
apes, bonobo, 81–82
Apple, 22, 35, 119, 137, 139
Aquinas, Thomas, 22, 180
Archimedes of Syracuse, 12
Argentina, 56, 143
Ariely, Dan, 18
aristocracy, 161, 194, 195
Aristotle, 22
Arno River, 141–42
Asia, 104–6, 172–73, 190
  financial crisis in, 182–83, 230
AT&T, 28
auctions, 20, 33
Augustine, Saint, 86
Australia, 11, 46, 50–51, 62, 90, 207
auto industry, 30–31, 116, 126

Babylonian code, 87
*Badalone, Il* (barge), 141–42
Bangladesh, 103, 208, 218–19, 224
banks, bankers, 42, 43, 114, 125–29,
    229, 232, 233, 236, 239
  earnings of, 120, 121, 125, 126,
    128, 129
  regulation of, 125, 128, 129,
    244–45
Bardot, Brigitte, 175
BarranquillasBest.com, 95
Barton, Joe, 212
baseball, 118
basketball games, 39
beauty, wages and, 115
Becker, Gary, 71, 86, 175
Beckham, David, 120